S0-AXE-240

art-SITES
BRITAIN &
IRELAND

contemporary art
+ architecture

sidra stich

san francisco

art-SITES BRITAIN & IRELAND
First Edition

PUBLISHED BY
art-SITES, 894 Waller Street, San Francisco, CA 94117

EDITOR
Fronia Simpson
DESIGNER
Lisa Schulz/Elysium
CARTOGRAPHER
Ellen McElhinny
PRINTED BY
Hignell Book Printing

© Sidra Stich and art-SITES 2000. Second printing 2003.
art-SITES™ is a trademark of Sidra Stich.

All rights reserved. No part of this book may be translated or reproduced, stored in a retrieval system or transmitted in any form by any means, electronic, photo-copying, recording or otherwise, except brief extracts for the purpose of a review, without written permission of the copyright owner.

Although the author and publisher have tried to make the information as accurate and current as possible, they accept no responsibility for any loss, injury or incon-venience sustained by any party as a result of errors, omissions or advice contained in this book.

Library of Congress Cataloguing-in-Publication Data
Stich, Sidra.
    art-sites Britain & Ireland : contemporary art + architecture handbook / Sidra Stich.
        p.   cm.
    Includes indexes.
    ISBN 0-9667717-2-9
    1. Art, British—20th century—Guidebooks. 2. Art, Irish—20th century—Guidebooks. 3. Architecture—Great Britain—20th century—Guidebooks. 4. Architecture—Ireland—20th century—Guidebooks.
    N6768.S75 2000
    709/.41/0904—dc21   00-699900
                                          CIP

Printed in Canada

COVER IMAGE
Antony Gormley, *Angel of the North*, 1998

table of contents

BRITAIN & IRELAND

SCOTLAND

Dundee

Glasgow
Edinburgh ★

North Shields
Newcastle   South Shields
Gateshead   Sunderland
Consett
Stockton
Middlesbrough
Darlington

Londonderry
NORTHERN
IRELAND
Belfast ★

Grizedale
Forest Park   Kendal

Bradford   Leeds   Hull
Halifax   West
Bretton
Salford
Liverpool   Manchester
Sheffield
Nottingham

Dublin ★

IRELAND

Norwich

Wolverhampton   Walsall
Birmingham

Cambridge
ENGLAND   Duxford   Ipswich
WALES   Milton
Keynes
Forest
of Dean
Swindon   Oxford
Cardiff ★
Llanarthne   Henley-on-
Bristol   Thames   London ★

Southampton   Goodwood

Exeter

St. Ives
Newlyn
St. Austell

Introduction

BRITAIN & IRELAND is the second book in the **art·SITES** series, following last year's inaugural publication of **art·SITES FRANCE**. We plan to produce many such books, eventually covering all the major countries and regions where contemporary art and architecture are flourishing. The aim is to identify and give a pithy commentary on the most significant sites where there is innovative, intriguing, top-notch work from the present and recent past. By providing background, analytic and practical information, we orient you to a place or project, both in advance and during a visit. The book is organized geographically so you can conveniently and efficiently arrange walking tours of a neighborhood or excursions to a region. Sites are keyed by number to detail maps and by icon to subject categories—museums, art centers (exhibition spaces), film and media centers, art galleries, architecture, public art, sculpture parks and bookstores. Recent exhibitions and artists associated with galleries are also named to broaden your knowledge of sites.

The **art·SITES** handbooks gather all sorts of pertinent material on what's happening here and now in the arts within a given city, region or country. Whether you have only a few hours or several weeks to spend on your travels, **art·SITES** is an invaluable resource. Especially if you want to get to know a place beyond the scope of the main museums or typical tourist monuments, these handbooks will open up a new world for you. We help you discover hidden treasures within major cities and the wealth of exciting exhibitions and artwork in places you may never even have heard of.

Tony Blair's Britain is constantly described with the terms "youthful," "newness" and "cool." Indeed, the UK has become an upbeat place where culture and media play a pivotal role. But this was hardly the case previously. During the years when Margaret Thatcher was prime minister, and thereafter under the government of John Major, support for the arts—especially innovative work by young, emerging artists—was wanting. Legendary British conservatism held sway. By default, artists had to take more control into their own hands and develop alternative means of asserting their presence and potency.

Y B A The spark that ignited the current burst of worldwide attention focused on the UK art scene flared in 1988 when Damien Hirst, then a student at Goldsmiths College in London, organized the exhibition *Freeze*. It took place in an abandoned Docklands warehouse and included work by Hirst and 15 fellow students (Steve Adamson, Angela Bulloch, Mat Collishaw, Ian Davenport, Angus Fairhurst, Anya Gallaccio, Gary Hume, Michael Landy, Abigail Lane, Sarah Lucas, Lala Meredith-Vulja, Stephen Park, Richard Patterson, Simon Patterson, Fiona Rae). But Hirst didn't simply present a show of student art: he produced a frenetic three-part spectacle composed of eccentric objects having irritating or mundane subject matter. Moreover, there was a glossy catalogue, an effective publicity campaign and unqualified sales success. Everything was sold! The phenomenon of the YBA—Young British Artists—was born.

The energy generated by *Freeze* funneled into myriad activities and events. It helped to have someone like Damien Hirst, a British version of an Andy Warhol or Julian Schnabel ringleader, sustaining the spotlight on himself and YBA. A skillful impresario, as well as a flamboyant, often boorish personality, he delighted the tabloids by popping up in the right places with the right people at the right time.

An apex in YBA history was reached in the fall of 1997 when artworks owned by the mega-collector Charles Saatchi went on display at the Royal Academy of Arts, London, in an exhibition titled *Sensation*. Some artists from *Freeze* as well as many others, who have since acquired star status, were included, among them, Darren Almond, Richard Billingham, Simon Callery, Jake & Dinos Chapman, Tracey Emin, Mark Francis, Mona Hatoum, Langlands & Bell, Chris Ofili, Marc Quinn, Jenny Saville, Sam Taylor-Wood, Gavin Turk, Mark Wallinger, Gillian Wearing, Rachel Whiteread.

Whereas *Freeze* had been a historic moment within the local art community, *Sensation* brought worldwide public attention to YBA. But many reviewers were not impressed. It was, in the words of one critic, a media carnival. "The exhibition jangles the nerve of physical confrontation and inflames the shock gland (which perhaps withers in the face of recurring shock tactics), although the lack of real substance is the most disconcerting thing. With some exceptions, the work reminds me of the shortest joke in the world: 'This seal walks into a club.' "

Indeed, much of the art on display (not unlike much contemporaneous art seen in New York, Germany and elsewhere) grovels in the audacious and scandalous, or, as the exhibitions chief of the Royal Academy (a YBA supporter) stated, the artists "go right for the jugular." As its title implies, the exhibition and its art aimed to capture attention, if not to incite and shock viewers. And this it did. There were protests, demonstrations (for and against) and a record-breaking crowd of over 350,000 visitors.

Apart from all the hype, *Sensation* presented art dealing with such big issues as life, death, sex and boredom and did so unabashedly in big, in-your-face objects. Typically there's a disturbing or provocative undercurrent. And yet, the imagery is not depressing. Using precocious theatrics, the work has a freshness, brazenness and spirit of defiance. It doesn't so much deal with personal expression as with irksome, common, familiar subjects. Content and images are accessible to a broad, non-art audience. They often are treated playfully and cleverly with wit or bold-faced irony. Like many contemporary artists, YBA show little reverence for traditional media, favoring instead non-art materials, photography and video. Notably, *Sensation* marked a decisive move away from the industrial aesthetic and the heavy, conceptual, theory-laden approach to art-making and curating—dominant forces during past decades.

POST-*SENSATION* What began as publicity-oriented exhibitions filled with self-indulgent one-liners and deliberately crude, outrageous art has emerged as a viable art scene. It's still energized by an upbeat mind-set and controversial projects, but now it encompasses greater diversity of expression and a degree of maturity. Many of the artists featured in *Sensation* have acquired star status but they are not the only ones contributing to the UK's new reputation as "Cool Britannia." Foremost among the younger generation not in *Sensation* are Helen Chadwick, Tacita Dean, Willie Doherty, Douglas Gordon, Steve McQueen, Cornelia Parker, Steven Pippin, Hannah Starkey, Jane & Louise Wilson. And there's also the older generation of ever-productive, notable artists—Anthony Caro, Tony Cragg, Grenville Davey, Richard Deacon, Ian Hamilton Finlay, Barry Flanagan, Lucian Freud, Gilbert & George, Andy Goldsworthy, Antony Gormley, Richard Hamilton, David Hockney, Anish Kapoor, Richard Long, Julian Opie, Richard Wentworth, Bill Woodrow.

A significant result of the hoopla surrounding *Sensation* has been the embrace of British artists by foreign galleries and museums and their inclusion in major international exhibitions. Attention to YBA has also elevated London's stature: it's now considered a leading hub of contemporary art activity. When the new Tate Modern opens in May 2000, the city's reputation will undoubtedly skyrocket. London is also awash with contemporary art galleries. During the late 1990s, the field greatly increased in number, asserting a concentration in both the established Bond Street area and the more artsy East End and Southwark communities. A welcome corollary has been the emergence of British collectors in what heretofore had been a market populated almost exclusively by Saatchi and very few others. In addition, new centers of art activity have been developing throughout the UK and in Ireland (Liverpool, Leeds, Gateshead-Newcastle, Glasgow, Dublin, etc.) These feed into the London scene even as they prosper independently.

With all the momentum, the timing couldn't have been better for the second splash of publicity from *Sensation*. This occurred when the show appeared in New York at the Brooklyn Museum of Art in the fall of 1999—two years after the initial showing in London.

If there's a downside to the YBA phenomenon and a weakness in the prevailing character of Britain's art scene, it's the perpetuation of UK insularity. Museum collections, exhibitions and gallery artists focus strongly, if not entirely, on homegrown talents, and public artworks and major buildings are pretty much all created by Brits. When little attention is paid to what has been and is happening in the outside world, it not only skews perceptions but also solidifies provincialism. Attempts to counter insularity are slowly taking root and hopefully will become increasingly apparent to sustain the dynamism in the current art climate in the UK.

PUBLIC ART Despite the preponderance of innovative artists working in sculpture and installation art, few have been commissioned to create permanent works in the public arena. Indeed, there are few world-class examples of public art in the UK and Ireland. (A notable exception is the active public art program in northern England—the Northumberland region.) There are, however, many temporary public artworks of a most extraordinary, innovative nature, at times interdisciplinary or collaborative, being commissioned in London and elsewhere. To find out about these, you need to check local listings and keep an eye out for posted announcements.

Several sculpture parks offer the opportunity to see art a natural environment, and there are projects like the C2C Cycle Route and Art Trail that are setting art in nonurban, out-of-the-way locations.

ARCHITECTURE During postwar era, the most radical reaction to conservative reconstruction efforts was New Brutalism, spearheaded by Alison and Peter Smithson. Permeated by a welfare mentality, this architecture favored truth to materials and a no-nonsense expressiveness derived from the mechanical and structural elements. Although Archigram, a collective of utopianist, fun-filled architects, challenged this approach during the 1960s by advocating a need to rethink the whole social fabric in light of modern technology, consumerism and science, they never realized any of their visionary ideas in actual buildings.

Not until the 1980s did the built landscape in Britain begin to include radical, innovative designs. But then there was a pause caused by the fiery, antimodernist criticism of Prince Charles (1984) and the storm of controversy that followed.

Finally, in the 1990s, after Prime Minister John Major put in motion a "renaissance and improvement" plan to mark the millennium, architectural activity really took off in the UK. Major's proposal—fueled by the mega-minded National Lottery, a strong economy and the support of Tony Blair, the "newness" prime minister—spawned widespread urban renewal projects, major new infrastructure buildings and expansion of transportation systems and their related buildings. A veritable building boom has taken hold and is dramatically transforming the appearance of London and other cities. Most conspicuous are the steel-and-glass towers that have been added to skylines and waterfront or dockland redevelopments. Canary Wharf (London) is a classic example.

At the top of the British architectural domain are two world-renowned figures: Norman Foster and Richard Rogers. Both are versed in high-tech design and favor structures that are spare but eye-catching and finely attuned to spatial and structural articulation. Other architects, who are core participants in the current wave of new building, include Arup, David Chipperfield, CZWG, Terry Farrell, Future Systems, Nicolas Grimshaw, Michael Hopkins, James Stirling, Michael Wilford.

Many of these architects were selected to design the 14 Landmark Millennium Projects. Ranging from the Tate Modern (an art project in London), to the Millennium Stadium (sports in Cardiff), to the Eden Project (botany in Cornwall), to the International Center for Life (science in Newcastle), to the Lowry Centre (theater and arts in Manchester/Salford), these grand edifices serve various realms of interest and activity and are located in every region of the UK. Comparable to President Georges Pompidou's *grands projets* in France, these buildings assert national prowess and aim to revitalize, expand, sustain or encourage preeminence in various fields.

There's a lively network of architectural associations in Britain whose purpose is to promote architecture through lectures, conferences, festivals, exhibitions, workshops, seminars, mass-media programs, tours, etc. The quality of the programs is quite high and usually intended for the general public. Well-known names in the field as well as emerging figures are featured in these programs.

ARTS COUNCILS National and regional arts councils are the mainstay of the arts in the UK. They develop, sustain and promote dance, music, drama, touring companies, contemporary art galleries and exhibitions, film and literature projects by distributing public (government) money and revenue generated by the National Lottery. Virtually all arts projects—big and small, artist-run or part of a major museum, radical or conservative—receive arts council funding.

Notably, the Arts Council of England only funds one contemporary art collection: artworks purchased for circulating exhibitions and administered by the Hayward Gallery. Its focus, and indeed the focus of art activity throughout the UK, is on exhibitions and artist projects. Though its resources underlie numerous and diverse projects, it also supports five noncollecting contemporary art institutions: Arnolfini (Bristol), Ikon Gallery (Birmingham), Oxford Museum of Modern Art (Oxford), Serpentine Gallery (London) and Whitechapel Art Gallery (London).

NATIONAL LOTTERY Created under a 1993 Act of Parliament, the lottery (and then the Millennium Commission which administers it), was established to fund "lasting monuments to the achievements and aspirations of the people of the UK." These include flagship projects and proposals to create a village green. By

January 1999 the commission had awarded £1.26 billion to 187 capital projects on more than 3,000 sites across Britain. Lottery awards were matching grants exclusively for infrastructure. In the visual arts, the grants supported the construction of new buildings and the renovation of old buildings for institutions that may or may not have existed before 1993. Some monies also went toward commissioning permanent works of public art.

The sudden availability of large sums of money caused a megalomanic outbreak. Museums, art centers and all sorts of arts organizations started thinking on monumental terms using superlatives like biggest, best, most comprehensive, all-inclusive, etc. Not surprisingly, a fair number of awards resulted in white elephants since attendance projections were unrealistic and operating costs could not be met. In some cases, matching funds were not forthcoming so projects had to be put on hold, downsized or canceled. Problem cases notwithstanding, the lottery has done wonders for the arts, if only to encourage activity, involvement and outreach in ways that were not previously even imagined.

ART TRUSTS In addition to arts council and lottery grants, many arts projects in the UK are beholden to art trusts. These are nonprofit (or to use the British term, "charitable") organizations that promote the creation and presentation of unusual projects, typically at unusual venues. They commission work that usually is temporary and in a public space outside the purview of a museum or gallery. Functioning like independent curators, high-echelon consultants, artist agents, project directors, event facilitators and conduits of art activity, they wield a great deal of power within and beyond the communities in which they operate. Among the most renowned—responsible for outstanding, innovative projects and new thinking about art and its role in contemporary society—are Artangel in London and the Henry Moore Trust in the Leeds-Yorkshire area. Again, to find out about the temporary exhibitions, performances and events developed by art trusts, you need to check local listings and keep an eye out for posted announcements.

ART CELEBRATIONS, FESTIVALS AND FAIRS In their effort to advance and promote the arts, the UK has increasingly been designating a particular theme for a year-long celebration. For example, 1996 was the Year of Visual Arts; 1999, the year of Glasgow—City of Architecture and Design; and 2000, the Year of the Artist. Each appellation gets widespread, impressive attention through such things as exhibitions, events, public art projects, lectures, seminars, artist residencies and publications. If you had been in Sheffield in 1998—the Year of Photography and the Electronic Image—you would have seen an array of "sight and sound" projects in 16 different venues. Or in Liverpool and Manchester, you could have gone to *Revolution98*, an incredible program of 100 new media projects and an international symposium. Assisted by national and regional funding, these "year of" celebrations have achieved considerable success in raising the profile of the arts in general and individual artists in particular.

The UK also has its share of special festivals and fairs devoted to the arts. Among the most renowned are the annual London Film Festival (November), the Edinburgh Festival (August), Belfast Festival at Queen's (November) and the **London Contemporary Art Fair**, held in late January at the Business Design Center (52 Upper Street, Islington, N1 0QH, 020-7288-6005).

PRIZES The Brits and Irish love prizes and seem to keep establishing them to honor the most talented artists and architects. Along with the prestige, many of the prizes award lucrative monetary gifts. An exhibition of all the short-listed candidates usually accompanies the announcement. Among the most esteemed awards are the Turner Prize, in association with the Tate Gallery (£20,000); NatWest Art Prize (£26,000); Jerwood Painting Prize (£30,000); Citibank Private Bank Photography Prize, in association with the Photographers' Gallery, London (£15,000); Stirling Prize for architecture (£20,000); and the Glen Dimplex Prize in Ireland (£15,000).

ART MAGAZINES There are several magazines with good coverage of contemporary art that give significant attention to artists and exhibitions in the UK. *Frieze* (£4.50), *Contemporary Visual Arts* (£4.95), *Art Monthly* (£2.95), *Untitled* (£2.95), *AN*—focuses on visual and applied art (£3); *Art Review* (£3.95), *Portfolio*—focuses on photography (£8.95/$25, biannual), *liveartmagazine*—focuses on performance and theater (free). In most cities or regions you can pick up a free listing of current exhibitions and events in the local galleries. Internet listings, like londonart. co.uk/listings, are also a source of information, albeit spotty and incomplete.

Practicalities

art·SITES BRITAIN & IRELAND has tried assiduously to present up-to-date and accurate information. Despite out best efforts, you're likely to find different admission prices, hours, new addresses and even sites that no longer exist. We apologize for the inconvenience and hope you will inform us of changes so we can make corrections and update the next edition.

HOURS Unlike most countries in Europe and America, many museums and commercial galleries in the UK are open on Mondays. Some galleries have shorter hours on Saturday and others are only open Thursday–Sunday. During the summer, galleries variously close on Saturdays, or for the entire month of August. There is no rhyme, reason or consistency. To avoid frustration and wasted time, check the current listings or call in advance.

HOLIDAY CLOSINGS Most galleries and museums are closed on the following days:
England and Wales New Year's Day, Good Friday, Easter Monday, May Day bank holiday (first Mon in May), spring bank holiday (last Mon in May), summer bank holiday (last Mon in Aug), Christmas, Boxing Day (Dec 26).
Scotland New Year's Day, Hogmanay (Jan 2), Good Friday, May Day bank holiday (first Mon in May), spring bank holiday (last Mon in May), summer bank holiday (first Mon in Aug), Christmas, Boxing Day (Dec 26).
Northern Ireland New Year's Day, St. Patrick's Day, Good Friday, Easter Monday, May Day bank holiday (first Mon in May), spring bank holiday (last Mon in May), Battle of the Boyne/Orangemen's Day (July 12), summer bank holiday (last Mon in Aug), Christmas, Boxing Day (Dec 26).
Republic of Ireland New Year's Day, St. Patrick's Day, May Day bank holiday (first Mon in May), June bank holiday (first Mon in June), summer bank holiday (first Mon in Aug), Halloween (last Mon in Oct), Christmas, St. Stephen's Day (Dec 26).

TELEPHONE NUMBERS The country code for the UK is 44, for the Republic of Ireland it's 353. When dialing within the UK or Ireland, preface the telephone number with 0. Omit the 0 when calling from abroad. As of June 1999 a new system of area codes went into effect in several cities, including London. Old numbers will no longer function after April 22, 2000. Although the new system imparts some consistency to telephone numbers in the UK, there are still many regions and cities where codes and exchanges have diverse systems and disparate numbers of digits.

In the new system, 020 is the area code for London, 023 for Portsmouth and Southampton, 024 for Coventry, 029 for Cardiff and 028 for Northern Ireland. These area codes, followed by a new prefix of one or two digits plus the old phone number, form an eight digit exchange. In London, the former codes 171 and 181 are now 7 and 8 respectively. The Portsmouth prefix is now 92, Southampton 80, Coventry 76, Cardiff 20 and Belfast 90. For example, 0171-333-4444 is now 020-7333-4444 (London) and 01703-666777 is now 023-8066-6777 (Southampton).

ADMISSION FEES Most museums and exhibition spaces in the UK and Ireland are free. There is, however, often a charge for special exhibitions with a reduced rate for children, students, seniors and various other categories. Where applicable, we note both regular and reduced fees (e.g. £5/3) for each site.

GEOGRAPHICAL NAMES Ambiguous, overlapping geographical domains are commonplace in the UK. Don't be surprised if you can't figure out relationships and actual boundaries between neighborhoods, districts, boroughs, cities, counties (shires) and regions. Moreover, old historic names and modern names are used interchangeably. Cities whose official names include the river on which they are located (Newcastle upon Tyne) are referred to with and without the qualifying designation, but a place like Kingston-upon-Hull is called Hull, not Kingston. And then there's the case of Londonderry and Derry, one city with two equally acceptable names. Best not to apply logic and prepare to be confused.

SITE ICONS The following icons are used to distinguish the sites in this handbook:

    🏛 museum   architecture

    🖽 art center or exhibition space   public art

    🎥 film or media center   sculpture park

    🖻 art gallery   arts bookstore

england

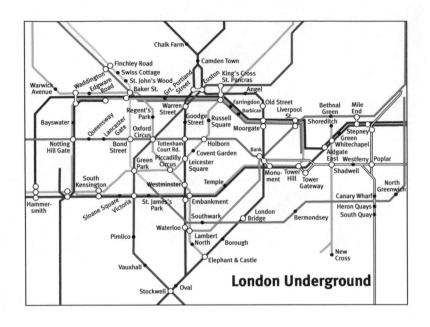

London Underground

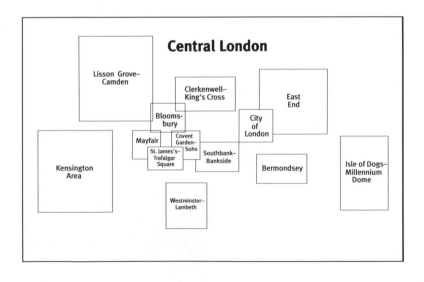

Central London

Lisson Grove–Camden

Clerkenwell–King's Cross

East End

Bloomsbury

City of London

Mayfair

Covent Garden–Soho

St. James's–Trafalgar Square

Southbank–Bankside

Kensington Area

Bermondsey

Isle of Dogs–Millennium Dome

Westminster–Lambeth

London

CURRENT ART LISTINGS *Time Out* magazine is the best all-around source of information about current programs and events in London's lively art, culture and entertainment spheres. Alternatively you can find a specific listing of gallery and museum shows in *New Exhibitions of Contemporary Art*, a free, foldout brochure published bimonthly and available in art centers and galleries. It's also online at www.newexhibitions.com.

LONDON UNDERGROUND Beware of the London tube map. There is absolutely no logic to its artfully arranged schema in terms of geography. Distances and relative locations were forsaken by the original designer in favor of easy readability. Thus, what seems walkable may be a major hike and what seems remote may be around the corner. Within the Underground system you can take an architectural tour by riding on the new Jubilee Line extension, getting off at each stop to explore the stations. Unlike the old stations, these have been designed by leading and hot-shot young architects without the requirement that they adhere to a consistent "house style." Moreover, the stations are wondrous, gigantic spaces, built for the future. In the following pages discussions about the most compelling designs (Westminster, Southwark, and North Greenwich) appear as noteworthy sites in the context of their respective neighborhoods.

ARTIST INITIATIVES Damien Hirst's legendary exhibition *Freeze* was one of many artist initiatives that are still a lively, important feeding ground for art activity in London. Artist-run galleries which are ongoing are discussed in the following pages. But there are other short-lived and on-again off-again exhibition spaces in artist studios, vacant warehouses or sundry other places that are readily available and cheap. Most are located in the East End, Southwark, Deptford and Lambeth—neighborhoods heavily populated by artists. There are also solo-artist projects and one-time events often promoted by catchy or ridiculous titles. It's not always easy to find out about such activities though it's here that you may see the most experimental, risky-taking work.

A patient attitude is mandatory when exploring artist initiatives since you're likely to wade through lots of raw, derivative work on the chance of finding a hidden gem. Past artist initiatives bode well for finding such gems. Some recent examples are Michael Landy's *Market* (1990), Rachel Whiteread's *Ghost* (1990) and *House* (1993), Damien Hirst's *In and Out of Love* (1991), Sarah Lucas & Tracey Emin's *The Shop* (1993), Anya Gallaccio's *intensities and surfaces (1996)* and the manic exhibitions like *Cocaine Orgasm* (1995) and *Stop short changing us. Popular culture is for Idiots. We believe in ART (1998)* by the collaborative BANK.

ART TRUSTS Artangel, Public Art Development Trust (PADT) and International Institute of Visual Arts (INIVA) are three leading art trusts, active in producing refreshing, intriguing temporary art projects within London's public space. These take the form of performances, films, television productions, contemporary dance programs, sound artworks, audio walks, street interventions, interdisciplinary collaborations, art installations in the Underground and airports, outdoor video projections, artist publications and much more. Details concerning these events can be found in the press, on posters and announcement cards distributed at museum and gallery reception desks.

Mayfair

Courtyard Sculpture
1 Projects

Royal Academy of Arts
Burlington House,
Piccadilly St, W1V 0DS
tube: Piccadilly Circus, Green Park

After you walk through the archway fronting Piccadilly, you enter a large, open-air, paved courtyard surrounded by the staid, Italianate architecture of Burlington House. Built in 1715–17 by the third earl of Burlington, the residence (considerably remodeled) became the headquarters of the Royal Academy of Arts (RA) in 1867. A notable addition

to the Academy's program occurred recently when it began using the courtyard for one-person sculpture installations, timed to coincide with major exhibitions. Not only do these enliven a somewhat dreary space, providing a subsidiary art experience for visitors waiting on line to see the blockbusters inside the RA, but they give contemporary sculptors the opportunity to show multipartite projects and large-scale objects in a prime public setting. Exhibitions have featured Eduardo Chillida, Tony Cragg, Richard Deacon, Antony Gormley.

Critical Mass by Gormley (1998) was particularly compelling because of the artist's potent use of the human body—or, more accurately, body posture—and

Antony Gormley, *Critical Mass*, 1998

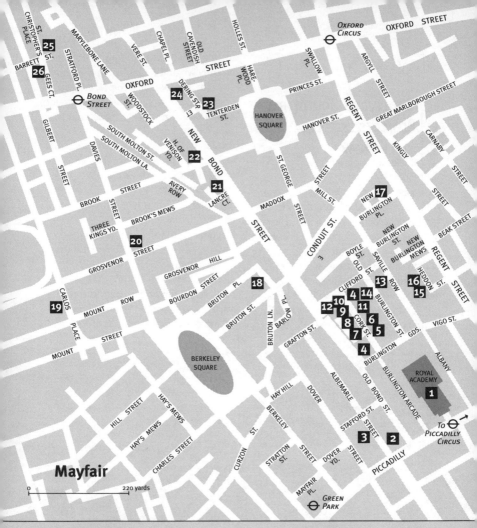

1. Royal Academy of Arts
2. Marlborough Fine Art
3. Faggionato Fine Arts
4. Waddington Galleries
5. Victoria Miro Gallery
   Michael Hue-Williams Fine Art
6. The Mayor Gallery
7. BAC Gallery
8. Entwistle Gallery
9. Atrium Bookshop
10. Helly Nahmad Contemporary
11. Alan Cristea Gallery
12. Bernard Jacobson Gallery
13. Rocket Gallery
14. Stephen Friedman Gallery
15. Sadie Coles HQ
16. Gagosian Gallery
17. Jason & Rhodes Gallery
18. Timothy Taylor Gallery
19. Hamiltons Gallery
20. Gimpel Fils
21. Jigsaw
22. Pleats Please (Issy Miyake)
23. Anthony d'Offay Gallery
    Annely Juda Fine Art
24. Anthony Reynolds Gallery
25. William Pye, *Christos*
26. Laurent Delaye Gallery

the physical environment of the court-yard. The installation included 60 solid cast-iron sculptures (almost one ton each), all the same size, shape and uniform black tonality. Forty-six lay abandoned on the ground, their bodies strewn about, some tightly curled up in a fetal position, one lying flat on its back with legs tautly vertical, and others stretched out on their sides or stomachs with arms and legs variously bent or extended. Frozen in states of anguish and pain, as if struck down by a horrendous force, they called to mind situations of mass oppression even as they aroused empathy for each victim. Awareness of the individual as part of, yet isolated from, the whole was vividly manifested by the 14 figures on the periphery of the courtyard. They were shown suspended in the midst of a fall, hanging by their heels or standing immobilized in an upright position.

Royal Academy
1 of Arts (RA)

renovation: Norman FOSTER, 1991
Burlington House,
Piccadilly St, W1V 0DS
020-7300-8000 f: 7300-8001
www.royalacademy.org.uk
daily, 10–6; Sun in summer,
10–8:30; some exhibitions are open
late on Fri
admission: £3/2.50–£7/6
(varies for each exhibition)
tube: Piccadilly Circus, Green Park

When you enter the narrow lobby, don't succumb to the temptation of climbing the majestic staircase directly ahead. You must purchase exhibition tickets at an inconspicuous counter in the ground-floor lobby before going up to the grand foyer, bookstore or galleries on the upper levels. However, to fully appreciate the building—especially Norman Foster's innovative design for the interface between two existing structures—it's better to skirt around the staircase off to the right, following signs for the café. You'll know you've arrived when you come to a narrow space (less than 16 1/2 ft—5 m—wide) bounded by exterior wall facings, three stories high and suffused with natural light from above. The café has a negligible presence in that it is totally overshadowed by the physicality of the space itself and the allure of the oval

glass elevator in its midst. Even if you have to wait, be sure and take the elevator to the top so you can experience the incredible simultaneity of openness and confinement. This route up also gives dazzling views of the antique Roman sculptures set along the walls and illuminated by sunlight filtered through a translucent glass roof. Well known for his use of glass and light, Foster outdid himself in the simple but effective design of this multifunctional corridor. He was also responsible for the renovation of the Sackler Galleries, entered at the summit of the corridor, and the adaptation of a second space between two buildings (off to the left side of the lobby) housing a diagonal-and-curve-shaped glass staircase.

The Royal Academy is an unusual organization with a vibrant exhibition and lecture program equal to the largest, richest museums anywhere in the world. But unlike its rivals, the RA is completely independent, receiving no government funding. Moreover, it is run by its members—a self-perpetuating board of 80 distinguished painters, sculptors, engravers, printmakers, draftsmen and architects. Promoting the visual arts is the sole purpose of the RA, and it fulfills this mission by mounting exhibitions, providing training in its schools, operating a library and developing a collection.

The collection, composed of British art from the 18th century to the present, showcases work by RA members (each is required to give an example of his or her work) or donations. The art hangs in private rooms throughout the building, accessible to the public on scheduled tours. However, you can always view the collection's famous treasure, Michelangelo's *Virgin and Child with the Infant St. John* (the *Taddeo Tondo*), in an open anteroom near the entrance to the Sackler Galleries.

Exhibitions at the RA are worth seeing even if you're not particularly fond of the artist or the subject. Since there are usually several shows running at the same time, you'll have a considerable choice. The list of some recent projects gives a sense of the breadth of art covered: *Africa—The Art of a Continent, Amazons of the Avant-Garde, Tadao Ando—Master of Minimalism, Chagall— Love and the Stage, Corot to Matisse— 100 Years of Collecting in Japan, Glory of Venice, Goya, Imperial Chinese Ceramics, Kandinsky, Living Bridges, Mantegna, Monet in the 20th Century, Picasso—Painter and Sculptor in Clay, Sacred Art of Tibet, Van Dyck.* In contrast to museum blockbusters that are mere compendiums of objects, the shows here tend to be well curated and astutely selected.

Although modern art is represented in the schedule, contemporary art had not garnered much attention until the arrival of *Sensation: Young British Artists from the Saatchi Collection* in the fall of 1997. Not only did this exhibition create an international stir but it set a new attendance record. The subsequent showing of *Joseph Beuys: The Secret Block for a Secret Person in Ireland* (summer 1999) suggests that contemporary art has become part of the RA program. Of course, there's the annual summer show—a juried exhibition that ends up as an exhaustive hodgepodge of every possible mode of current art making with a smattering of vanguard creativity thrown in. Anyone paying £17 can submit a work (up to 3 works per person), and as evidenced by the checklist of 642 artists and 1,202 objects in the 1998 exhibition, many do. Unquestionably, there's a great incentive in addition to the RA imprimatur: numerous cash prizes are awarded, the largest of which is £25,000 ($40,000)! Should you go to see this exhibition, don't be surprised to find huge crowds, since it's extremely popular with the general public.

A part of the RA program not to overlook is the evening lecture series. It includes superb speakers from a range of different disciplines who discuss the art, artist or a topic related to one of the current exhibitions. The architecture talks are especially rewarding. Admission: variable, from 0 to £17—the price may include drinks and a private viewing or guided tour of the exhibition.

2 | Marlborough Fine Art

6 Albemarle St, W1X 4BY
020-7629-5161 f: 7629-6338
www.marlboroughfineart.com
mfa@marlboroughfineart.com
Mon–Fri, 10–5:30; Sat, 10–12:30
tube: Green Park

This longstanding gallery represents some of Britain's mainstream masters of the late 20th century as well as various mid-career artists who take a somewhat staid approach to figuration or abstraction. Artists: Frank Auerbach, Christopher Bramham, Steven Campbell, Lynn Chadwick, Chen Yifei, Stephen Conroy, Christopher Couch, John Davies, Daniel Enkaoua, Karl Gerstner, Dieter Hacker, Maggie Hambling, John Hubbard, Bill Jacklin, Ken Kiff, R. B. Kitaj, Christopher Le Brun, Raymond Mason, Thérèse Oulton, Victor Pasmore, Celia Paul, Keith Piper, Sarah Raphael, Paula Rego.

3 | Faggionato Fine Arts

49 Albermarle St, W1X 3FE
020-7409-7979 f: 7409-7879
106755,1733.com
Mon–Fri, 9:30–5:30; closed Sat
tube: Green Park

Located on the first floor in a quite limited space, this gallery shows a diverse range of artists—established and unknown in Britain, modern and contemporary, European, Asian and American. Care is taken with the selections so you often see choice or unorthodox examples of an artist's work. Recent exhibitions: *Francis Bacon, Barbara Ess, Lucian Freud, Julio Gonzalez, Carlo Guaita, Donald Judd, Rodrigo Moynihan, Yan Pei Ming, Robin Tewes, Jean Tinguely, Rosemarie Trockel, Sixties Sculptures, Surrealist Decalcomania*.

| Cork Street

Just around the corner from Bond Street (in the zone where Old Bond becomes New Bond) is the unassuming, one-block-long Cork Street, sometimes called "the art street" because it is chock-full of galleries. Indeed, the whole area bordered by Piccadilly, Regent and Oxford Streets is awash with galleries and related shops. Since the streets tend to be short, often L-shaped or dead-ended and sharing the same "family name" (Burlington Street, Gardens, Mews, Arcade, and New Burlington Mews, Street, Place), be prepared to get lost and hopelessly confused.

4 | Waddington Galleries

11, 12 & 34 Cork St, W1X 2LT
020-7437-8611 f: 7734-4146
waddington-galleries.com
Mon–Fri, 10–5:30; Sat, 10–1
tube: Piccadilly Circus

This is one of London's stalwart galleries where you can see some of the classics from the modern era by celebrated British artists as well as midcentury and current work by British and international figures. American art from the 1960s generation is a particular strength. Waddington's operation is spread among three spaces and is somewhat like a department store, where you have a multiplicity of offerings with something always an attention-getter. On the corner (#34) there's a selection of paintings by gallery artists. At #11 you'll typically find a mixed bag of work in various genres by renowned and little-known artists. And at #12, the exhibitions are one-person shows—new work by a leading young star (like Fiona Rae) or a particular series by an established name (like Andy Warhol's paintings after Giorgio de Chirico).

Artists: Craigie Aitchison, Peter Blake, Patrick Caulfield, John Chamberlain, Michael Craig-Martin, Ian Davenport, Barry Flanagan, Donald Judd, Peter Halley, Barbara Hepworth, Patrick Heron, Roger Hilton, Ivon Hitchens, John Hogland, Zebedee Jones, Lisa Milroy, Henry Moore, Ben Nicolson, Mimmo Paladino, John Piper, Fiona Rae, Robert Rauschenberg, Lucas Samaras, Stanley Spencer, Frank Stella, Graham Sutherland, Antoni Tapies, William Turnbull, Jack B. Yeats.

5 | Victoria Miro Gallery

21 Cork St, W1X 1HB
020-7734-5082 f: 7494-1787
vicmir@dircon.co.uk
Mon–Fri, 10–5:30; Sat, 11–1
tube: Piccadilly Circus

Don't be misled by the small space of this gallery. It has one of the most high-powered programs in London. Exhibitions are fine-tuned and precisely installed to engage the viewer and showcase individual objects. And the objects are often extraordinary works of both conceptual and visual creativity. Hardly shrinking from sensational or satirical imagery, the gallery organizes noteworthy group shows with provocative themes. Such was the case with *Heads Will Roll*, a 1998 exhibition presenting compelling work by Ian Hamilton Finlay, Robin Lowe, Dawn Mellor, Lars Nilsson, Chris Ofili and Keir Smith.

To its credit, the gallery has a strong history of supporting emerging and little-known artists, especially British talents, who then rise to higher levels of prominence. Artists: Marina Abramovic, Doug Aitken, Cecily Brown, Thomas Demand, Peter Doig, Ian Hamilton

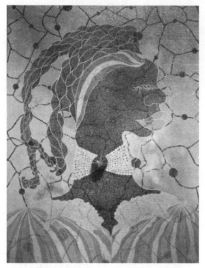

Chris Ofili, *Dreams*, 1998

sentations and considerations of space, light and time. The artists exhibited (usually in one-person shows) have worldwide reputations even though they may not be familiar names outside their own countries and specialties. The slant is less British than elsewhere and the gallery doesn't traffic in the splashy, sensational images of the YBA.

Artists: Tony Bevan, Thomas Joshua Cooper, Stephen Cox, Susan Derges, Andy Goldsworthy, Per Kirkeby, Langlands & Bell, Garry Fabian Miller, Jaume Plensa, Jose Maria Sicilia, Hiroshi Sugimoto, James Turrell, John Virtue, Michael Young.

Finlay, Andreas Gursky, Alex Hartley, Chantal Joffe, Isaac Julien, Udomsak Krisanamis, Yayoi Kusama, Abigail Lane, Brad Lochore, Robin Lowe, Nicholas May, Dawn Mellor, Tracey Moffatt, Chris Ofili, Gary Perkins, Hadrian Pigott, Inez van Lamsweerde, Stephen Willats.

In June 2000, the Victoria Miro gallery will move to spatious new quarters at 16–18 Wharf Road in the East End (see p. 105).

5 | Michael Hue-Williams Fine Art

⬡ | 21 Cork St, W1X 1HB
020-7434-1318 f: 7434-1321
mhw@btinternet.com
Mon–Fri, 9:30–5:30; closed Sat
tube: Piccadilly Circus

Located on the first floor with its exhibition space in one modest, well-proportioned room lined along one side by windows and a long bench, the gallery provides a comfortable, relaxed environment in which to see and contemplate art. Appropriately, the art shown here has a conceptual base and meditative edge related to nature, portrait repre-

6 | The Mayor Gallery

⬡ | 22a Cork St, W1X 1HB
020-7734-3558 f: 7494-1377
artnet.com/mayor.html
mayor.gallery@virgin.net
Mon–Fri, 10–5:30; Sat, 10–1
tube: Piccadilly Circus

Dating back to 1925, the Mayor Gallery was the first art gallery on Cork Street. It introduced many modern masters to Britain, including those associated with Dada and Surrealism. The gallery is still a surrealist stronghold (incomparable in terms of its holdings and knowledge of British Surrealism), though it also has a penchant for Pop art and 1950s British painting with a kitchen-sink sort of gritty realism expressing an attitude somewhat like the Beat poets or characters in *Look Back in Anger*. Depictions of working-class, postwar culture presented from a socialist point of view are favored though an exhibition featuring a playful, ribald installation by a contemporary artist may occur simultaneously.

Recent exhibitions: *Ivor Abrahams— Exits and Entrances, Bank—Dead Life, Pauline Boty—The Only Blond in the World, Antony Donaldson, Jean Hélion, Georgie Hopton & Tanya Ling, Marina Karella, Man Ray, Jane Mulfinger,*

Patrick O'Reilly—The Broken Wing, Grace Pailthorpe & Reuben Mednikoff, Portraits—In Honor of the 30th Anniversary of Mr. Chow, Thierry Renard, Victor Skrebneski, Surrealism in Britain, Tom Wesselmann.

7 | BCA (Boukamel Contemporary Art)

9 Cork St, W1X 1PD
020-7734-6444 f: 7287-1740
www.bca-gallery.com
BCA@netcomuk.co.uk
Mon–Fri, 10–5; Sat, 10–1
tube: Piccadilly Circus

Through its previous affiliation with the Raab Gallery in Berlin, BCA established itself as the London showplace of German neo-expressionist painting. The gallery also shows European artists who emerged during the mid-1970s. Artists: Elvira Bach, Philip Braham, Luciano Castelli, Sandro Chia, Francesco Clemente, Ken Currie, Hélène Delprat, Rainer Fetting, K. H. Hödicke, Markus Lüpertz, Joumana Mourad, E. R. Nele, Cyril Olannier, Ernesto Tatafiore, Gerard Traquandi.

8 | Entwistle Gallery

6 Cork St, W1X 2EE
020-7734-6440 f: 7734-7966
Mon–Fri, 10–5:30; Sat, 11–4:30
monica@entwistle.net
tube: Piccadilly Circus

Entwistle may give the impression of a Madison Avenue gallery owing to its well-polished, upscale appearance, but the work shown here is venturesome, cutting-edge art mainly by the young generation of British and European upstarts. If you're curious about one of the latest rubrics, the so-called neurotic realism, ask to see some paintings by Nicky Hoberman. Her images of sweet but coy children, skillfully delineated with supple and wiry contours and colored with rosy and acidic tones, are intensely expressive, all the more so because they are in compressed or vacuous settings and suggestive poses or odd groupings.

Artists: Sue Arrowsmith, Charles Avery, Jason Brooks, Nicole Eisenman, Paul Finnegan, Luke Gottelier, Siobhán Hapaska, Nicky Hoberman, Edward Lipski, Peter Newman, Tim Sheward, Tomoko Takahashi, James White. Recent exhibitions: Holding Court (international sculpture), Painting Lab (British painting), Anselm Kiefer—Works on Paper.

Nicky Hoberman exhibition, 1998

9 | Atrium Bookshop

5 Cork St, W1X 1PB
020-7495-0073 f: 7409-7417
bookshop@atrium.co.uk
Mon–Fri, 10–6; Sat, 10–4
tube: Piccadilly Circus

If you're searching for a specific art book or just want to poke around and see the gamut of British publications, this is the perfect place. Book addicts should beware that they'll undoubtedly discover stacks of unknown gems and lose all sense of time when they start sifting through the tightly packed shelves. Don't despair if perchance you can't find what you're after here. London—and the entire realm of Great Britain—has incredible bookstores, many with mind-boggling selections in terms of both quantity and quality.

10 | Helly Nahmad Contemporary

2 Cork St, W1X 1PB
020-7494-3200 f: 7494-3355
gallery@hellynahmad.ndirect.co.uk
Mon–Fri, 10-6; Sat, 10–1
tube: Piccadilly Circus

Unlike the modest size of many London galleries, this one has an extralarge space at street level and a second expanse below. More like a museum than a commercial gallery, it presents a single exhibition for a full season or two months. The shows are often grand retrospectives of major 20th-century artists, mainly modern masters. However, a spring 1999 exhibition featured five of the most radical YBA stars.

Exhibitions typically comprise works of superb quality such as you might find in major museums. For example, the fall 1998 exhibition, *Picasso: Artist of the Century*, was an extraordinary survey of over 100 works from all of Picasso's periods, styles and media. It even included some choice objects never displayed before in public. This well-heeled

gallery (the Nahmad family of power-house Lebanese dealers has for years had a gallery in New York on Madison Avenue) also publishes catalogues to accompany its projects. Other exhibitions: *Damien Hirst, Angus Fairhurst, Gary Hume, Keith Coventry, Joan Miró, Marc Quinn; Modern Masters; The New Painting—New Visions in Modern Art (1835-1956).*

11 | Alan Cristea Gallery

31 Cork St, W1X 2NU
020-7439-1866 f: 7734-1549
Mon–Fri, 10–5:30; Sat, 10–1
tube: Piccadilly Circus

If you like prints and want to see masterful examples by artists of every stripe, unknown or renowned, this is the place to visit. The gallery shows work from the portfolios it publishes in addition to organizing historic exhibitions—such as its demonstration of Matisse's whole repertoire of printmaking techniques (summer 1998) or its comprehensive showing of prints by Josef Albers (April 1999).

In commissioning original prints, Cristea's aim is to have artists "create memorable 'images' which exploit the various printmaking media and which are literally inconceivable in any other form." This goal is exemplified in recent work by Gillian Ayres, Patrick Caulfield, Michael Craig-Martin, Jan Dibbets, Jim Dine, Richard Hamilton, Howard Hodgkin, Langlands & Bell, Ian McKeever, Lisa Milroy, Julian Opie and Mimmo Paladino. Particularly notable are Dibbets's *Ten Windows* and *Ten Cupolas*, two portfolios of gripping, contemplative photographs concerned with perception, light and form; and Hamilton's prints made with the computer and unprecedented combinations of media.

The large collection of prints in stock includes works by Georg Baselitz, Chuck Close, Hamish Fulton, David Hockney,

Donald Judd, Roy Lichtenstein, Bruce Nauman, Robert Mangold, David Salle, Kiki Smith, Frank Stella, Bill Woodrow.

12 | Bernard Jacobson Gallery

14A Clifford St, W1
020-7734-6440 f: 7495-8575
bernard-jacobson@slad.org
Mon–Fri, 10–6; Sat, 10–1
tube: Green Park, Piccadilly Circus

The emphasis here is on British painting from older generations steeped in traditions of modernism or figuration, though some contemporary art, albeit by established artists (British and otherwise) who gained recognition during the 1960s, is also shown. Exhibitions often present a mix of gallery artists and occasionally feature a non-gallery artist, like the fall 1999 showing of Jules Olitski paintings.

Artists: Ivor Abrahams, David Bomberg, Ivon Hitchens, Donald Judd, Phillip King, Peter Lanyon, Sol LeWitt, Ben Nicholson, Robert Rauschenberg, William Scott, Richard Smith, Derek Sprawson, Frank Stella, Graham Sutherland, William Tillyer, Marc Vaux, Glynn Williams.

13 | Rocket Gallery

13 Old Burlington St, W1X 1LA
020-7434-3043 f: 7434-3384
js.rocket@btinternet.com
Tues–Wed, Fri–Sat, 10–6;
Thurs, 10–8; closed Mon
tube: Piccadilly Circus

In its compact space, Rocket presents extremely varied exhibitions, ranging from abstract art in an utterly minimalist, reductive mode to a floor-to-ceiling installation of disquieting, garishly colored photographs depicting global products of modern consumerism. Thematic exhibitions—like *Young Photography, Childlocked, Chicago Hip, Hanging Out, LA Cool, Monomania*—are also part of

the program. With its international flair and support for artists who have not received widespread publicity, the gallery offers the chance to see unfamiliar work, often of a genre different from that in other local galleries. It's an uneven mix, some quite intriguing, some a bit sophomoric or too derivative. Don't overlook the closetlike inset in the wall near the office (named the "Photo Booth"), where photographs and photographic books are displayed.

Artists: Augusto Alves da Silva, Thomas Ankum, Brian Blow, Stefan Eberstadt, Fred Fehlau, Charlotte Gibson, Michelle Grabner, Charles Christopher Hill, Jus Juchtmans, Philip Mead, Douglas Melini, Martin Parr, Carter Potter, Edda Renouf, Terry Smith, Amy Wheeler, John Zinsser.

14 | Stephen Friedman Gallery

25–28 Old Burlington St, W1X 1LB
020-7494-1434 f: 7494-1431
Tues–Fri, 10–6; Sat, 11–5;
closed Mon
frie@dircon.co.uk
tube: Piccadilly Circus

This is one of the galleries that brought new life to the London scene in the mid-1990s by presenting a rich program of challenging artists from abroad who had not previously received due attention in Britain. The gallery also shows work by young British artists. Whether painting, sculpture, photography, video or mixed media, the art shown here expands the parameters of subject matter, expression, meaning and context, usually with subtlety rather than bombast.

Artists: Stephan Balkenhol, Geneviève Cadieux, Tom Claassen, Lucky DeBellevue, Peter Fraser, Tom Friedman, Kendell Geers, Betty Goodwin, Angela Grauerholz, Arturo Herrera, Jim Hodges, William Kentridge, Nikki S. Lee, Beatriz Milhazes, Yoshitomo Nara, Rivane

William Kentridge, *Weighing...and Wanting*, 1998

Neuenschwander, Vong Phaophanit, Richard Phillips, Alexander Ross, Michal Rovner, Yinka Shonibare, David Shrigley, Kerry Stewart, Kara Walker.

15 | Sadie Coles HQ

35 Heddon St, W1R 7LL
020-7434-2227 f: 7434-2228
Tues–Sat, 10–6; closed Mon
tube: Piccadilly Circus

Although only a stone's throw from the Cork St maze, Heddon St is inaccessible therein. You must walk around to Regent St and look for an inconspicuous entry into what seems to be a dead-end alley. Number 35 is close to the corner where the street turns, adding another short block to its existence.

An upbeat outlook and ambitious plans characterize this young gallery. Brashness, vigor, humor, satire and a no-holds-barred energy typify the art it favors. It's a gallery shaped by the late 1990s and infused with an irrepressible spirit of youthful adventure. In its brief history (open since April 1997), Sadie Coles has presented a stream of American and British upstarts, including some of the current notables from the emerging generation. The gallery also organizes off-site projects, like the *GCSE Examination* exhibition by Jake and Dinos Chapman in an scruffy East End storefront (actually the artists' house). Recent exhibitions: *Don Brown, Jeff Burton, Liz Craft & Pentti Monkkonen, John Currin, Keith Edmier, Angus Fairhurst, Saul Fletcher, Jim Lambie, Sarah Lucas, Danny Oates, Laura Owens, Simon Periton, Elizabeth Peyton, Richard Prince, Gregor Schneider, Nicola Tyson, Sue Williams, T. J. Wilcox, Andrea Zittel, Contemporary Fine Arts Berlin, Young Scottish Artists.*

16 | Gagosian Gallery

8 Heddon St, W1
20-7665-6645
tube: Piccadilly Circus

Gagosian Gallery, one of the big players in the art world with galleries in New York and Los Angeles, will open this space in the spring of 2000. The fact that this gallery has decided to establish a presence in London speaks strongly for the current importance of the city's art scene. The gallery's exhibitions here will be similar to its American program featuring such artists as Cecily Brown, Chris Burden, Francesco Clemente, Walter De Maria, Mark di Suvero, Eric Fischl, Ellen Gallagher, Frank Gehry, Maya Lin, Annette Messager, Ed Ruscha, David Salle, Richard Serra, Frank Stella, Phillip Taaffe, Robert Therrien, Cy Twombly, Andy Warhol, Elyn Zimmerman.

17 | Jason & Rhodes Gallery

4 New Burlington Pl, W1X 1SB
020-7434-1768 f: 7287-8841
jasonrhodes@compuserve.com
Mon–Fri, 10:30–6, Sat 10:30–1
tube: Piccadilly Circus,
Oxford Circus

Located within one of the confounding street patterns bearing the name Burlington, this gallery (begun in 1994) is committed to promoting British art and the British scene. If you ask about an artist, you're likely to get an impassioned response that goes well beyond sales talk or the latest critical gibberish. It's more the voice of a committed patron determined to realize an ideal and further the careers of particular artists, be they emerging, midlevel or historic modernists.

With its large, two-story space, the gallery can display an ample selection of art. Though photography is not a specialty, a fair number of exhibitions feature photographic work by young artists exploring imaginative approaches to the medium and distinctive imagery. Artists: Kate Belton, David Bomberg, Jesse Dale Cast, Calum Colvin, Robert Davies, Jessica Dismorr, Frank Dobson, Geraint Evans, William Gear, Eric Gill, Michael Ginsborg, John Greenwood, Paul Huxley, Chris Jones & Phillip Jones, Ansel Krut, John Minton, Eduardo Paolozzi, Marianne Ryan, Paul Storey, John Tunnard, John Virtue, Rose Warnock, Mark Wright, Brian Wynter.

18 | Timothy Taylor Gallery

1 Bruton Pl, W1X 7AD
020-7409-3344 f: 7409-1316
www.timothy-taylor-gallery.com
ttgal@zoo.co.uk
Mon–Fri, 10–6; closed Sat
tube: Bond Street, Green Park

Located on a tiny street off Bruton St just past the intersection with New Bond St.

After entering a cramped area and proceeding along a narrow corridor hung with art, the main gallery with its high-pitched roof and skylights is a pleasant surprise. The squarish room, amenable to about five paintings, does justice to the art and is a comfortable place that almost makes you forget you're in a commercial gallery in the middle of a bustling city. Most exhibitions are of midcareer and established stars from the international circuit, some of whom have had little visibility in London. Even if you are familiar with a particular artist's work, a visit here is well worth the effort since you'll probably see unusual or new compositions of notable quality.

Artists: Craigie Aitchison, Michael Andrews, Miquel Barcelo, Jose Bedia, Nick Danziger, Lucian Freud, Julio Galan, Philip Guston, Howard Hodgkin, Guillermo Kuitca, Jonathan Lasker, Henry Moore, Julian Schnabel, Sean Scully, Ray Smith, Juan Uslé.

19 | Hamiltons Gallery

13 Carlos Pl, W1Y 5AG
020-7449-9493 f: 7629-9919
www.art-online.com/hamiltons
nicole@hamiltonsgallery.demon.co.uk
Tues–Sat, 10–6; closed Mon
tube: Bond Street

The focus here is photography and the gallery shows many of the outstanding 20th-century masters in the field as well as established contemporary figures. Though you will see work by several artists who are experimenting with new techniques or radical imagery, this is not the main direction of the gallery. Artists: Richard Avedon, David Bailey, Lillian Bassman, Cecil Beaton, Alan Delaney, Robert Doisneau, Elliott Erwitt, Garry Fabian Miller, Huger Foote, Adam Fuss, Horst P. Horst, Kenro Izu, André Kertész, William Klein, Peter Lindbergh, Don McCullin, Frances McLaughlin, Robert Mapplethorpe, Duane Michals, Helmut Newton, Norman Parkinson, Malcom Pasley, Irving Penn, Herb Ritts, Willy Ronis, Tomio Seike, Hiroshi Sugimoto, Ellen Von Unwerth, Javier Vallhonrat, William Wegman, Joel-Peter Witkin.

20 | Gimpel Fils

3 Davies St, W1Y 1LG
020-7493-2488 f: 7629-5732
www.slad.org/gimpelfils
gimpel@compuserve.com
Mon–Fri, 10–5:30; Sat, 10–1
tube: Bond Street

Located a bit away from the Bond Street maze, this upscale, refined gallery with an impressive history dating back to 1946 is run by the fourth generation of Gimpel sons. The program follows a tradition of selling modern masters to finance and support contemporary art. Though this enabled the showing of vanguard work in the past, now exhibitions are rather conservative. Artists: Robert Adams, Gillian Ayres, Charles Beauchamp, Reg Butler, Alan Davie, Andrea Fisher, Pamela Golden, Albert Irvin, Peter Kennard, Peter Lanyon, Louis Le Brocquy, Antoni Malinowski, Bernard Meadows, Niki de Saint-Phalle, Christopher Stewart, Annelies Štrba, Jenny Watson.

21 | Jigsaw

architect: John PAWSON, 1996
126 New Bond St, W1
tube: Bond Street

This fashionable boutique with a fully glazed facade bears the markings of high minimalist design. Clearly, the architect wanted the store to have a clean, starkly luxurious image with the clothing barely visible behind tall, hand-etched acrylic screens positioned to create wide side aisles and a sequence of uniform, geometrized spaces down the center of the space. Unfortunately, the intended effect—and the presence of elegant walnut furnishings designed by Pawson—has been greatly diminished by displays of merchandise cluttering the walls, front and open areas. A nice feature is the lateral placement of a narrow double staircase going down to the lower level. It conserves space even as it adds airiness and a touch of grandeur to a basement space.

22 | Pleats Please (Issy Miyake)

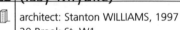

architect: Stanton WILLIAMS, 1997
20 Brook St, W1
tube: Bond Street

Miyake's boutiques are typically expressions of fine-tuned visual theater and this one is no exception. Should you walk by and cast an innocent glance inside, you'll probably be startled enough to inspect the scene more closely and perhaps enter, if only to experience the ambience of such a serenely seductive, nearly empty environment. It's an utterly unostentatious, tiny, narrow shop in which every inch of space is carefully determined but unenclosed. Your eyes wander freely, following contours and surfaces while stopping to see things in isolation or to view them from various angles. Architectural details, like the steel floor on the right and the glass shelves floating above a cutout segment in the floor (a transparent juncture between the ground and lower levels of the shop), serve as complements to the merchandise. Only one or two mannequins in the window, an array of thinly distributed clothes hung from a suspended pole along the right wall and a few articles sparsely laid out on the shelves present Miyake's designs. And yet the display conveys the nature of his famous pleated garments with their streamlined, simple shapes that open out into rhythmic flows of movement through space.

Anthony
23 d'Offay Gallery

9, 21 (ground and 1st floors), 23 (1st floor), 24 Dering St, W1R 9AA
020-7499-4100 f: 7492-4443
www.doffay.com
Mon–Fri, 10–5:30; Sat, 10–1
tube: Bond Street, Oxford Circus

Like Cork Street, Dering Street—a narrow T-shaped street with easily missed entries from both New Bond and Oxford Streets—is a major gallery zone. Most particularly, it houses the five exhibition spaces of the Anthony d'Offay Gallery—the Big Daddy of London's contemporary art scene. Here you will see some amazing exhibitions of new and historic work by leading art-world figures from both current and past eras. At times a single artist occupies several of the gallery spaces; sometimes two or three artists have one-person shows simultaneously; alternatively, there are group shows that provocatively bring together the work of several renowned artists.

D'Offay's operation is nothing short of extraordinary. It embraces artists from all over the globe working in a diversity of media and disparate conceptual and stylistic orientations. If you want to see work by top-notch British artists, ask about Liza May Post or Rachel Whiteread. Even if you can just see installation photos of Whiteread's 1998 show at the d'Offay Gallery, which featured exploratory sculptures relating to the Viennese Holocaust Memorial she designed, you'll get a good sense of her work and the incredible nature of the exhibitions presented here.

Artists: Carl Andre, Georg Baselitz, Joseph Beuys, Christian Boltanski,

Rachel Whiteread, Untitled (*Book Corridors*), 1997–1998

Francesco Clemente, Ellen Gallagher, Gilbert & George, Richard Hamilton, Howard Hodgkin, Jasper Johns, Ellsworth Kelly, Anselm Kiefer, Yves Klein, Willem de Kooning, Jeff Koons, Jannis Kounellis, Roy Lichtenstein, Richard Long, Bruce McLean, Mario Merz, Tatsuo Miyajima, Reinhard Mucha, Bruce Nauman, Gabriel Orozco, Richard Patterson, Sigmar Polke, Liza May Post, Gerhard Richter, Ed Ruscha, Kiki Smith, Smith/Stewart, James Turrell, Cy Twombly, Bill Viola, Andy Warhol, Boyd Webb, Lawrence Weiner, Rachel Whiteread.

23 | Annely Juda Fine Art

23 Dering St, W1R 9AA
020-7629-7578 f: 7491-2139
ajfa@annelyjudafineart.co.uk
Mon–Fri, 10–6; Sat, 10–1
tube: Bond Street, Oxford Circus

The gallery occupies the 4th and 5th floors showing two different exhibitions at once. The space on the top floor, designed for its previous tenant by the illustrious Japanese architect Arata Isozaki, has wonderful light from above and a spare but pleasing layout.

From its active participation in European art fairs and its trove of early 20th-century art—mainly abstraction, especially Russian Constructivism—this gallery has established an international reputation. Objects from the collection of modern masters are shown annually, usually in a summer exhibition. Otherwise, the gallery presents a program of contemporary work, mainly by veteran abstract, minimal or conceptually oriented artists.

Artists: Roger Ackling, Anthony Caro, Martyn Chalk, Alan Charlton, Eduardo Chillida, Christo and Jeanne-Claude, Prunella Clough, Nathan Cohen, Gloria Friedmann, Hamish Fulton, Katsura Funakoshi, Gotthard Graubner, Alan Green, Nigel Hall, Noriyuki Haraguchi, Christine Hatt, Werner Haypeter, Al Held, David Hockney, Gottfried Honneger,

Malcolm Hughes, Yoshikuni Iida, Menashe Kadishman, Peter Kalkhof, Tadashi Kawamata, Leon Kossoff, Darren Lago, Edwina Leapman, Catherine Lee, Ciaran Lennon, John McLaughlin, Michael Michaeledes, François Morellet, David Nash, Alan Reynolds, Yoshishige Saito, Toko Shinoda, Yuko Shiraishi.

24 | Anthony Reynolds Gallery

5 Dering St, W1R 9AB
020-7491-0621 f: 7495-2374
Tues–Sat, 10–6; closed Mon
tube: Bond Street, Oxford Circus

Counter to the impression you may get from the smallish, somewhat scruffy, low-key nature of this gallery's space, Anthony Reynolds has a long history and steadfast commitment to supporting adventurous, radical art. Among the most interesting exhibitions are those presenting work that deftly raises awareness of unsettling realities and disquieting practices within contemporary society. Though you might assume this art will be somber and didactic, quite the contrary; it tends to be assertive, visually gripping, sensorial, surreal, if not heavily laced with wry wit or satirical irreverence. Projects by Richard Billingham, Steve McQueen, Georgina Starr or Mark Wallinger are especially strong exemplars.

In actuality, the gallery shows a wide range of art with no single approach dominating. To be responsive to new things, it keeps its exhibition schedule flexible and open. It also takes special pride in its spontaneous, thematic shows, presented every now and again. One such show came about because Reynolds serendipitously discovered there were a fair number of artists named Keith. He therefore organized What's in a Name—a group exhibition whose only common thread was the arbitrary fact of a shared personal name.

Keith Farquhar exhibition, 1998

Be sure to check out the lower level, where you'll usually find a few additional objects on display as well as a very crowded office area often alive with art-world conversation. Should you join in or ask a question, you're likely to learn a lot about what's going on in London. Artists: Eija-Liisa Ahtila, Mark Alexander, David Austen, Richard Billingham, Ian Breakwell, Tony Carter, Erik Dietman, Keith Farquhar, Leon Golub, Paul Graham, Georg Herrold, Thomas Lawson, Matthew McCaslin, Steve McQueen, Andrew Mansfield, Alain Miller, Lucia Nogueira, Susana Solano, Nancy Spero, Georgina Starr, Jon Thompson, Amikam Toren, Keith Tyson, Mark Wallinger, John Wilkins.

25 | William Pye

Christos, 1993
Barrett St and St.
Christopher's Pl, W1
tube: Bond Street

This tree-laden mews one block north of Oxford Street (or two hops east of Selfridge's) is a delightful place to relax on a pleasant day. Undisturbed by traffic, you can window shop in the boutiques or luncheon at one of the café-restaurants that take over the pavement. You can also sit on the marble seats surrounding the small fountain by William Pye. Composed of bell-shaped elements with water flowing from them into drainage grates at ground level, the sculpture's simple, soothing design is perfectly suited to the environment.

26 | Laurent Delaye Gallery

22 Barrett St, W1M 5HP
020-7629-5905 f: 7491-1248
delayegallery@clara.net
Tues–Fri, 10–6; Sat, 12–6;
closed Mon
tube: Bond Street

Look carefully for the stairway door alongside the storefront and go up to the 1st floor. The gallery is a very small room with display space for only a few works of art. But selections are choice and the objects shown would hold their own anywhere. The gallery tends to specialize in figurative or pictorial

James Rielly, *Still Life*, 1998

St. James's–Trafalgar Square

The Economist Building

1

🏢 architects: Alison and Peter SMITHSON, 1961–64

🚇 25 St. James's St, SW1
020-7830-7105
daily, 10–8
admission: free
tube: Green Park

You can enter from St. James's, Ryder or Bury Sts.

work—the kind riven with provocative underpinnings and narrative, surreal, erotic or emotional potency. One-person shows focus on UK artists though group shows include intriguing newcomers from elsewhere.

If you're not familiar with the work of James Rielly, check it out. He makes very sketchy-looking paintings of children, teenagers and families, often as group composites with single figures or faces on separate canvases. At first, the images seem calm, subdued, withdrawn. Yet there's always something lurking beneath the surface—expressions of pain, suffering, guilt, menace, fear, vice. The combination of superficial blandness and deep psychological penetration gives the depictions a gnawing presence. It's a masterful blend of countercurrents taking advantage of seminal aspects of both abstraction and representation.

Artists: Mark Dean, Machiko Edmondson, Paul Emmanuel, Simon English, Milo Garcia, Rut Blees Luxemburg, Chad McCail, Wendy McMurdo, James Rielly.

This project furnished a model in post–World War II London of how a modern high-rise could be compatible with the scale and character of existing 18th-century buildings. Monolithic towers and slab-on-podium forms had already begun to desecrate London's cityscape, so the Smithsons' approach was a welcome alternative.

What they did was to locate the three components of the project—offices for *The Economist* newspaper, apartments and a bank—in separate buildings around a central plaza. Because the plaza is elevated above street level and provides outlets and vistas to adjoining streets, it adds open public space that is readily accessible but somewhat secluded. And although the three buildings are differing heights—the 17-story one is set back and the outer ones echo the height of neighboring structures—they share a common design articulated by its oblique-angled corners and a facade of single-pane, variously sized windows set in a grid framework covered with a light gray rough stone.

The exhibitions, which are installed in the lobby of the main building, vary greatly in their focus and content. Occasionally, they feature art or archi-

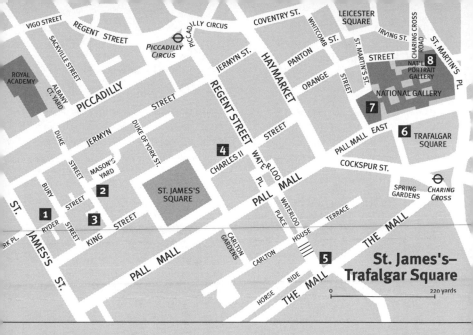

St. James's–
Trafalgar Square

0 ————— 220 yards

1. The Economist Building
2. 11 Duke Street
3. Jay Jopling/White Cube
4. Emily Tsingou Gallery
5. Institute of Contemporary Arts
6. Fourth Plinth Sculpture
7. National Gallery
8. National Portrait Gallery

tectural objects. Sometimes sculptures are also displayed outdoors in the plaza. For example, during the fall of 1998, a delightful group of monumental bronzes by Barry Flanagan—variations on his signature rabbit imagery—enlivened the spaces between and around the buildings.

The ARCHITECTURE FOUNDATION (020-7839-9389), at the corner of Ryder and Bury Streets, is a goldmine of information and illustrations on most of the proposed, in-process or recently completed buildings in London. Their computer databases are a great resource.

2 | 11 Duke Street

⌂ 11 Duke St, SW1Y 6BN
020-7976-2733 f: 7976-2744
duke@aol.com
Mon–Fri, 10–6 only for
special exhibitions
tube: Green Park

You may wonder if you're at the right address since it looks like a proper, old town house. Climbing up the wood-paneled stairwell, landing at the door of a minuscule office laden with book-shelves only to find a maze of small res-idential-looking, empty rooms does little to assure you that you're in an art gallery rather than a barrister's sanctum or a set for a detective film. In fact, this gallery mainly functions privately and is open to the public only once or twice a year when it showcases a few objects by hot-shot artists. The works are from the sec-ondary market (i.e., consigned or pur-chased for resale) but tend to be superb examples of adventurous creativity, well worth seeing. Check in the gallery list-ings to see if there's an exhibition.

Artists in past exhibitions: Wim Delvoye, Damien Hirst, Jeff Koons, Robert Mapplethorpe, Raymond Pettibone, Charles Ray, Cindy Sherman, Andy Warhol, Christopher Wool.

Jay Jopling/
3 White Cube

⊡ 44 Duke St, 2nd floor
St. James's, SW1 Y 6DD
020-7930-5373 f: 7930-9973
www.whitecube.com
Fri–Sat, 12–6; closed Mon–Thurs
tube: Green Park

You don't expect to find a radical, contemporary art gallery in the midst of a neighborhood populated by old master galleries displaying rare coins in velvet-lined cases in the window and gilded-framed marine and horse paintings on wainscoted, dark oak walls. Nor would you think that the hottest vanguard gallery in London would be identified by an insipid signboard. Odder still, you enter a commonplace door, climb a scruffy, narrow staircase and come to a tiny room, barely big enough to hold one or two paintings. Soon you realize this is it. Nothing big and splashy, not even a chic space for the receptionist who sits across the hall in a compressed, dentist-office-like cubicle crowded with file cabinets.

Marc Quinn, *Reincarnate*, 1999

Joplin has in fact turned the tables on the conventional gallery concept by having a small "project room" instead of a grand "showroom." Rather than present numerous objects in a museum or merchandising format, the aim of White Cube is to promote the close viewing of and personal experience with a particular artist's work in a space that is literally a white cube. "The central concern when establishing the program was to create an intimate space in which an invited artist might present a single important work of art or a coherent body of work within a very focused environment." This approach is similar to that of Gallery Pièce Unique in Paris but otherwise it stands apart.

In its short existence (it opened in May 1993), White Cube has both catapulted some of the most creative (and provocation-oriented) young talent to fame and presented some of the best new work by underrecognized, midcareer international artists.

Gallery artists: Darren Almond, Itai Doron, Tracey Emin, Antony Gormley, Marcus Harvey, Mona Hatoum, Damien Hirst, Gary Hume, Sarah Lucas, Sarah Morris, Marc Quinn, Marcus Taylor, Sam Taylor-Wood, Gavin Turk, Cerith Wyn Evans. Exhibitions: Franz Ackermann, Nobuyoshi Araki, Ashley Bickerton, Sophie Calle, Jake and Dinos Chapman, Gregory Crewdson, Carroll Dunham, Brian Eno, Angus Fairhurst, Peter Fischli/ David Weiss, Anna Gaskell, Nan Goldin, Gary Hill, Michael Joo, Clay Ketter, Suchan Kinoshita, Sean Lander, Damian Loeb, Esko Männikkö, Walter Niedermayr, Jack Pierson, Lari Pittman, Richard Prince, Paul Ramirez Jonas, Doris Salcedo, Christian Schumann, Glen Seator, Jessica Stockholder, Hiroshi Sugimoto, Luc Tuymans, Patrick van Caekenbergh, Jeff Wall, Terry Winters.

In April 2000, White Cube will expand to a second location in Hoxton Square (see p. 105). Finally, the gallery will have room to present large work and more inclusive exhibitions. The Duke Street gallery will remain as a project space.

4 | Emily Tsingou Gallery

⬒ 10 Charles II St, SW1Y 4AA
020-7839-5320 f: 7839-5321
Tues–Sat, 10–6; closed Mon
tube: Piccadilly Circus

Located between Regent Street and St. James's Square, this young gallery is carving out its territory by representing artists not shown elsewhere in Britain. Especially the foreign artists (from Europe and America), who have attained considerable recognition abroad (even cult status), have received only minimal attention in London.

The gallery tends to favor photographic work—the big, brightly colored kind—with images mainly pertaining to the body, urban street life, sex, violence, seduction, youth, identity, alienation from societal norms and black humor. Curiously, the expressive and thematic zone that the artists explore here is not so different from that of the YBA, yet the sensibility is quite different. Most exhibitions are monographic, and the occasional group show mixes gallery artists with others pursuing similar ideas. For instance, a quirky interpretation of intransigence and repetition was the subject of *Time after Time*, which included work by Michael Ashkin, Vanessa Beecroft, Henry Bond, Larry Clark, Fischli and Weiss, Karen Kilimnik, Martin Kippenberger, Ugo Rondinone, Jim Shaw.

The gallery location may be a bit off the beaten track but you won't be sorry if you go the extra few blocks to check it out. Artists: Michael Ashkin, Henry Bond, Kate Bright, Larry Clark, Gregory Crewdson, Lukas Duwenhögger, Karen Kilimnik, Elke Krystufek, Peter Pommerer, Collier Schorr.

Institute of Contemporary Arts (ICA)

5

📠 The Mall, SW1Y 5AH
020-7930-3647 f: 7873-0051
🎥 www.ica.org.uk
info@ica.org.uk
📖 galleries: daily, 12–7:30. other areas: Mon, 12–11; Tues–Sat, 12–1am; Sun, 12–10:30
admission: £1.50 weekdays, £2.50 Sat and Sun
tube: Charing Cross, Piccadilly Circus

You can easily walk right past the ICA and miss it. That's because there's no eye-catching signage at its inconspicuous entrance located at the end of a long, one-story stone platform topped by a balustrade and having the aura of a security wall. (It's actually the platform of the terraces built onto Carlton House—George IV's residence—by the famed architect John Nash in 1827–32.) Look for a simple double door with ICA printed on a window panel and you will be at one of the stalwart (it began in 1947), cutting-edge art centers in the world. More than just showing daring, new art, the ICA brazenly and continuously reconstitutes its mission, repeatedly challenging the way art is presented and conceived. With its blank-slate definition of "art," the ICA embraces all sorts of objects, technologies, performances, installations, projects, activities and ventures.

If you're accustomed to a museum ambience for viewing art, be prepared for a change. The layout has a makeshift character, and a casual, unpretentious atmosphere prevails. As much as this is a place to see art, it's also a place to relax, hang out, meet friends or sit and think. Almost every inch of space has been resourcefully appropriated as an exhibition space. These include the lobby; a roomy, high-

Steve McQueen, *Deadpan*, 1997

ceilinged gallery off the lobby; a long hallway ("the concourse") leading back to the bar-café; the bar-café itself; a theater; two conference/event halls; several galleries situated around the top of a steep balustered staircase; and a cinema. Beware: since the path to the upper galleries is indirect and somewhat hidden down a corridor leading away from the café, you can unknowingly neglect part or all of an exhibition.

Exhibitions are either one-person, group or theme projects focused on work by innovative artists, designers, architects and filmmakers. Whereas many art institutions claim to show avant-guard art, the ICA truly pays attention to emerging currents, often presenting the first glimmers of future trends from artists at home and abroad. (The ICA played a role in developing the YBA craze by giving Gary Hume and the Chapmans their first "museum" shows.) Don't be surprised to see work that seems experimental or conceptually unresolved. The ICA doesn't shy away from presenting the exploratory stage wherein a certain rawness exists together with a creative potency. It also gives artists considerable latitude, sanctioning many on-site projects that are not object-based. For example, in a 1998 exhibition, *Surfacing: Contemporary Drawing*, Richard Reylond created a huge drawing that sprawled across the entrance door onto the walls of the lobby. Informative catalogues—ranging from small brochures to well-illustrated books—accompany most exhibitions.

In addition to its gallery exhibitions, the ICA supports a world-class Cinémathéque that screens three to four classic or new films daily; an exciting performance and lecture schedule; and Club Nights featuring informal, cross-arts, audiovisual events. Also contributing to the mix of activities is the New Media Centre, a collaboration with Sun Microsystems. It makes the latest digital technology available to the ICA, putting it at the forefront of experimentation with yet another realm of creativity.

A distinctive aspect of the ICA is the central place occupied by the bar-café. Physically, it encompasses an expansive, two-leveled space, larger in scale than the galleries. More significant, it is a meeting, work and entertainment space, where artists, students and all sorts of people come, whether or not they plan to see an exhibition or attend an event. Like everything else at the

ICA, the ambience here is extremely low-key and comfortable.

Be sure to include time at the bookshop, located in the front lobby. (It's open 12–9.) It's a fabulous place to browse with a rich selection of magazines and museum catalogues as well as books on film, video, new media and critical theory. A good plan is to visit the bookstore to get something to read while you savor some quiet moments or people-watch in the bar-café. Better still, plan to stay awhile and go to an evening event.

Recent exhibitions: *Assuming Positions, Miriam Bäckström, Belladonna, Vija Celmins, Chapmanworld, Crash, Die Young Stay Pretty, The Golden Age (Johnny Spencer, Neo Rauch, Graham Fagen), Urs Fischer, Imaginaria '99—Digital Art, Rem Koolhaas, Steve McQueen, Billy Name, Gabriel Orozco, Pandaemonium, Private Streak—Fashion Meets Science, Thomas Scheibitz, Stealing Beauty—British Design, T. J. Wilcox.*

6 | Fourth Plinth Sculpture

Trafalgar Sq

Marking the actual center of London from which distances to all places in the UK are measured, Trafalgar Square is a large open area invariably congested by buses, tourists and pigeons. In the middle is Nelson's Column and at the four corners are massive granite plinths, three of which bear bronze statues. The fourth (near the entrance to the Sainsbury Wing of the National Gallery) has remained empty for more than 150 years despite various attempts to set something permanent on it.

Currently a competition, administered by the Royal Society of Art and Sculpture at Goodwood, is trying to place a contemporary work of art on the plinth. Three finalists—Mark WALLINGER, Rachel WHITEREAD, Bill WOODROW—have been chosen. Each artist will install his or her proposed work in situ for six to nine months. At the end of this period, a committee will decide which work will be permanently installed—assuming financial issues and politics don't get the upper hand. It remains to be seen whether the current effort will fare any better than in the past or if public opinion will decry the official choice.

On July 21, 1999, the first work, *Ecce Homo* by Mark Wallinger, was unveiled. Unlike the grandiose, pompous statues on most monuments, this one is life size and actually looks quite tiny in comparison to the mammoth base on which he is positioned. Moreover, the image of Christ appears very humble and human, even vulnerable as he stands at the edge of the plinth with his hands behind his back. Apart from the crown

Mark Wallinger, *Ecce Homo*, 1999

of gilded barbed wire and loincloth, he's a relatively conventional-looking man with a clean-shaven face and muscular body. The image recalls the scene when Pontius Pilate thrust Christ before the crowd declaring "Ecce homo" ("Behold the man") and then ordered his execution. But here the figure also has the guise of a modern man and we are implicated as spectators in his drama.

By depicting Christ in this manner as the subject of a civic monument, Wallinger provokes thinking about contemporary values and the conventions of public sculpture. He raises questions about the way Western civilization has tended to aggrandize, transform, elevate, distort, manipulate, emotionalize and dramatically re-create figures considered to be leaders (spiritual or political) and/or heroes. The shock of Wallinger's sculpture is not so much what it is but what it's not. As in most all his art—as when he bought a thoroughbred racehorse and called it *A Real Work of Art*—Wallinger cynically and cleverly confronts us with our perceptions and beliefs. His choice of Christ for the Trafalgar plinth is particularly telling in this era of millennial hype. The year 2000 ostensibly marks the date of Christ's birth, yet one is hard pressed to find the slightest reference to this event in any of the gala programs and commemorative literature associated with the millennium.

In January 2000, a giant bronze titled *Regardless of History* by Bill Woodrow will take its place on the plinth. This sculpture features a leafless tree and human head seemingly crushed by a book. According to the artist, it refers to "the never-ending cyclical relationship between civilizations, knowledge and the forces of nature."

The final entry is Rachel Whiteread's upside-down cast of the plinth. Constructed in semitransparent resin, its purity and elegance contrast dramatically with the cold, bland solidity of the stone base. Though it calls atten-

tion to architectonic form, it also has an enigmatic, poetic aura that is especially potent in an urban setting.

7 | National Gallery

architects (Sainsbury Wing):
VENTURI SCOTT BROWN, 1986–91
Trafalgar Sq, WC2N 5DN
0207-839-3321
www.nationalgallery.org.uk
information@ng-london.org.uk
Mon–Tues, Thurs–Sat, 10–6;
Wed, 10–8; Sun, 12–6
admission: free, special exhibitions
£5.50/3.50
tube: Charing Cross

This is one of the great museums of the world, housing a staggering collection of Western European paintings spanning the years 1260–1900. (Art created after the cutoff point is in the Tate Britain and Tate Modern.) You will, however, find examples of 20th-century—even contemporary—art in some of the special exhibitions held here. A recent instance was *Mirror Image*, a superb show examining the way artists from different periods—including Lucian Freud and Helen Chadwick—expressed their fascination with the effects of light and reflective surfaces.

If you're intent on focusing on recent creativity, spend time perusing the new Sainsbury Wing, located to the left side of the main building. It and contemporary architecture became the subject of heated debate in 1984 when a glass-and-steel design won the second competition for the extension to the National Gallery—a 19th-century stone building. Prince Charles revved up the controversy by stigmatizing the proposal as "a monstrous carbuncle on the face of a much-loved and elegant friend." (For those not familiar with royal jargon, Webster's defines *carbuncle* as "a painful local purulent inflammation of the skin and deeper tissues with multiple openings for the discharge of pus and usually necrosis and sloughing of dead tissue.") The acrimonious battle ended with the cancellation of the project. But a year later, enabled by a funding offer from the Sainsbury brothers, another competition brought forth a postmodern design by the Philadelphia architects Robert Venturi and Denise Scott Brown. This proposal, finally, got implemented. As might be expected after so much rancor, the building has a rather lackluster exterior, so pseudo-classicized that it seamlessly fits with the other dull facades bordering Trafalgar Square.

Abiding by the thesis of his influential book, *Complexity and Contradiction in Architecture (1966)*, Venturi designed a structure with five different styles that merge, interpenetrate and oppose one another, sometimes set apart as hyperbolic forms or ironic, superfluous remnants from the past. Borrowing the architectural citations from nearby buildings and spicing them up with a few modernist and vernacular features (the black glazed wall, skylighted roof, billboardlike display of the museum's name, etc.), the Sainsbury Wing exemplifies the eclectic discontinuity of postmodern aesthetics.

In contrast, the galleries (located at the top of the grand, polished marble staircase) are perfectly proportioned, logically organized and totally orchestrated to enhance the art and facilitate a visitor's experience. Care taken with vistas from room to room and the architectural framing of paintings, not to mention the lighting, are but some of the outstanding elements. In addition to the galleries, the Sainsbury Wing includes various 20th-century museum accouterments—a theater, souvenir-and-book shop, restaurant and counter for renting portable CD sound guides. There is also a 21st-century domain: the Micro Gallery where you can (courtesy of Microsoft) sit at a workstation and see the entire National Gallery collection without ever looking at a "real" work of art!

National Portrait Gallery

8

🏛 2 St. Martin's Pl, WC2H 0HE
0207-306-0055 f: 7306-0056
📖 www.npg.org.uk
Mon–Sat, 10–6; Sun, 12–6
admission: free
tube: Charing Cross, Leicester Square

The National Portrait Gallery abuts the National Gallery on its right and back sides. The main entrance is just off the northeast corner of Trafalgar Sq.

Even if you're not particularly interested in seeing likenesses of famous British men and women, you're likely to enjoy this museum's display. The focus on famous people encapsulates the country's history and culture in a thought-provoking way, often reconfiguring events and emphases. Hopefully the staid aura will disappear when the new wing (designed by Jeremy DIXON and Edward JONES) is completed. It will provide additional display space, a new entrance hall, rooftop restaurant, café, bookshop and lecture hall.

Late-20th-century portraits are located on the ground floor, organized in groupings: Politics and the Establishment from 1960; Public Figures; Science, Technology and Business; and Arts. The selection is uneven in terms of artistic quality and quite curious in terms of the people represented. Among the contemporary portraits are photographs of rock and film stars by Richard Avedon and Annie Leibowitz, a painting of Sir David Webster by David Hockney and images of Joan Collins, Mick Jagger and Queen Elizabeth by Andy Warhol. From time to time, special exhibitions in the photography and Wolfson Galleries also feature work by contemporary artists or about the contemporary era (e.g., *Icons of Pop*). In addition, the museum has commissioned some video portraits, such as a mesmerizing 11-monitor installation showing the swimming skills of Olympic gold medalist Duncan Goodhew (by Marty St. James and Anne Wilson, 1990).

Covent Garden –Soho

1 Embankment Place, Charing Cross Station

architect: Terry FARRELL, 1987–90
Charing Cross, WC2 IJ77
tube: Embankment

Like several other railroad stations in London, Charing Cross has redeveloped its site by taking advantage of air rights. This has entailed replacing a 19th-century shed by office buildings suspended over the platforms. Here the offices have added significance since the architecture contributes a monumental presence to the riverfront and London skyline at one end and a prominent frontage to a major city intersection at the other. Depending on the direction of your approach, you'll perceive the structure as a massive, basically symmetrical edifice with an arched, central expanse set between four corner towers; or an irregular conglomerate variously clad in granite, concrete, brick and glass with its flat surfaces interspersed with thin steel tension cables and interrupted by quirky elements— such as giant circular hollows cut into walls and green-painted steel (a pseudo-copper effect) and glass canopies, balconies and room extensions projecting from them.

The best way to get a sense of the eccentricities of Farrell's design is to walk toward Embankment Place from the footpath on the Hungerford Railway Bridge. (The path connects to South Bank Centre across the Thames.) An initial perspective of grandeur shifts dramatically when the walkway abruptly ends, affording a glimpse of greenery in Victoria Embankment Gardens, access onto Villiers Street—a bustling, oldfangled side road lined with storefront eateries—and zigzig passage into the interior expanse of the station's main concourse. You'll experience radical scale changes and odd juxtapositions, like the pairing of classical references with an industrial aesthetic. In good postmodern form, Farrell borrowed many features from neighboring buildings. He aimed to contextualize his design by recognizing the potency of stylistic multiplicity and disunity.

2 Courtauld Gallery

Somerset House, Strand,
WC2R 0RN
020-7873-2526 f: 7873-2589
Mon–Sat, 10–6; Sun, 2–6
admission: £4/£2, free after 5
tube: Covent Garden, Temple

You won't find any contemporary art here, but you should squeeze in a visit if only to refresh your mind about historic precedents. The Courtauld is chock-full of gems, including major paintings by Cranach, Bellini, Botticelli, Tintoretto, Rubens, Gainsborough as well as numerous outstanding works by Manet (e.g., *Bar at the Folies-Bergère*), the impressionist and post-impressionist masters. A recent renovation and reinstallation has placing more art on view with improved lighting, though many Londoners complain that the display is too crowded and stark.

3 Royal Opera House

redevelopment: Jeremy DIXON and
Edward JONES, 1997–99
Covent Garden, WC2E 9DD
020-7240-1200 f: 7212-9502
tube: Covent Garden

The prime location of opera houses on a main city thoroughfare or at the apex of vistas and converging avenues aptly coheres with the pomp and spectacle of operatic performance. In the case of London's Royal Opera House (ROH), situated on a back street in the midst of a

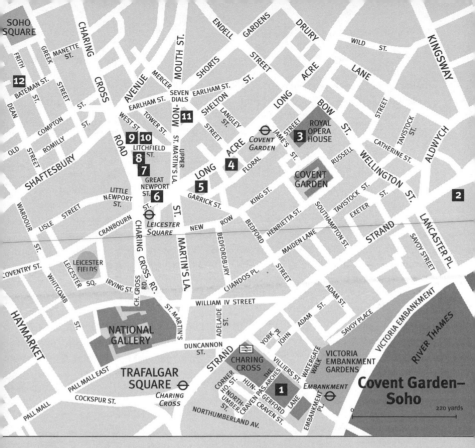

1. Embankment Place, Charing Cross Station
2. Courtauld Gallery
3. Royal Opera House
4. Stanfords Maps + Books
5. Dillons Art Bookshop
6. Photographers' Gallery
7. Ian Shipley Bookshop
8. Zwemmer Media Arts
9. Zwemmer Arts Bookshop
10. The Ivy
11. Comyn Ching Triangle
12. Frith Street Gallery

densely occupied, labyrinthine neighborhood, the siting is decidedly nonmajestic, indeed quite mundane. Even its new size—it underwent massive renovations and expansion,1997–99—has not set it apart as an imposing entity, largely because its heterogeneous, partite makeup undercuts its physical presence. A "street" arcade cutting through the building further accentuates the integration of the structure into its surroundings, making it part of the urban context and enabling the lively atmosphere of Covent Garden to permeate its walls. Indeed, there were political battles during the construction about the opera house's role in the public realm. Particularly because of enormous cost overruns and administrative scandals, media attention focused on the inequity of a publicly subsidized venue for an art form associated with the rich. As a result, great attempts were made to assert how the opera and its new home were accessible to the general public. (Despite its name, the ROH is actually home to both the opera, its orchestra and chorus, and the Royal Ballet.)

If you go to Bow Street, you'll see the old stone building created by E. M.

BARRY, 1857–58 with its raised, six-column portico. Both the exterior and the beloved horseshoe auditorium were essentially kept intact during the recent redevelopment project. Around the corner and behind Barry's theater sits a white filigree cast-iron-and-glass enclosure whose sweeping, arch-shaped facade extends back as a barrel roof over an airy expanse of space. Although originally constructed as a place for selling flowers to operagoers (à la *My Fair Lady*), it became a storage for scenery after the site's roof was destroyed by fire in the 1950s. In its current incarnation as the social heart, refreshment center and auxiliary performance area within the new Opera House, the hall adds grandeur to the complex. Configured as a foyer with exalted escalators, it is also a passage zone. Besides providing access to the theater, it connects with a sequence of foyers leading to a covered open-air loggia overlooking the refurbished Covent Garden Piazza.

As is evident when you walk around the exterior, the ROH now fills the entire irregularly shaped block behind the original building. The expansion added a new ballet studio with seating for 200, a Studio Theater with 420 seats and enhanced rehearsal, storage, set, costume and broadcasting facilities. Other than an extension down Floral Street, added in 1982, all else was developed in the last few years by Dixon Jones. Going beyond the diversity of styles and materials in the existing structures, they exaggerated the premise of difference by borrowing various and variant architectural modes from disparate eras. For example, the facade on the piazza side appropriates 18th-century London stonework; an arcade of shops and restaurants in postmodern classicism distinguishes the frontage along Russell Street; and alignments of metal-framed windows and austere balcony extensions in modernist design articulate the outer wall on Floral Street.

Even if you don't attend a performance, you can see many of the interior spaces. Some are open to public use during the day and others can be visited on tours.

This area (and London as a city) is paradise for book lovers. Prepare to be overwhelmed by the availability of new and used books and the number of speciality bookstores. You're bound to find many enticing titles you've never seen before. Best to pace yourself so you don't spend all your money in the first store you visit!

4 Stanfords Maps & Books

12–14 Long Acre, WC2E 9LP
020-7240-3611 f: 7240-8171
Mon, Sat, 10–6; Tues–Fri, 9–7
buyers@stanfords.co.uk
tube: Covent Garden, Leicester Square

Should you need any sort of map, atlas, gazetteer or travel book, you'll find it and lots else in this amazing emporium.

5 Dillons Art Bookstore

8 Long Acre, WC2E 9LH
020-7836-1379
Mon, Wed–Sat, 9:30 am–10 pm;
Tues, 10–10; Sun, 12–7
tube: Covent Garden, Leicester Square

Whatever your art penchant, you're sure to find a slew of books on the subject here. Just browsing through the compendious selection is a great way to acquaint yourself with British and European contemporary visual culture. The magazine collection is also worth a look. Should you have questions, don't hesitate to ask the well-informed staff, even though they'll probably be frenetically running around trying to respond to the never-ending stream of customers in the store. If you want a taste of the London literary-arts scene, check the events calendar and attend one of the basement readings or launch parties.

The Photographers' Gallery

6

🚏 5 and 8 Great Newport St, WC2H 7HY

📖 020-7831-1772 f: 7836-9704
www.photonet.org.uk
info@photonet.org.uk
Mon–Sat, 11–6; Sun, 12–6
admission: free
tube: Leicester Square

Hellen van Meene, Untitled, 1998

This is a very popular place attracting a mixed audience of photography lovers, misplaced tourists, students and raucous tour groups. It's often crowded and noisy, factors exacerbated by the unaccommodating layout: two separated town houses only minimally adapted as art venues for the public. Unfortunately, scruffy conditions and poor lighting also weaken the viewing experience, critically diminishing the character and visibility of the art.

At the #5 address, exhibition objects are on display in the reception hall, along the corridor walls, in the café (a favored hangout and meeting locale) and in one small space at the top of the stairs. One of the former bedrooms on the upper level, moreover, houses Print Sales, a shop presenting one-person shows and making a large, eclectic collection of work by both renowned and unknown photographers available for purchase. The main exhibition space is actually at #8, a few doors down the street. A bookstore—with a good selection of anthologies, artist monographs and catalogues on still images, video, film, electronic media and theory—is also located at the #8 address.

The Photographers' Gallery approaches photography from many perspectives, showing classical, documentary, fashion, installation, mixed-media and video work. Despite the poor setup, the exhibi-

tions feature challenging, high-quality art and are accompanied by informative small brochures. For example, the summer 1999 showings of haunting images by the East Village artist Francesca Woodman and young girls in staged portrayals by the Dutch artist Hellen van Meene were incredible exhibitions, the first solo shows in Britain for both these photographers. Lectures, films, workshops and community projects are also part of the program.

Every year (around February–March), the gallery hosts an exhibition of the five shortlisted candidates for the Citibank Private Bank Photography Prize (£15,000). The prize (founded in 1996) rewards the individual judged to have made the most significant contribution to the medium of photography over the preceding year. The exhibition, which presents an outstanding body of work by each artist, is not to be missed. The finalists for 2000 included James Casebere, Anna Gaskell, Jitka Hanzlová, Tim Macmillan, Tracey Moffatt. Previous winners were Richard Billingham, Andreas Gursky, Rineke Dijkstra.

Recent exhibitions: *Asia City, Dominique Blain, Blue Suburban Skies, Robert Capa, Circulating Cities, Paul Fusco, Sergio Larrain, Ulf Lundin, May Day—Communities/Communications, Christopher Muller, Jean-Luc Mylayne, Near & Elsewhere, Speed, Annelies Štrba, Jürgen Teller, Piotr Uklanski, Hellen van Meene, Francesca Woodman.*

7 | Ian Shipley Bookshop

70 Charing Cross Rd, WC2
020-7836-4872 f: 7379-4358
tube: Leicester Square

With its specialty in art history and criticism, this bookstore is a bit more for the academic-minded. It looks like and is a classic, old-style book haven where the sellers and customers have a deep knowledge and love of art from centuries past. Contemporary art is not a particular strength. In addition to new books, it has a good selection of used books including some hard-to-find exhibition catalogues.

8 | Zwemmer Media Arts

80 Charing Cross Rd, WC2H 0BB
020-7240-4157 f: 7240-4186
Mon–Fri, 10–6:30; Sat, 10–6
tube: Leicester Square

This tightly organized shop specializes in books on photography, design and cinema. You'll find books from all around the world, which, especially in the case of photography, are rarities not available elsewhere. It's a delight just to thumb through some of the sumptuous volumes.

9 | Zwemmer Arts Bookshop

24 Litchfield St, WC2H 9NJ
020-7379-7886 f: 7836-7049
Mon–Fri, 10–6:30; Sat, 10–6
tube: Leicester Square

Located around the corner from the Media Arts store.

You'll find art books aplenty here, especially the big, well-illustrated ones on individual artists and styles. Art per se is on the ground floor, and architecture and design are on the lower level. Compared with Dillons (see above), this store has a more mainstream collection featuring books by the major publishers.

Sometimes photography exhibitions, such as Larry Clark and Edward Weston, are held here.

10 | The Ivy

1–5 West St, WC2H 9NE
020-7836-4751 f: 7240-9550
tube: Leicester Square

The Ivy is a very chic restaurant populated by those who like to see famous faces and be seen. The cuisine has a superb reputation (reservations are hard to come by), service is first-rate and the decor is tastefully peppered with art by Patrick CAULFIELD, Eduardo PAOLOZZI, Allen JONES, Howard HODGKIN, Peter BLAKE, Joe TILSON and Barry FLANAGAN. Even if you can't get in past the front door, you can at least see Caulfield's stained glass, prominently installed on the corner facade. (Best to view this after dark.) The composition is a spare, midnight blue field sprinkled with stars and a crescent moon. It represents a cliché vision of a romantic sky except that the upper borders are framed by bare yel-

Paul Caulfield, stained glass window

low light bulbs. The reference thus shifts from nature to stage set, quite appropriate for a window in Soho, London's celebrated theater district.

Comyn Ching Triangle
11 (Ching Court)

renovation: Terry FARRELL, 1984–90
19 Shelton St, WC2
tube: Covent Garden,
Leicester Square
Entrances between 13 and 17
Shelton St and at 45 Monmouth St.

This block of late-17th- and early-18th-century brick houses, named for the architectural ironmongers who occupied the site, is part of the Seven Dials area, infamous during the Victorian era as one of London's most wretched slums. Inadvertently saved from demolition (grand-scale redevelopment of the area collapsed), the old buildings were converted to a mixed-use complex of shops, offices and flats. Central to the scheme was the redesign of the triangular interior space as a public courtyard. It's a puzzling place, where the well-aged backs of ordinary buildings juxtapose oddly with new towerlike structures in the three corners, chic—albeit subdued and playful—stepped curvatures in the pavement and ruby red, faux-lacquer embellishments done up in a Chinese-Art Deco style. It's not that the elements clash but that the courtyard itself seems so out-of-sync with its environment. Indeed, the entrances are very concealed, hardly opening the space up to the public.

12 Frith Street Gallery

59–60 Frith St, W1V 5TA
020-7494-1550 f: 7287-3733
Tues–Fri, 10–6; Sat, 11–4;
closed Mon
tube: Tottenham Court Road

Ensconced in two interconnected Georgian houses with exhibitions spread out in four separate rooms, the Frith Gallery presents a distinctive viewing experience. To see the art, you wind your way down narrow corridors, through doors, around corners and in and out of spaces still bearing the marks of their former domestic existence. Depending on the art on display, the setting is either an enhancement or a distraction. Some artists take advantage of the space by creating intimate installations.

The gallery began 10 years ago by showing works on paper by various international artists. It continues this initial direction intermittently with superb drawing exhibitions by the likes of Juan Muñoz or Thomas Schütte. The main focus now, however, is midcareer British artists and some rising stars from the younger generation. Artists: Fiona Banner, Dorothy Cross, Tacita Dean, Marlene Dumas, Bernard Frize, Craigie Horsfield, Callum Innes, Jaki Irvine, Cornelia Parker, Giuseppe Penone, John Riddy, Bridget Smith.

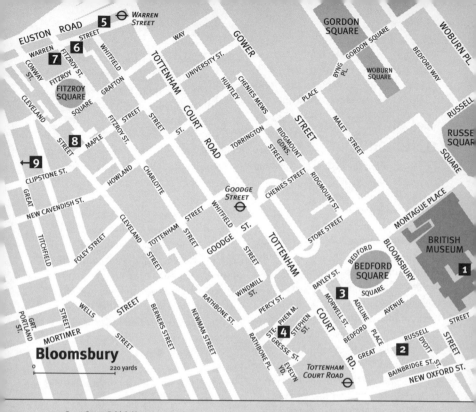

1. Great Court, British Museum
2. Cinema Bookshop
3. Architectural Association
4. British Film Institute
5. Magnani Gallery
6. Corvi-Mora Gallery
7. greengrassi
8. Lotta Hammer Gallery
9. RIBA Architectural Centre

Bloomsbury

Great Court, British Museum

1

🏛 renovation: Norman FOSTER, 1998–2000

🏛 Great Russell St, WC1
020-7636-1555
Mon–Sat, 10–5; Sun, 2:30–6
admission: free,
special exhibitions £5/3
tube: Tottenham Court Road,
Russell Square

Norman Foster, the 1999 winner of the Pritzger Prize (considered the Nobel Prize for architects), has designed a two-acre public square enclosed by a lattice-framed glass roof as the new Great Court at the heart of the British Museum. (This is one of the Millennium Projects funded in part by the Heritage Lottery Fund.) Previously this area, with the incredible, round Reading Room at its center, was occupied by the British Library. The library's move to new accommodations in 1997–98 permitted restoration of the original courtyard plan—considered a great neoclassical monument of the mid-19th century Greek Revival. Not only does the recent construction again establish the courtyard as the museum's central circulatory space, but it encircles the Reading Room with two monumental staircases that lead to a new elliptical structure in back, which in turn connects by a bridge to the upper galleries of the main building. In addition to the new open-access reference library and database facility in the Reading Room, the Foster design locates a temporary exhibition gallery and terrace restaurant in the rear structure and the Center for Education and Sainsbury African Galleries in excavated space beneath the courtyard.

If you've never been inside the Reading Room, it's well worth a visit. Especially now, you'll experience the full power of a spectacular domed space that inspired many writers—among them Karl Marx who sat in row G when composing *Das Kapital*. In the museum itself, you might also want to see the Rosetta Stone, Elgin Marbles and other ancient treasures.

2 | Cinema Bookshop

13–14 Great Russell St, WC1 B3NH
020-7637-0206
Mon–Sat, 10:30–5:30
tube: Tottenham Court Road

This unassuming little shop is so jam-packed with books, magazines and cinema collectibles that it's hard to move around. Within the clutter you'll find theory and history texts, actor and director monographs, anthologies and critical studies about a particular theme or film. The selection includes new, used and out-of-print materials. If you're a film buff or hunger for a book on Greta Garbo, Mia Farrow or François Truffaut, or if you simply like to burrow through disorder to find unexpected treasures, this is a place you'll enjoy.

3 | Architectural Association (AA)

34 Bedford Sq, WC1B 3ES
020-7887-4039 f: 7414-0782
www.aaschool.ac.uk
Mon–Fri, 10–7; Sat, 10–3
admission: free
tube: Tottenham Court Road,
Goodge Street

The Architectural Association and its School of Architecture (the only private architectural institute in Britain) are located in two adjacent Georgian town houses: proper, four-story brick residences whose elegantly ornamented interiors are preserved though well-worn, scruffy and overrun by their present-day occupants. Despite the incongruous setting, the AA presents an exciting, diversified lecture series as well as exhibitions, symposia, book launches and conferences with workshops on a broad range of arts-related topics.

The main gallery (actually three attached parlors) is on the ground floor to the left of the front door. The bar, front member's room and photo library on the 1st floor are also used variously for displays. To appreciate the exhibitions—which require skillful negotiation of a maze of narrow corridors, stairs and semienclosed spaces often crowded with people and things—you have to abandon a museum mind-set. Don't be misled by the amateurish, low-key character of the installations, for the content is top-notch. And don't be turned off by the overly long, too-didactic labels. Just concentrate on the imagery in the models, photographs, drawings, plans, books and other materials. These objects reveal the creative impulses and basic premises of a particular situation or architectural project, and the projects are conceptually fascinating. Typically, they either approach some mundane subject from a new angle or focus attention on a controversial topic.

Recent exhibitions: *Berlin Free University, Lacaton & Vassal, Robert Le Ricolais, Living Room—The Residential Building as an Artistic Station, Mississippi Horizons, Motel Interiors—Josef Pausch, Pipe Dreams (Mark Lucas, Jane Thorburn, Richard Wilson), Joze Plecnik, Reconstructing Space—Architecture in Recent German Photo-*

graphy, *Sauerbruch Hutton, Space Stories (Naomi Tracz), Travels in Modern Architecture (F. R. Yerbury)*.

If a talk by a creator or thinker who is in the forefront of the current, global avant-garde (architects, video and performance artists, photographers, designers, historians, landscape and garden planners, critical theorists, sociologists, urbanists, filmmakers, installation sculptors, musicians, choreographers,...) excites your fancy, be sure to check the events schedule (020-7887-4111) and arrive early at the door (well before the starting time of 6:30). Unfortunately, the lecture room is small and AA students are admitted first. There are no tickets (except on rare occasions), but if you call in advance to the membership chair and make a convincing plea you may be able to secure a place. The speakers may not yet be famous names though they are the crop of movers and shakers who are making inroads where and when it counts. Guaranteed, you'll be captivated if not inflamed by what they say, and you'll leave London craving a lecture series like the AA's in your hometown.

For example, speakers during the spring of 1999 included Cecil Balmond, Gordon Benson, Thomas Demand, Digital Tsunami, Lynda Fairbairn, William Firebrace, Gigon & Guyer, Mona Hatoum, Jacques Herzog, John Koermeling, Rem Koolhaas, Anne Lacaton, Diane Lewis, Carlos Libedinsky, Daniel Libeskind, Akos Moravanszky, Laura Mulvey, Josef Pausch, Vong Phaophanit, Alex de Rijke and Michael Mack, Tom Sachs, Esther Shalev-Gerz, Grahame Shane, Bernard Tschumi, Thomas van Leeuwen, Wouter Vanstiphout/Crimson.

4 | British Film Institute

21 Stephen St, W1P 1PL
020-7255-1444 f: 7436-0437
www.bfi.org.uk
tube: Tottenham Court Road

Begun in 1933, the British Film Institute (BFI) is an amazing institution that "exists to encourage the development of film, television and video in the United Kingdom and to promote knowledge, understanding and enjoyment of the culture of the moving image." To

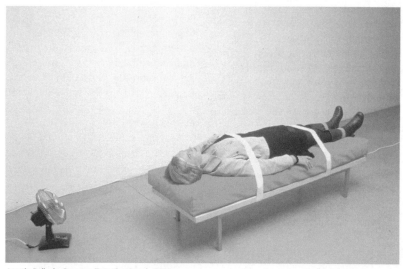

Angela Bulloch, *Strap on Zone Out Bench*, 1996

fulfill this mission the BFI curates first-rate film programs and exhibitions; presents daily screenings (see below, National Film Theatre and IMAX, South Bank); collects and preserves films, television programs, videos—including video games, stills, posters, artifacts and designs; organizes the London Film Festival; presents a full calendar of workshops, conferences and lectures; produces and distributes films and videos; engages in research, publishing (including the impressive magazine *Sight and Sound*) and education; grants fellowships to filmmakers; co-runs a doctoral program; and operates the Museum of the Moving Image, BFI National Library and John Paul Getty, Jr., Conservation Center.

Despite its incredible development and achievements, the BFI functions pretty much on a shoestring, inefficiently running its various departments and activities from locations scattered across London. Plans for consolidation in a single National Cinema Centre have been repeatedly thwarted for one reason or another. The government has recently tightened the reins of BFI by implementing organizational changes, the effects of which are not yet fully apparent. During the next several years, access to resources in the BFI archives may be temporarily curtailed. It is not yet clear how or if programs at the National Film Theatre and Museum of the Moving Image will be modified.

5 | Magnani Gallery

60–61 Warren St, W1P 5PA
020-7916-6366 f: 020-7916-6369
tube: Warren Street

In December 1999, the Robert Prime Gallery, located at this address and co-directed by Gregorio Magnani and Tommaso Corvi-Mora, ended its life. The gallery represented both emerging and established international artists whose work tended to make reference to non-art themes and issues. Objects and exhibitions were challenging, inevitably arousing a strong response by being irreverent, deadpan, crudely made or spiked with social commentary. You're likely to see the same or similar art in the new Magnani and Corvi-Mora Galleries.

6 | Corvi-Mora Gallery

22 Warren Street, W1P 5DD
020-7383-2419 f: 7383-2429
tube: Warren Street,
Great Portland Street

See Magnani Gallery above.

7 | greengrassi

39c Fitzroy St, W1P 5HR
020-7387-8747 f: 7388-3555
Tues–Sat, 11–6; closed Mon
tube: Warren Street,
Great Portland Street

This new, still emerging gallery, located on the second floor of a town house (just off the corner of Warren Street), has at its helm an ambitious, lively director with strong Italian and American connections. Though it has only a very limited space in which to show art, greengrassi's choice of objects is first-rate and its artists are notable talents, albeit not (yet) familiar names in British art circles. A 1998 exhibition by the young Italian Margherita Manzelli, for example, presented just three paintings. But each was a riveting, haunting self-portrait, and the three together gave a clear sense of the artist's approach even as they made you want to see more.

Artists: Tomma Abts, Stefano Arienti, Jennifer Bornstein, Steve Doughton, Samuel Fosso, Joanne Greenbaum, Margherita Manzelli, Kristin Oppenheim, Alessandro Pessoli, Lari Pittman, Charles Ray, Allen Ruppersberg, Frances Stark, Jennifer Steinkamp, Lisa Yuskavage, Pae White.

8 | Lotta Hammer Gallery

⌂ 51 Cleveland St, W1P 5PQ
020-7636-2221 f: 7436-6067
clever@easynet.co.uk
Tues–Fri, 11–6; Sat, 12–4
tube: Goodge Street

Within a compact space—two small rooms on the ground floor and another below—this high-energy gallery presents paintings, video, artist's books and other creations by young artists. The variation in the character of art is so broad that each show is an island onto itself. They tend toward the eccentric, which means they can be uniquely fantastic or quirkily awful. More than support a specific group of artists, the gallery presents a string of exhibitions, each introducing new work or artists never before shown in London.

Recent exhibitions: *Liz Arnold, Martin Boyce, Roddy Buchanan, Jason Coburn, Jeremy Dickinson, Cheryl Donegan, Moyna Flannigan, Vincent Gallo, Graham Gussin, Jonathan Hammer, Stephan Jung, Flora Neuwinth, Charlotte von Poehl.*

9 | RIBA Architectural Centre

▭ 66 Portland Pl, W1N 4AD
020-7307-3699 f: 7307-3703
📖 www.riba.org
admin@inst.riba.org
exhibitions: Mon, Wed, Fri, Sat, 8–6; Tues, Thurs, 8–9
admission: free
tube: Regent's Park,
Great Portland Street

RIBA (Royal Institute of British Architecture) is the official architectural organization in the UK, and this imposing building—a 1930s mix of Art Deco and sterile grandeur—is its headquarters. Though the exterior style (it bears a likeness to that developed by Albert Speer for the Nazi state) also characterizes parts of the interior, the scale and effect are somewhat subdued. This is particularly true of the café-bar, an elegant setting spread around the top of a majestic staircase. Decorative, finely crafted furnishings and wall patterns define the space and create a unified, period setting.

There are usually several different architectural exhibitions presented at any given time in the RIBA Centre. The main gallery is on 1st floor behind the staircase and café-bar. A second gallery, on the same level in a long room facing the street, and two additional rooms on the ground floor are also used. Exhibitions cover the gamut of styles and topics. Among the most popular are those displaying the finalists for major UK or RIBA architectural prizes. Though exhibitions are not installed with much panache and are either devoid of helpful signage or fashioned like a textbook, the designs themselves provide illuminating perspectives on contemporary and historic architecture. Recent exhibitions: *Architecture of Oman, Displaced Grid, The Inflatable Moment—Pneumatics and Protest in '68, Manifesto—Fifty Years of British Radicals, Oscar Niemeyer, Twentieth Century British Housing.*

If your schedule has an opening on a Tuesday evening, you might enjoy hearing a talk in the RIBA lecture series (6:30; admission, £5.50/3). Among the distinguished guests who have appeared are Tadao Ando, Peter Cook, Elizabeth Diller, Terry Farrell, Tony Fretton, Nicolas Grimshaw, Jacques Herzog, Dan Kiley, Wolf D. Prix, Richard Sennett, Alvaro Siza, Peter Zumthor.

For anyone with even a glimmer of curiosity about architecture, the place not to miss is the RIBA bookstore. It is one of the world's best bookstores on architecture, landscape architecture, gardens, urban planning, interior design and related subjects. Located on the

Willie Doherty, *Contemplating the Consequences of Political Failure (the surveillance scene)*, 1998

right side of the ground floor, it extends the length of the entire building. Some books are placed in a display area in the front, separated from the store itself, so be sure to visit both sections.

Lisson Grove–Camden

1 Lisson Gallery

🗔 renovation: Tony FRETTON, 1992
52–54 Bell and 67 Lisson Sts, NW1 5DA
020-7724-2739 f: 7724-7124
www.lissongallery.com
contact@lisson.co.uk
Mon–Fri, 10–6; Sat, 10–5
tube: Edgeware Road

If you like the utterly cool, white-box environments of designer-chic galleries, you'll feel right at home here. As a result of a two-phase renovation by Tony Fretton, there are three ample spaces on the lower level and additional exhibition spaces upstairs on the office level. The environment may be sterile, but the light is good and the sparse installations allow you to take in each work alone or in comparative groupings without extraneous interference.

This is one of London's premier galleries, renowned internationally for its long-standing commitment to conceptual and minimal art. Leading artists associated with the early phases of these movements are still shown, though the program now includes members of younger generations who have branched off in diverse directions. Since European heavyweights are well represented, this is a good place to become acquainted with some key artists often omitted from an Americanized history of the last 40 years. Whether presenting new or historic work, the selections at Lisson are consistently museum-quality with at least a few objects causing a rethinking of assumptions and values. The gallery sells small catalogues related to its exhibitions as well as a variety of related publications.

Artists: Edward Allington, Francis Aÿs, Art & Language, John Baldessari, Pierre Bismuth, Christine Borland, James Casebere, Mat Collishaw, Tony Cragg, Grenville Davey, Richard Deacon, Lili

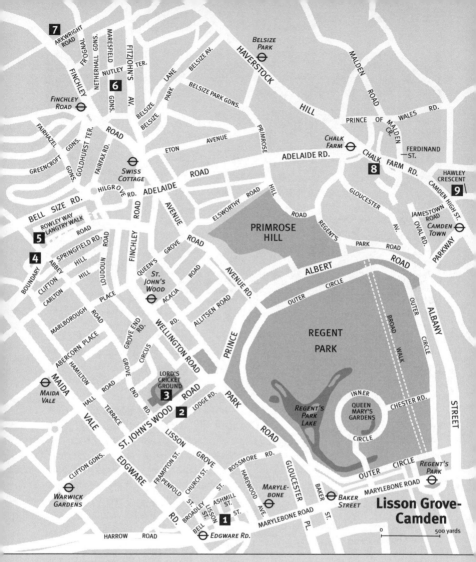

1. Lisson Gallery
2. Anish Kapoor, Holocaust Memorial
3. Lord's Cricket Ground
4. Saatchi Gallery
5. Public housing
6. Freud Museum
7. Camden Arts Centre
8. Roundhouse
9. MTV Europe

Dujourie, Ceal Floyer, Douglas Gordon, Dan Graham, Rodney Graham, Mark Hosking, Shirazeh Houshiary, Peter Joseph, Donald Judd, Anish Kapoor, On Karawa, John Latham, Sol LeWitt, Allan McCollum, John McCracken, Robert Mangold, Jason Martin, Jonathan Monk, Anna Mossman, Juan Muñoz, John Murphy, Avis Newman, Julian Opie, Tony Oursler, Guilio Paolini, Simon Patterson, Thomas Schütte, Lee Ufan, Jan Vercruysse, Richard Wentworth, Franz West, Jane & Louise Wilson.

Anish Kapoor, *Holocaust Memorial*, 1996

2 | Anish Kapoor

Holocaust Memorial, 1996
Liberal Jewish Synagogue
28 St. John's Wood Rd, NW8 7HA
Mon–Thurs, 9–5; Fri, 9–3; closed
Sat–Sun
admission: free
tube: Warwick Avenue

To enter, go to the door at the end of the walkway on the right side of the building, not the main door facing the street.

A 1920s colonnaded portico serves as the formal entrance to the synagogue, though the building behind, from a later date, is of generic modern design. Kapoor's sculpture hangs on the foyer wall facing and on axis with the sacred ark at the front of the congregational hall. Like many of his works, it is a large stone mass having a hollow, indeterminate space as its interior. In this case, a square windowlike cavity has been cut into a rough-hewn block of black Irish limestone, and the inner realm is a deep, dark, unnerving vacuum whose highly polished surface dimly reflects your own image. The paradox of the incredible physicality of the stone and the mystical, undefinable void is haunting, all the more so because color and luminosity—features common to the interior of Kapoor's sculptures—are absent and the title alludes to an unfathomable reality of death, destruction and the attempted annihilation of a people.

3 | Lord's Cricket Ground

St. John's Wood Rd, NW8
architects: Mound Stand—Michael HOPKINS, 1985–87; Indoor Cricket School—David MORLEY, 1994–95; New Stand—Nicholas GRIMSHAW, 1995–98; Media Centre—FUTURE SYSTEMS, 1996–98
020-7289-1611 f: 7286-9545
www.lords.org
tube: St. John's Wood

Located across the street from the Liberal Jewish Synagogue.

This is the hallowed home of cricket —the UK's national sport—and the famed MCC (Marylebone Cricket Club)—the ruling body for the game. League and cup matches, including the Tests (cricket's World Series), are played here on the most immaculate, impeccably groomed pitch (playing field). During the past 10 years, Lord's has totally renovated its facilities, hiring Britain's top architects to design each component. Though you can't enter the site unless you're attending a match, it is possible to get a look if you walk up St. John's Wood Road to the northernmost gate, which gives access to the Lord's Shop. (This tony sports store is open Mon–Sat, 10–5, and Sun, 12:30–5 from Apr–Sept; and Mon–Fri, 10–5 from Oct–Mar.) Using the guise of wanting to browse through the latest cricket attire or equipment in the shop, you can thus gain admittance behind the brick boundary wall and get an overview of the site. Since this may well be your only chance to glimpse the cricket phenomenon up close, go for it!

The most incredible (and bizarre) feature of the game of cricket is its length and pace. Games last from one to five days and it's an exaggeration to say they typically have high-intensity moments. The comedian Robin Williams captured cricket's essence when he described it as "baseball on Valium."

The centerpiece of the Lord's complex is the main pitch, which is bordered by a mix of separate stands and pavilions (as opposed to a single, unified stadium), with a viewing place for the press at one end. The recent upgrades conserve the previous arrangement of the stands as they developed over 150 years, despite the fact that the arrangement wasn't particularly appealing or purposeful. However, it reeked of British tradition and cricket's original, village-green roots. Hence, it was endowed with inestimable value, not readily forsaken. Behind the main ground are indoor facilities and offices in the school building, and a second field used for practice matches and training, called the Nursery Ground. (Terminology that sounds odd to Americans is another characteristic of cricket.)

Michael Hopkins spearheaded the master plan and first phase of Lord's renovation with his design for the Mound Stand. The new stand follows the curve of a ground-level brick wall and structural arcade, c. 1890. An open terrace of seating extends in front; private boxes are set within a white-painted steel structure above; and a second terrace on top culminates in a mast-supported roof of white tensioned fabric. The masts are also the endpoints of six structural steel columns. The whole, crowned by the tentlike, suspended roof, appears quite light and festive.

When Nicholas Grimshaw created the New Stand, which faces the Mound Stand, he reiterated the mast imagery. But he used only one central mast as his prime support element. Tension rods extend from it to a lattice beam, running the length of the stand, which in turn supports the canopy roof. One crit-

ic suggests that the image is aeronautic with the roof appearing as a wing.

The latest addition to the main ground is the Media Centre: an egg-shaped structure of white aluminum resting atop two tall towers. Because the towers (support columns as well as elevator and staircase shafts) are hidden behind stands so as to be nearly invisible, the building seems to float above the field. From the front, where the egg is sliced open with the resultant long, svelte plane entirely configured as a picture window, the center looks like a spacecraft from another planet. It's just what you'd expect from an architectural firm named Future Systems. The interior, designed to accommodate 300 print and broadcast journalists, has a bar and restaurant in back and a two-floor layout compartmentalized into workstations in front. The slanted, glazed facade provides unimpeded, nonreflective views of the entire field from all seats.

The Indoor Cricket School, located to the side of the main ground, echoes the airy lightness of the new main-ground buildings. It is a big, white, barrel-vaulted hangar whose facade is glazed, with an open terrace on the upper level and a scalloped roof overhang. The architect David Morley also designed the sides with sliding walls to enhance ventilation and indoor-outdoor seamlessness in the summer.

Taken together, the conglomerate of buildings is a jumble of individual statements with threads of commonality, held in check by the fields of lush green grass.

4 | Saatchi Gallery

renovation: Max GORDON, 1985
98A Boundary Rd, NW8 ORH
020-7624-8299
Thurs–Sun, 12–6; closed Mon–Wed
admission: £4/2
tube: St. John's Wood

Saatchi Gallery, *Young Americans 2*, 1998

Located just off Abbey Rd—yes, it's the one made famous by the Beatles. Turn left (west) onto Boundary Rd and then, from the right side of the street, go into the nondescript gravel driveway behind the gray steel gate. You won't see anything that looks like a gallery since the building is in back of a row of houses and shops fronting the street. It's easy to miss.

This is not a commercial gallery but an exhibition space displaying works from the large, ever-expanding, private collection of Charles Saatchi. Beginning in the 1970s with an initial focus on minimalist art, Saatchi has expanded in diverse directions, amassing an enormous number of extraordinary works of art. (The collection originally belonged to Charles and his wife, Doris, but after their divorce in 1988, the gallery became his exclusive province.) The choices invariably represent the most vanguard, and often subversive, modes of contemporary creativity. Unquestionably, his support of young British artists has been the single most important factor in elevating the profile of the London art scene in the 1990s and in advancing the success of British contemporary art internationally. Seminal aspects in this were the six grand-scale exhibitions, *Young British Artists*, at the Boundary Road gallery and the worldwide media-splash produced by *Sensation*, the exhibition of YBA from the Saatchi Collection held at the Royal Academy (and subsequently at the Hamburger Bahnhof—National Gallery, Berlin and the Brooklyn Museum of Art). The presence of the Saatchi Gallery in London and its displays of exemplars of the latest art trends (British and otherwise), have, moreover, had a strong impact, especially on aspiring students.

Charles and his brother Maurice founded the powerhouse global advertising agency Saatchi & Saatchi, which has produced momentous campaigns for commercial products as well as for such politicians as Margaret Thatcher and John Major. Fair to say, the marketing and promotional acumen of Charles Saatchi's business also permeates his art activities—for better and for worse. On the one hand, his purchases and exhibitions have attained superstar status, at times because he packages an individual or group of artists under a catchy label or shocking image to create a phenomenon. On the other hand, his treatment of art like stock investments, bought in bulk and sold abruptly at hyped-up auctions for great financial gain, has been a source of anguish in the art world. (Major Saatchi sell-offs have occurred twice: in 1989–91 and again in 1999.)

Contrary to Saatchi's flair for creating eye-catching ads and purchasing bold works of art, the entrance and gray exterior of his gallery are supremely understated. The building, formerly an industrial warehouse, was transformed in 1985 by Max Gordon into a place where Saatchi could showcase his collection. It was the first of such barebones, chic art spaces in Britain and added to Saatchi's reputation as a renowned patron and collector.

When you first enter the gallery, the drama of its space is not apparent. The reception area and contiguous hall are unassuming and modestly scaled. But when you step into the main hall, you're likely to gasp and remain frozen in place as you take in the sheer volume of space. It's like an airplane hangar, a totally empty expanse with a concrete floor and bounded by blank, windowless white walls. Apart from the size, the natural light, streaming in through an industrial roof of glass and steel, is the dominating feature. Within this no-context, anti-expressionist space, each artwork has plenty of room to breathe and can exist as a self-contained, autonomous object. Nothing detracts from its being seen as an object unto itself without interference or reference to extraneous, external elements. Thus, the space manifests the ultimate in minimalist design. Unfortunately, it is also a cold, inhospitable vacuum that establishes a certain aura, sustaining aloofness in the viewing experience regardless of the content or character of the art.

Exhibitions at the Saatchi Gallery focus on a single artist or group of artists who share a particular creative bent or national identity. Objects are typically museum quality and indicative of a recent or current hot trend. For example, *Young Americans 2* (fall of 1998) included a diverse range of work by Michael Ashkin, Ashley Bickerton, John Currin, Carroll Dunham, Tom Friedman, Martin Kersels, Clay Ketter, Robin Lowe, Josiah McElheny, Sarah Morris, Laura Owens, Elizabeth Peyton, Monique Prieto, David Salle, Jessica Stockholder, Brian Tolle, Sue Williams, Terry Winters, Lisa Yuskavage.

To the rear of the main space is another large gallery with two additional rooms alongside it. Be sure to see the permanent installation of *20:50* (1987) by Richard WILSON, off to the left of the break between the two big galleries. Only one person at a time enters this experiential artwork which consists of a path running into the middle of a room filled with a dark, utterly still, seemingly liquid or viscous, very reflective substance. Or is it all mirrored? You have the sense of being on a pier looking down into a boundless, extremely deep, enigmatic space. Either you'll obsess on what's creating the effects, or else you'll just savor the wondrous experience.

Recent exhibitions: *Thomas Demand, Reneke Dijkstra, Duane Hanson, Gary Hume, Alex Katz, Esko Männikkö, Neurotic Realism (I and II), Fiona Rae, Ugo Rondinone, Tomoko Takanashi, Juan Uslé, Young Americans, Young German Artists*.

5 | Public housing

architect: Neave BROWN, 1969–79
Langtry Walk, NW8
tube: Swiss Cottage

Located between Abbey Rd, Boundary Rd, Loudoun Rd and Rowley Way. If you cross Abbey Rd from the Saatchi Gallery, just ahead—before you reach the railroad bridge—you'll come to a pedestrian street bordered by housing units. This is Langtry Walk, site of the controversial housing project confusingly known as Alexandra Rd.

Neave Brown, public housing

Adopting the brute look of raw, reinforced concrete, Neave Brown created low-cost, high-density housing (520 units for some 1,660 residents) without, however, succumbing to the common tower-block design of the sixties. Though making no attempt to make the buildings blend with existing housing in the area, the architect was extremely attentive to the railroad track bordering the plot on the north and to light, space and privacy considerations.

The layout consists of attached dwellings forming alignments of four and six stories facing one another across a slightly curving, pedestrian street nearly one-half mile long. Stepped-back facades with generous terraces enhance the appearance even as they produce a more communal, sun-filled central passageway. The aura of public housing is further reduced because staircases are decentralized, set between paired dwellings, and elevators are dispersed at intervals throughout. At the rear of the north side, a parking garage occupies the hollow undersection of the housing and a solid upper wall functions as a noise barrier. In contrast, the south side gives onto a park area with four playgrounds, each for a different age group.

Units vary from studio to three-bedroom size, and care has been taken to endow them all with good proportions and strong detailing. Nevertheless, the whole bears an overriding look of repetitive sameness, exaggerated due to the nonstop, extreme length of the layout. Some critics have also harped against the fixed arrangement of rooms since this doesn't accommodate complex social needs.

Viewing the housing today, it is impeccably clean, kempt and variously diversified by plants and personal touches. Fortunately, its current state belies its history. Camden Housing Council neglected the Alexandra Road development for years and it became rundown and crime-ridden. In frustration, the residents recently joined forces and took over the maintenance of the property. Repairs, security cameras, guards and a new brick street path have not only improved the appearance but instilled pride in the community. There is still work to be done: shops (at the east end) remain abandoned and the community center could use a general revamping. (Brown did not design these buildings or the school for handicapped children which is also part of the neighborhood.)

6 | Freud Museum

20 Maresfield Gardens, NW3 5SX
020-7435-2002 f: 7431-5452
www.freud.org.uk
freud@gn.apc.org
Wed–Sun, 12–5; closed Mon–Tues
admission: £4/2
tube: Finchley Road, Swiss Cottage

Beyond the Swiss Cottage intersection, walk up (north) Finchley Rd on the right side; turn into a small passageway, Trinity Walk; at the top of the hill turn left onto Maresfield Gardens. The museum is a block and a half ahead on the right.

This is the house where the famous father of psychoanalysis and his family lived after escaping the Nazi invasion of Vienna in 1938. The next year, Freud died. The house has been preserved—with his library, antique collection, Biedermeier and Austrian country furniture—close to the way it was during his life.

On an irregular schedule, the museum presents exhibitions by contemporary artists. These tend to show images or themes related to or directly influenced by Freudian concerns, like the unconscious, jokes, pleasure, pain, dreams, sex, family relationships or death. An exhibition titled *Appointment* by Sophie Calle (1999), for example, placed texts, many of which were irreverent, and unlikely objects, like a stripper's wig, throughout the house as if they were being used by Freud and were integral parts of his environment. Other recent exhibitions featured erotic and fetishized nudes by the young South African artist Marlene Dumas, *Trousers for the Brain* by Weiner Reiterer, *Living in a Paradox* by Gabrielle Rifkind, *Childhood Fragments* by Helen Wilks.

7 | Camden Arts Centre

Arkwright Rd, NW3 6DG
020-7435-2643 f: 7794-3371
info@camdenarts.demon.co.uk
Tues–Thurs, 11–7; Fri–Sun, 11–5:30; closed Mon
admission: free
tube: Finchley Road

The Camden Arts Centre may be a bit off the beaten track but it's a "must-visit" site in London. Located in a residential neighborhood with a mixed affluent and working-class population, it presented a program of art classes and local exhibitions from its founding in 1968 until 1990, when the current director, Jenni Lomax, arrived. Since then, exhibitions have featured artists from the international vanguard, and a broadened range of educational activities—seminars, lectures, workshops, on-site installations, off-site projects, artist residencies, art courses, teacher-training discussions—have been creatively integrated with the exhibitions. Camden is a first-rate operation with its values in the right place, strong leadership and a rare sensitivity to its audience and innovative modes of art making.

After entering the building, a former public library, walk back and you'll come to a lobbylike space with a reception desk and small but superb bookshop. (The selection includes books and catalogues mainly related to artists who have shown work at the center, art criticism and a wealth of magazines.) Behind the lobby area is a fresh, new space comprising two flexible, skylit galleries, totally white—including a white linoleum floor. This addition, which postdates the main building, was constructed to replace a section bombed out during World War II. Off the right end of the lobby is a single large room often used for video installations. Camden's program nicely balances emerging and established artists, shows focused on a single body of work, one-person retrospectives, contemporaneous solos of three different artists and

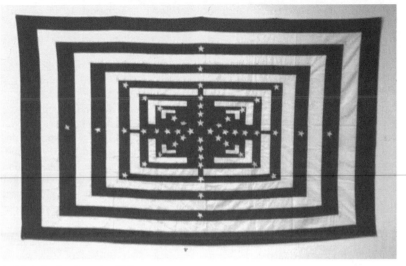

Paul Thek, *Flag from Procession*, 1977

group surveys. A general theme loosely threads together all the exhibitions and projects of a given year.

The building also contains studios for resident artists. These are open to the public once a week so that visitors can see work in progress and speak with the artists. At times, these artists develop projects outside the building, as in the North London Link Project (1999–2000) where six artists (or artist teams) created a work along the North Link railroad line in a train station, hospital, bingo hall and the like.

Recent exhibitions: *Orla Barry, Bernd & Hilla Becher, Anna Best, Kathrin Bohm & Stephan Saffer, Marie José Burki, Sophie Calle, Juan Cruz, Marlene Dumas, European Painting Show, Laura Ford & Jacqueline Poncelet, Felix Gonzalez-Torres, Jim Isermann, Kim Lim, Len Lye, Object Relations, João Penalva, Simon Periton, John Riddy, Select—Video Digital Program, Paul Thek, Thinking Aloud*.

Pending lottery funding, Camden Arts Centre may close for about a year beginning April 2001. During the renovation period, there will be no exhibitions on-site but off-site projects will continue.

8 | Roundhouse

Chalk Farm Rd, NW1
tube: Chalk Farm

Originally an engine shed and turn-round building for trains, it became a hippie gathering and pop music place in the 1960s. Events like a secret jam session by the Beatles (1968) have made the Roundhouse legendary as a site of artistic inventiveness.

For the last 30 years, it's been used on and off for performances and visual arts projects. In 1998, for example, Ilya and Emilia Kabakov created *The Palace of Projects* at Roundhouse. Sponsored by Artangel, this very popular exhibition was an installation or rather, a series of installations "made by melancholics and misfits, absurd hobbyists and down-to-earth dreamers." In the fall of 1999 another art project—this time sponsored by the South London Gallery and installed in the labyrinth of subterranean tunnels—took place at Roundhouse. It was a collaborative venture linking primordial forms by Mimmo Paladino with a unique sound-and-light production by Brian Eno.

Pending financing and final approval,

the building may soon be transformed into a performing center for young people. Should this not transpire and should artists continue to use Roundhouse as a venue, you can learn about any current exhibitions or events in the local press and art calendars.

9 | MTV Europe (former TV-am studios)

renovation: Terry FARRELL, 1981–83
Hawley Crescent, NW1
tube: Camden Town

In his conversion of an old garage into studios for a breakfast-time television station, Farrell enlivened the building with witty forms and glitzy elements that gave it an upbeat character. On the street front, the giant sculpted letters "TVam" were stacked at the ends of a windowless facade sheathed in corrugated metal with a few sunrise-colored lines running down its length. A flamboyant, neon-lit steel framework shaped like a grand arch marked the entrance. The back of the building, which borders a canal, was decorated with a saw-toothed roofline topped by blue-and-white egg cups containing golden eggs. Indeed, the "eggs on the roof" became the beloved, well-known logo of the station. With its jokey symbols and industrial materials, the building was a prime British exemplar of the anticlassical, antipurist strain of postmodern architecture. This spirit also shaped the interior, where forms or sets denoting distant, exotic places—a temple, ziggurat, desert—embellished the atriumlike space running through the center of the building.

When TV-am died in December 1992, having lost its bid for franchise renewal owing to an unfortunate political snafu, its home was occupied by MTV Europe. The TVam letters were blocked out and the sunrise colors were painted over. But other features—including the "eggs on the roof"—were retained and still distinguish the building.

Kensington Area

1 | Serpentine Gallery

Kensington Gardens, W2 3XA
020-7402-6075 f: 7402-4103
www.serpentinegallery.org.uk
daily, 10–6
admission: free
tube: South Kensington,
Lancaster Gate

Located in the southwest section of Kensington Gardens off the (West Carriage Dr) Ring and Flower Walk, and overlooking the west bank of the Serpentine lake.

Cornelia Parker, *30 Pieces of Silver*, 1998

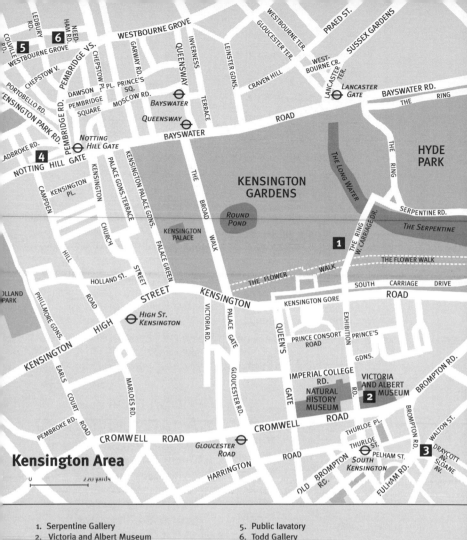

1. Serpentine Gallery
2. Victoria and Albert Museum
3. Michelin Building
4. Pharmacy
5. Public lavatory
6. Todd Gallery

Kensington Area

Formerly this building was the royal tea pavilion. But since 1970 it has been a prime London venue for special exhibitions of contemporary art. The royals must have been daffy to give up this charming garden house with its high-ceilinged, wonderfully skylit room in the center. Though not designed for art, it's a great place in which to see it, or maybe it just seems so since most all the exhibitions are first-rate. The Serpentine has a knack for organizing shows that capture the best of experimental, avant-garde creativity by emerging and renowned artists, as well as some cult figures from the early 20th century. Works are judiciously selected and well installed to enable independent viewing and provoke correspondences. If you want to read something about the art, artist and works on display, buy a broadsheet, available for 20p. It's written in plain English (not highfalutin artspeak) and provides a good orientation to an exhibition. More extensive information is of course found in the exhibition catalogue: these are also a good buy. If you really want to be saturated with the latest thinking about the featured artist, you can go to an exhibition symposium. Check at the reception desk (or on their web site) to get the particulars.

Recent exhibitions: *Ken Adam, Louise Bourgeois, Richard Deacon, Anya Gallaccio, Andreas Gursky, Tadashi Kawamata, William Kentridge, Yayoi Kusama, Piero Manzoni, Chris Ofili, Bridget Riley, Jane & Louise Wilson*.

Be sure to save time for perusing the excellent bookstore. It has lots of artsy knickknacks but also has a top-notch collection of theory, philosophy and criticism books related to contemporary culture.

1 | Ian Hamilton Finlay

pavement, benches,
tree plaques, 1998
Serpentine Gallery grounds

As part of the major renovation of the Serpentine (1996–97), the Scottish artist Ian Hamilton Finlay was commissioned to develop a permanent work for the area around the gallery. For part of his project, he placed eight benches on the side lawn. These are a great addition to the gallery since they make it possible to sit, relax, read or eat in a lovely setting before or after seeing an exhibition. The artist also shaped the setting by inscribing the benches with pastoral poetry and putting a plaque with a line from Virgil on a nearby tree ("Home, goats, home, replete, the evening star is coming." *Ecologue X*). All the written elements are in both English and Latin. As is his custom, Finlay sought to remove art from its object orientation and instead create works that arouse a nature and culture sensibility within a particular environment. The idea of moving out of the gallery and having art relate to non-art

(noncompositional, nonformalistic) issues attained a widespread following in the 1970s and 1980s.

Another part of Finlay's project is located on the ground in front of the entrance to the gallery. It's another inscription, this time set within the rings of a large concentric circle of paved slate. The writing contains the names of trees found in Kensington Gardens and a quotation from the philosopher Francis Hutcheson (1725): "The beauty of trees, their cool shades, and their aptness to conceal from observation, have made groves and woods the usual retreat to those who love solitude, especially to the religious, the pensive, the melancholy, and the amorous." At the circle's center is a dedication to Diana, Princess of Wales, who was the Serpentine Gallery Patron from 1993 to 1996.

2 | Victoria and Albert Museum (V&A)

new addition: Daniel LIBESKIND,
c. 2001
Cromwell Rd, SW7 2RL
020-7938-8500
www.vam.ac.uk
Mon, 12–5:45; Tues, Thur–Sun,
10–5:45; Wed, 10–5:45 and
6:30–9:30 (seasonal evening hrs)
admission: £5/3, free after 4:30
tube: South Kensington

Located on the corner of Cromwell and Exhibition Roads in a huge, multipartite building, the V & A is the National Museum of Art and Design. Encompassing some 146 galleries and extensive collections of decorative art objects from numerous cultures and epochs, at any given time you will see an incredible selection of ceramics, glass, furniture, woodwork, metalwork, textiles, fashion, jewelry, silver, sculpture, books, prints and photographs. In addition, there are special monographic and thematic exhibitions.

The contemporary era is represented in most of the collections. Of particular note because of its preeminent position within the avant-garde of recent decades is photography. Though the museum began to buy photography in the 19th century and to present photography exhibitions in the 1960s, only since May 1998 has it devoted a permanent space to the collection. The Canon Photography Gallery, situated on level A, room 38, to the right (east) side of the garden, is a bland, adequately sized hall furnished with beige, mass production wall dividers that can best be described as tacky eyesores. What a disservice to the art!

The V & A's photo holdings include over 300,000 fine art, documentary, commercial and digital prints. Among them are pioneering works by such conceptual, mixed-media, installation and technique-based artists as Bernhard and Hilla Becher, Richard Billingham, Marcel Broodthaers, Hamish Fulton, Adam Fuss, Nan Goldin, David Hockney, Gabriel Orozco, Cindy Sherman. The gallery always presents a general survey highlighting major names. Usually there is also a second exhibit focused on a particular body of work. For instance, Helen Chadwick's acclaimed installation, *The Oval Court* (1986) was shown in the summer and fall of 1998, followed by Henri Cartier-Bresson's photographs from the Americas and Asia.

A radical transformation of the V & A will occur when its very controversial extension opens about 2001. Designed by Daniel Libeskind in a daring, innovative style that rivals Frank Gehry's Bilbao Guggenheim Museum, the new building—called the Spiral—will itself be a signature image of outstanding art and design. Sandwiched between existing buildings, it rises up seven stories in a series of dynamic, zigzagging planes clad in glittering ivory tiles. Appropriately, the structure will be the contemporary wing of the museum displaying the most adventurous creations shaped by new forms, unusual materials and advanced technology.

3 | Michelin Building

 restoration: Terence CONRAN, 1984–89
91 Fulham Rd, SW3
tube: South Kensington

Located at the intersection of Fulham and Brompton Rds on the corner between Sloane Ave and Draycott St.

This eye-catching building was designed in 1905–11 for Michelin, the tire manufacturer, and carefully restored in the 1980s by Terence Conran, the designer and founder of a home furnishings empire. It has been called "an exuberant and delightful freak of a building . . . [with] style, verve and craftsmanship!" Not only do the richly tiled facades create a colorful, excessively decorative exterior, but illustrative panels and architectural motifs make playful references to Michelin's products. Thus, the stained-glass mural features a tire-bodied man (the Michelin trademark) riding a bicycle, and the illuminated corner turrets are shaped like a stack of tires. Be sure to walk into the entrance area, where a series of tile panels portrays the early history of motoring.

In its current incarnation, the building houses the Conran Shop and Bibendum restaurant. Enticing flower and fresh seafood vendors who sell their goods in the entryway typify Conran's idea of bringing food and retailing together in a high-style setting. If you walk back along Sloane Avenue (right side), you'll see how the renovation added two set-back office floors onto the original structure and clad part of the facade with window walls.

4 | Damien Hirst

 Pharmacy
150 Notting Hill Gate, W11 3QG
020-7221-2442
tube: Notting Hill Gate

Both the facade and the interior decor of glass cabinets stacked with medicines (actually empty drug packages) give the impression of a real-life, traditional pharmacy. But it's an artwork functioning as a restaurant by the YBA maverick Damien Hirst. As in his Pharmacy sculptures, he cynically creates an excessively ordered, sterile image that simply duplicates a given reality having no ostensible art value or interpretive clarity. Thus he reasserts Marcel Duchamp's claim that "it's art if an artist says it is" even as he challenges the time-honored idea that representational accuracy is a prime standard of high quality. As absurdly nonsensical as the pharmacy theme may appear, considering the embrace of drugs by many in the art world, the subject is not really so far-fetched.

Hirst reiterates the pharmacy theme in the restaurant's DNA logo, wallpaper depicting pills in all shapes, sizes and colors, barstools shaped like giant Tylenols, waiters wearing surgical aprons, spices served in mortars and ashtrays depicting molecular diagrams. There are also butterfly "paintings"—reminiscent of the real butterflies Hirst used in an installation called *In and Out of Love* (1991)—which whimsically shift and further confound the specimen orientation by presenting dead butterflies stuck to monochrome canvases.

In case you're wondering, the food (modern French cuisine) is delicious. If you prefer the downstairs bar, the menu is "things on toast."

5 | Public lavatory

architect: Piers Gough (CZWG), 1993
Westbourne Grove
tube: Notting Hill Gate

If you go to the Saturday antique flea market at Portobello Road, take a short detour to see this cleverly designed public lavatory. It's just one block east of upper Portobello where Colville Road crosses Westbourne Grove. As an added

Piers Gough (CZWG), public lavatory

incentive, you can enjoy a delicious meal at one of the small restaurants across the street.

At first you may not realize that the picturesque little building on the island in the middle of the street is the site in question. Its long, svelte, triangular form sheathed in shiny aquamarine glazed bricks and crowned by a fanlike glass canopy is nothing like the mundane box design of a routine port-a-potty or the multitude of civic projects considered too lowly to warrant serious architectural attention.

Piers Gough has turned the public toilet into a prideful neighborhood landmark having all the pizzazz of an esteemed monument. Toward the rear, white panels painted with jaunty male and female silhouettes flare from the side walls to mark the entrances into the facilities. A big, round clock protruding out from the structure further sets a lighthearted tone. Most ingenious is the seamless merger of the lavatories with a flower shop, which occupies a small glass-enclosed space at the front but mainly displays its brightly hued blossoms and greenery around the long platform extending forward from the building like a ship's prow. So pleasant is the site that it serves as a popular setting for eating-on-the-run, people-watching and rendezvousing.

6 | Todd Gallery

1–5 Needham Rd, W11 2RP
020-7792-1404 f: 7792-1505
toddgallery@compuserv.com
Wed–Fri, 11–6; Sat, 11–4;
closed Mon–Tues
tube: Notting Hill Gate, Bayswater

Walk two blocks down Westbourne Grove, turn left and you'll be at Needham Road. The gallery has a modest but well-lit space and represents some highly respected teachers from London's art schools, some classic minimalists and younger-generation artists

working in various ways with painting, video and installations. The art tends to have a conceptual basis without the assertiveness or rebellious challenge of much contemporary expression.

Artist: Mac Adams, Basel Beattie, Mark Fannington, Katherina Grosse, Marcia Hafif, Jene Highstein, Maria Lali, Rosa Lee, Simon Lewis, Mark Pimlott.

The Ark

architect: Ralph ERSKINE, 1989–92
201 Talgarth Rd, W6
tube: Hammersmith

Located alongside the Hammersmith flyover across from the Broadway Shopping Centre.

Imagine one of the most incredible office buildings, designed on a remnant plot of land squeezed between rail tracks and an elevated highway (A4), and you have identified the Ark. It may be a bit removed from central London but it's well worth the tube ride if you have even a smidgin of curiosity to see architectural creativity that surpasses style-conscious trendiness or in-your-face innovation.

Ralph Erskine, The Ark

Accommodating the limitations of the site, Erskine developed the building as a curved nine-story structure whose sides slant upward, thereby skirting the highway without wasting precious airspace. By alternating tones of window glass and marking floor divisions with copper panels, he reduces the bulkiness of the structure's Noah's Ark (or ocean-liner) shape. And by cutting a slit through the facade at the entrance, by forming stepped, inset and brick sections on the side facing away from the road and by suspending a glass conference room (the Crow's Nest) above the roof, he accentuates a simple design with stylish idiosyncrasy. (In case you're wondering about the noise factor, the perimeter is triple-glazed.)

The Ark became the UK headquarters of Seagrams in 1996. Although it is not open to the public, ask the receptionist if you can just stand in the atrium for a moment to get a glimpse of the extraordinary interior. This is not your typical office atrium with repeating rows of overhanging floors, a glass roof fully visible above and tall trees on the ground floor. Instead, a view up into the center space reveals a diversity of curved, straight and angular forms, planted terraces, bridges, white-painted walls with cutout openings, glass-enclosed rooms, winding corridors, a flood of natural light from a skylight strip running through an elegant timber-lined ceiling. It's a conglomerate of open and closed, large and intimate spaces under one roof. The concept behind the design is "the office as a community." In addition to the social areas interspersed throughout the work space, the building also houses a café and bar, fitness and lifestyle center, conference suites, an art collection and a tasting room on the top floor.

Westminster– Lambeth

Patrick Heron with
1 Julian Feary

Wind Screen, 1996–98
Stag Pl, SW1
tube: Victoria

This work of public art was part of a landscaping project for a privately owned plaza. The work, placed at the pedestrian entrance to the plaza, had to control and reduce the strong winds that made the setting unappealing and essentially uninhabitable.

Heron's screen is designed to baffle the wind by having a supporting mast structure interwoven with layers of perforated metal. The flat metal elements are actually part of the painted composition: giant splotches of blue, red, green and orange, colored and positioned so they read from both sides and all angles. The screen itself, a five-story-high transparent surface, visually fills the gap between the two tall buildings at the plaza's entrance and serves as an enlivening landmark for the area.

Channel 4
2 Headquarters

 architect: Richard ROGERS, 1990–94
124 Horseferry Rd, SW1
tube: St. James's Park

Even if this high-tech building didn't stand out owing to to its location in the midst of Westminster's older, traditional architecture, its flamboyant entrance (at the corner of Chadwick Street) virtually screams for your attention. Like other structures by Rogers (Lloyd's of London, the Pompidou Center in Paris), an ostentatious display of industrial materials and sophisticated construction technology are wedded to aesthetics. But

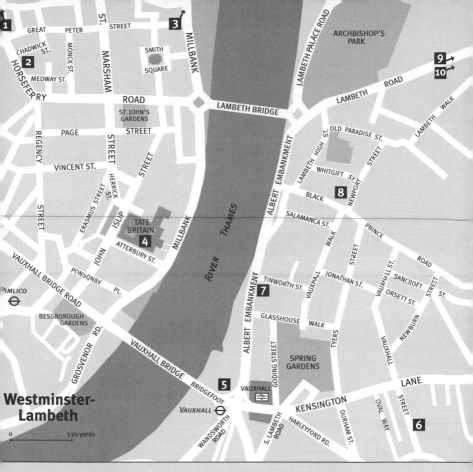

1. Patrick Heron, *Wind Screen*
2. Channel 4 Headquarters
3. Westminster Underground
4. Tate Britain
5. Vauxhall Cross

6. Gasworks
7. Milch
8. Beaconsfield
9. Imperial War Museum
10. salon3

whereas his other buildings entirely embrace this design mode, here it is reserved for the main facade. The four wings bordering the block, in contradistinction, have a rather commonplace, modernist appearance.

As you approach, you'll probably be drawn to the odd-looking service tower prominently located at the right front of the building. It's a conglomerate including a circular stairwell enclosed in polished metal; four stories of glass-and-steel-framed lobbies topped by a row of very tall and slender pipes; three rounded glass elevator cars suspended from a

red steel frame and surmounted by a double layer of box-encased heating and cooling units; a soaring transmission spire. Opposite this tower is another configuration composed of a duplicate stairwell attached to a stack of conference rooms, each a metal-and-glass-clad box set within a frame of red steel beams. Between these two structures, an open plaza spreads out to the street and back to a concave glass curtain rising to rooftop height and hanging from a steel-beam canopy. To enter the main lobby, which lies behind the curtain wall, you must walk across a

Richard Rogers, Channel 4 Headquarters

bridge over a glazed surface: suggestively a pool of water and actually the roof of a basement studio.

Although television studios and offices occupy the wings extending directly out from the theatrical entrance, the back wings form a residential complex of 100 apartments.

All the wings face into a central garden and there is parking underground.

3 | Westminster Underground

⬛ architect: Michael HOPKINS, 1999

This new station on the Jubilee Line of the Underground was an enormous challenge since the location beneath historic buildings with inadequate foundations necessitated the construction of a very deep shaft. Michael Hopkins rose to the occasion by using banks of escalators and the high columns supporting them as perspecti-

val forces that create a mind-boggling space. Rather than trying to hide the amazing depth and scale of the enormous hole, he emphasized and dramatized them. As one critic observed: "This may be just an Underground station, but it as exciting a spatial experience as you will find anywhere in the world."

4 | Tate Britain

🏛 architects (Clore Gallery): James STIRLING and Michael WILFORD,
⬛ 1982–85
Millbank, SW1P 4RG
📖 020-7887-8000
www.tate.org.uk
Sun–Thurs, 10–6; Fri–Sat, 10–10
admission: free, special
exhibitions—variable (£7.50/5,
£6.50/4.50, £5.50/4)
tube: Pimlico

Shuttle buses and boats link the Tate Britain with the Tate Modern.

The former Tate Gallery is in the midst of a transition phase that will escalate during the spring of 2000 when the Tate Modern opens at Bankside. (See p. 82-84) The new building will house the Tate's extraordinary collection of international modern and contemporary art and present special exhibitions. The Millbank location, rechristened the Tate Britain, will focus exclusively on British art from the 16th century to the present. The museum's new identity will be officially launched on March 24, 2000. However, renovation work on the west wing—which will increase display space for the collection, provide a new entrance on Atterbury Street and create new galleries for temporary exhibitions—will continue until 2001.

The transformed Tate is part of a reorganization and growth scheme that began with the construction of the Clore Gallery (1982–85) and was fol-

Sterling & Wilford, Clore Gallery

lowed by the opening of Tate outposts in Liverpool (1987) and St. Ives (1993). The Clore wing accommodates the important Turner Bequest—a large collection of paintings, drawings and watercolors by J.M.W. Turner. Attached to the main building as an L-shaped extension on the east side, the Clore has become a venerable part of the museum and an exemplar of postmodern architecture. In their design, Stirling and Wilford configured the front facade with latticelike delineations and a foreground landscaped with a lily pond to convey the impression of a garden pavilion alongside a grand house. They also utilized the practice of borrowing or contextualizing—a signature aspect of postmodernism—by shaping the Clore entrance as a pitched-roof form after the pediment-and-frieze configuration of the Tate's main entry. Translated into an utterly geometric, stark silhouette, their recessed entrance dominates the facade. It is, however, complemented by other striking elements: a solitary, tiny arched window; mullions and door frames painted lime green; oddly positioned V-shaped bay windows; red trellis beams and benches; abrupt changes

from mustard-toned stone to red brick within the grid across the wall surface.

If you walk around the outside of the Clore Gallery, you'll see additional borrowings from the architecture of neighboring buildings. Different styles converge, and conspicuous details accentuate the heterogeneity of the whole structure. Though the interior also includes some emphatic geometricization and appropriated architectural elements, it basically provides comfortable, well-proportioned, skylit rooms for displaying art. Even where bright colors are used—as in the hot pink, purple, turquoise and tangerine decor of the bookshop—they are suited to the space. Not to be missed are the upper-level galleries specially fitted for light-sensitive works on paper.

You can either pass directly from the Clore into the main building or you can exit, perhaps taking a break in the front garden, and reenter the Tate through its grand portal. Beyond the reception area is a small rotunda with paths leading off to galleries straight ahead and on either side. A restaurant and café are in the basement on the front left side, and a

Mona Hatoum, *Incommunicado*, 1993

jam-packed museum shop is to the right of the rotunda.

In addition to its extensive Turner holdings, the Tate has a superior collection of Pre-Raphaelite paintings; wondrous creations by William Blake; classics by Gainsborough, Reynolds, Constable and Hogarth; telling objects by British surrealists; prime sculptures by Henry Moore and Barbara Hepworth; and superb examples of David Hockney and Francis Bacon. Though some post-1900 works by British artists will be moved to the Tate Modern, displays at Millbank will always include a broad selection from the modern and current era. Indeed, the increase in space will bring rarely seen works out of storage and give rise to new dynamics within the installations.

The Tate has been at the forefront in rethinking the conventional practice of arranging the collection chronologically and stylistically. The new installations at both the Tate Britain and Tate Modern will dramatically revise tradition by exploring art across history in a series of thematic groupings interspersed with in-focus galleries and monographic displays. At Millbank, major works from five centuries of British art (paintings, sculptures and works on paper) will be shown alongside one another organized topically under the headings Portraits, Home Life, The City, The Inspiration of Literature, Fantastic Art, Visions, British Landscape, Artists Abroad, Images of War, Painters in Focus and Nudes.

In addition to highlighting contemporary art within the collection galleries, the Tate Britain will feature both group and solo exhibitions relating to the 20th and 21st century. *Mona Hatoum*, the first of a new series of annual sculpture exhibitions, will be presented when the museum reopens in March 2000, and *New British Art 2000* will inaugurate a new, grand-scale triennial project in the summer of 2000.

Every year on November 30, the Tate awards the Turner Prize—£20,000 ($32,000)—to an outstanding British artist under 50. It is the most prestigious accolade in the UK art world. In addition to the prize, the four short-listed finalists are the subject of a popular museum exhibition. This will continue to be held at the Tate Britain. Should you be in London during the fall season, this talk-of-the-town show provides an excellent snapshot of rising stars. In 1999 Steve McQueen won over Tracy Emin, Steve Pippin and the sister-duo, Jane & Louise Wilson.

If you, like most museum visitors, find their shops irresistible, there's a new group of items to check out at the Tate's book-gift store. On sale now at prices from $10–80 are lamps, fruit bowls, bath towels, a coat peg, garden tools, etc., designed by nine well-known British artists: Angela Bulloch, Tony Cragg, Richard Deacon, Antony Gormley, Anish Kapoor, Permindar Kaur, David Mach, Richard Wentworth, Alison Wilding. These classy household goods are the result of a 1999 collaboration between the Tate and Homebase—a "do-it-yourself" superchain. Just in time for the millennium, the final stage in the 20th-century collapse of the wall separating high and low culture. Should we call it a bang or a whimper?

5 | Vauxhall Cross

architect: Terry FARRELL, 1989–93
80–85 Albert Embankment, SE11
tube: Vauxhall

Should you not have the time to see this building close-up, walk to the riverbank in front of the Tate and you'll at least get a glimpse from afar. If it's a nice day and you're fantasy-minded, the walk across the Thames to the south end of Vauxhall Bridge where it's located, or even to the middle of the bridge where you'll get a good view, is advisable. Alternatively, if you plan to visit the new Covent Garden Flower Market, you can make an easy side trip to Vauxhall Cross.

You'll have no trouble identifying the building in question. It's the mammoth white one that looks like a Mayan ziggurat crossbred with a Disney castle spliced with a Grand Hyatt Hotel ensnared by a medieval fortress adorned with details from Art Deco and topiary masters regurgitated by a postmodern facsimilist! The vision is even more spectacularly curious when you consider that this ultra-conspicuous structure was specifically designed as the headquarters of MI6—otherwise known as the Secret Intelligence Service (S.I.S.), the bureau responsible for running secret agents overseas (à la James Bond)!

In fact, the architect has done a masterful job of camouflaging an office building and concealing its humongous mass. On the one hand, the interlocking terraces and emphatic white profile shift attention from the tower blocks behind. On the other hand, the play of rhythms from stone to glass, light to dark, solid to void, cylinder to cube enliven the utterly symmetrical facades. Should you have time to walk around the building, you'll discover that the back (the palatial waterfront side) is totally unlike the front, and that the sides have dynamically structured elevations in their own right.

Terry Farrell, Vauxhall Cross

6 | Gasworks

155 Vauxhall St, SE11 5RH
020-7735-3445 f: 7582-0159
gasgal@gasworks1.demon.co.uk
Fri–Sun, 12–6; closed Mon–Thurs
tube: Vauxhall, Oval

Deriving its name from the nearby industry, this low-key exhibition space is off the beaten track but in a neighborhood scattered with artists' studios. Gasworks is actually in a studio building operated by the Triangle Arts Trust, an international organization sponsoring guest residencies for artists, with special attention paid to the Third World. Though the gallery is part of the trust's program, it shows work by unaffiliated artists. For the most part, it's not radical vanguard art but fine-tuned creativity with a strong concept or formal base. Group projects are especially strong with unexpected interpretations of themes and astute selections. Recent exhibitions: *Duty Free, Eliminate the Negative, Janice Kerbel, Andrew Moszynski, The Nylon Salon, Passion, Projection—Video Magazine.*

7 | Milch

2-10 Tinworth St, SE11 5EH
020-7735-7334
milchgallery@yahoo.com
Wed–Sun, 12–6; closed Mon–Tues
tube: Vauxhall

Located off Albert Embankment directly across the river from the Tate Britain.

This nonprofit space takes an open, multidisciplinary approach responding to creative practices that may not fit within established, particularized categories. It commissions new work and presents art and projects from outside the UK. By placing equal emphasis on exhibitions, events and publications, Milch aims to offer a broader cultural perspective and to encourage dialogue. Housed in a warehouse (an old elevator factory) with a large public space and seven studios, it is able to accommodate all sorts of art objects, installations, performances, films, talks, music, a reading room and perhaps even a bookshop. Recent exhibitions: *Marisa Carnesky, Steve Farrer, Gift, New Art from the Baltic States, Emma Rushton and Derek Tyman, Keith Wilson.*

8 | Beaconsfield

Newport St, SE11 6AY
020-7582-6465
tube: Vauxhaul, Lambeth North

Located off Black Prince Road, just east of Albert Embankment near Lambeth Bridge.

The main gallery in this exhibition space is a double-height room with great lighting, perfect for video, painting or sculpture shows. There is no regular, ongoing program here, but it is used for traveling exhibitions or special projects.

9 | Imperial War Museum

Lambeth Rd, SE1 6HZ
020-7416-5320 f: 7416-5374
iwm.org.uk
mail@iwm.org.uk
daily, 10–6
admission: £5.20/4.20,
free after 4:30
tube: Elephant & Castle,
Lambeth North

For those who like oddities, they abound here. This is the national museum memorializing the two world wars and subsequent conflicts; the building formerly housed the infamous 19th-century insane asylum known as Bedlam. Displayed alongside the guns, bombers and military vessels are artworks from the museum's extensive holdings—England's second largest collection of 20th-century British art, mainly commissioned from war artists.

Periodically, the museum organizes exhibitions of contemporary art. They tend to present provocative statements about and against war and are often quite compelling. Recent art exhibitions: *Jananne Al-Ani, Helen Chadwick, Ian Hamilton Finlay, From the Bomb to the Beatles, Bill Furlong*.

10 | salon3

Unit 318, Elephant & Castle
Shopping Centre, SE1 6ZP
020-7252-4661
salon3@hotmail.com
tube: Elephant & Castle

If you arrive at unit 318, one of the street-side stores, and find there is no visible exhibition there, don't panic. salon3's projects are installed elsewhere in the shopping center or nearby. Just ask in the office or look for an announcement posted in the window.

Although a shopping center—especially an ugly one made of concrete and painted bright pink—is a kitschy address for a gallery, the location makes sense. It's an area with a mushrooming population of artists' studios. Because Elephant & Castle is surrounded on all sides by road and rail networks, it's also an accessible and very public location with lots of off-site potential for artist projects.

Only open since December 1998, salon3 is not your typical exhibition-oriented gallery. It primarily sponsors artist activities and projects. In addition, it organizes interdisciplinary discussions, book launches and screenings and publishes artist monographs.

Recent projects: *Dunne & Raby, Gunilla Klingberg, Out in the Isles, Plug In, Bojan Sarcevic*.

South Bank– Bankside

1 | Waterloo International Terminal

architect: Nicholas GRIMSHAW, 1988–93
tube: Waterloo

If you travel between London and Paris or Brussels, you depart from or arrive at Waterloo Station on a classy Eurostar. The terminal, a captivating design by Nicholas Grimshaw, more than matches the creative and engineering genius of a high-tech speedtrain. This is particularly evident in the extremely long, vaulted roof that runs the full length of the platforms (1/4 mile, 400 m), winding around like a snake through high grass. Shaped in an asymmetrical, tapering form, it fully exposes an intricate stainless-steel frame loosely covered with panes of glass. All appears spacious and rhythmic. There's no awareness that the sinuous path of the structure was dictated by the need to squeeze the five new canopied tracks and platforms between existing buildings and roadways with little room to spare.

The terminal is actually a two-story curved building with a parking garage at the bottom and the track-platform zone on top. More like an airport than a train station, passenger lounges and customs control are located down below. The large number of departing and arriving passengers are quickly moved on and off the platforms.

Though Grimshaw adjoins but separates the International Terminal from the rest of Waterloo Station, this causes some confusion and inconvenience, especially since the primary entrance is quite a distance from the new addition.

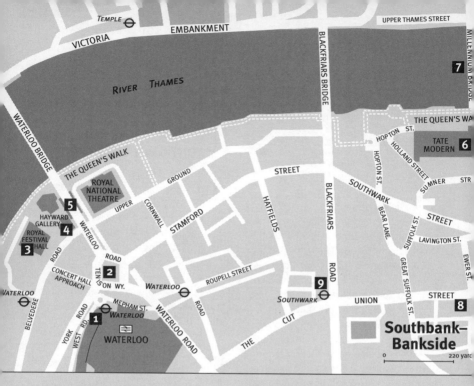

1. Waterloo International Terminal; Vilmouth (public art)
2. BFI London IMAX Cinema
3. Royal Festival Hall
4. Hayward Gallery
5. National Film Theatre and
   Museum of the Moving Image
6. Tate Modern
7. Millennium Bridge
8. Jerwood Gallery
9. Southwark Station

1 | Jean-Luc Vilmouth

Channel Fish, 1993–95
Waterloo International Terminal

It also seems incredible that only one art work was commissioned for such a large project as Waterloo. And as with most public art commissions for new buildings, the artist was not involved in the design process and only began his work when the building was nearly finished. Nevertheless, *Channel Fish*, created by Jean-Luc Vilmouth (a Frenchman), harmonizes with the architecture, adding a humorous touch and welcome reference to nature in an otherwise totally man-made environment. Arranged in a line floating in space, his 10 gigantic fish sculptures with their long silvery turquoise bodies comple-

ment Grimshaw's roof. Of course, they also relate to the path of the Eurostar trains through the Chunnel, and more particularly they bear a likeness to sand eels, a species indigenous to the English Channel.

From the narrow ground-floor lobby above which they hang, the fish are far too high up to be noticed. However, should you walk along the departure platform that looks down into this lobby, you would be on a level with them. The installation gives the illusion of an aquarium or fish swimming in the sea itself, especially since a window wall serves as the backdrop. To enhance this impression, Vilmouth has wired their resin parts so they gently wriggle at varying speeds.

Jean-Luc Vilmouth, *Channel Fish*

BFI London
2 IMAX Cinema

architect: Brian AVERY, 1997–99
I Charlie Chaplin Walk, SE1 8XR
020-7902-1234
www.bfi.org.uk/imax
imax.cinemas@bfi.org.uk
show times Sun–Thurs, noon–8:45;
Fri–Sat, noon–10
admission: £6.50/5.50
tube: Waterloo

Positioned on axis with Waterloo Bridge and set in the middle of a busy traffic circle, IMAX is a dazzling new landmark on the south side of the Thames. With its multistory cylinder set inside a frameless, glass-enclosed shell and raised above a public plaza (it looks somewhat like an exalted merry-go-round), the building is perfectly suited to its location. In fact, it serves as a beacon, visible from all directions. This is especially true at night when colored lights illuminate the form and show the lustrous, wraparound mural painted by Howard HODGKIN on the exterior wall. Even during the day, greenery trailing down from the first floor and a perimeter of plants differentiate IMAX from other buildings in the area.

Despite the building's being visually well situated, the architect faced major hurdles due to the location next to railroad and Underground train lines and encircled by a high-volume roadway. To provide safe and convenient access, he created subway passages with direct links to cross streets and nearby points of interest. He also insulated the building from vibrations and noise by setting the drumlike structure atop 90 spring-loaded pillars.

It's hard to imagine now that the site was a haven for vagrants and the demimonde right up to the time construction began on the cinema. Known as Cardboard City—a reference to the community of homeless who lived in throwaway cartons under the ruins (stone arches) of the derelict rotary—and the Bullring—so called either because of its shape or perhaps as a namesake of the infamous bear- and bull-baiting pits that flourished in the neighborhood from medieval times until the 1830s—the notorious locale was a punching bag for generations of politicians. Needless to say, the opening of IMAX in the spring of 1999 went a long way toward brightening the bleak landscape around Waterloo Station and the South Bank complex. Of course, the crowds coming to see films or to shop and eat in the stores and café-restaurants on the lower level of the cinema building are also contributing to the socioeconomic regeneration of the area.

IMAX theaters are becoming ubiquitous in major cities, each trying to outdo the others. This one, with its 10-stories-high silver screen (66 x 85 ft; 20 x 26 m) and 482-seat auditorium, claims distinction as the largest in the UK. Size and state-of-the-art technology—including a 360° sound system—aim to give viewers the impression of being "inside" the film. Only films specially produced for a large format, in either 2-D or 3-D, are shown at IMAX but the number of available selections is rapidly growing. These include destination films such as Grand Canyon, Antartica and Destiny in Space; natural history—The Living Sea, Tropical Rainforest; science fiction—Cosmic Voyage; entertainment-based—Encounter in the Third Dimension, Rolling Stones; adventure—Dolphins, Titanica; and animation—Fantasia 2000.

Apart from size and architectural design, this IMAX is truly unique in being affiliated with the high-profile British Film Institute (see p. 52-53). Similar to the National Film Theatre and Museum of the Moving Image (located a stone's throw away; see below), IMAX profits by BFI's programming expertise and experience in developing incredible outreach and educational activities.

3 | Royal Festival Hall

South Bank Centre, SE1
020-7960-4242
daily, 10 am–10:30 pm
admission: free
tube: Waterloo, Embankment

A pedestrian walkway on the Hungerford Bridge connects the Embankment to South Bank.

The ground-level foyer of this concert hall is a large, open expanse accessible to the public throughout the day. Cafés and bars, book, record and CD shops occupy the space, and often live music performances take place at lunchtime and after work. The back section of the foyer, an area designated as the ballroom, doubles as an art exhibition space. It's not a great place to show art (sculpture works best), and the quality of the projects varies considerably. The artists tend to be career beginners from London or artists from elsewhere who are not yet known in the UK. If you're in the area it's worth making a detour to see what's going on. Unfortunately, the space isn't always used for an art project and the shows are not included in media listings. Recent exhibitions: Angela de la Cruz, Jorge Pardo, Vong Phaophant, Darrell Viner.

4 | Hayward Gallery

South Bank Centre, Belvedere Rd, SE1 8XX
020-7928-3144 f: 7633-0946
www.hayward-gallery.org.uk
sbiggs@hayward.org.uk
Mon, Thurs–Sun, 10–6:
Tues–Wed, 10–8
admission: £6/4
tube: Waterloo, Embankment

This is one of the most inhospitable, dreary buildings you'll ever encounter. Constructed in the mid-1960s as an art exhibition space, it exemplifies the brutalist style of no-nonsense, functional architecture. Don't be surprised if you end up walking in circles through the ridiculous circuit of windy pedestrian decks, stairs and bridges before you find the humdrum entrance door. And when you finally get inside, don't expect an improvement. Here, too, the aura of a windowless bunker holds sway. The absence of natural light combined with raw concrete walls and a wildly illogical layout of intersecting levels is nothing short of unappealing and disorienting. Fortunately, the five galleries are large and flexible. With the addition of temporary walls and imaginative installation design, the spaces can be made to accommodate most exhibitions.

In fact, the Hayward's program is quite varied. It comprises historical shows, retrospectives, thematic exhibitions and art from other cultures. The contemporary era is well represented though the focus is not on emerging trends or experimental projects. To its credit, the Hayward has an open attitude toward the definition of art. It therefore explores visual creativity from diverse perspectives as evidenced in such exhibitions as *Addressing the Century—100 Years of Art & Fashion*, *Art of the Insane—The Prinzhorn Collection*, *Cities on the Move*, *Material Culture—The Object in British Art of the 1980s and 90s*, *Spellbound—Art and Film*. One-person shows also cover a wide gamut of approaches and stylistic directions: *Francis Bacon*, *Henri Cartier-Bresson*, *Patrick Caulfield*, *Chuck Close*, *Lucio Fontana*, *Howard Hodgkin*, *Anish Kapoor*, *Bruce Nauman*.

A plentiful selection of events and lectures accompanies each exhibit, and the bookshop supplements shows with related publications from various disciplines.

National Film Theatre (NFT) and Museum of the 5 Moving Image (MOMI)

South Bank Centre, SE1 8XT
020-7928-3232
www.bfi.org.uk
NFT—daily, variable hrs;
MOMI—daily, 10–6
admission: NFT—£6/4.50;
MOMI—£6.25/4.50
tube: Embankment, Waterloo

Located under Waterloo Bridge and tightly abutting the Hayward Gallery is a confusing maze of concrete structures housing the NFT and MOMI. You won't have much difficulty finding the building, however. Blowups of film stars appear around the riverfront Film Café, which is the entrance to the NFT, and a blue-crowned Statue of Liberty backed by space capsules and gory figures stands guard at the front door of MOMI.

The NFT has the best repertory film program in London and is world renowned for offering a unique insight into the world of film through its topical series and special events. These include cycles showing the work of a particular director, actor, country or genre; exclusive previews; on-stage interviews with such guests as Ralph Fiennes, Whoopi Goldberg, Samuel L. Jackson, Martin Scorsese, Quentin Tarantino, Sigourney Weaver; and festivals—highlighted by the prestigious London Film Festival. Film selections run the gamut from blockbusters to B-movies, classics to new releases, cult movies to comedies, silent films to musicals. All told, the NFT shows over 2,000 films each year in its three auditoriums (one large and two modest-sized).

If you want to learn about the history of cinema and television, beginning with 4,000-year-old Javanese shadow puppets and ending with the latest special-effect wizardry, you won't find a better way to do so than to visit the Museum of the Moving Image. This isn't your dry, academic presentation of dates and facts but an engaging 44-room emporium where film comes to life through props and costumes, film and TV clips, actor guides, a working cinema, a television studio and hands-on installations where you can fly like Superman, become a news anchor or audition for a Hollywood chorus line! This may sound like kid stuff, but even 60-year-old kids find MOMI absolutely riveting. The museum also curates special exhibits (e.g., *40 Years of Great British Comedy*), organizes programs (e.g., the Newsreel Conference, [Jack the] Ripper Day) and presents noontime lectures (first Tuesday of the month) on such topics as Animated Advertising, Cinderella Superman, The Disappearance of America's First Television Network, Hitchcock—A Sense of Place, Indian Cinema, Sex and the Single Girl.

To continue the museum experience, spend time at the MOMI store, where you'll find a fantastic array of gifts, posters, games, books, videos and film-related things to answer your every craving or serious need about cinema and TV. There is also an NFT Bookshop with an excellent inventory of publications on films, film criticism, history, theory, technique, filmmakers, actors and related subjects. Should you want a break after your visit, the Film Café is a great place to grab a snack, have an informal meal or just sit and relax.

As part of the Millennium development of the South Bank, a new British Film Institute complex is being planned. Preparations have necessitated the closure of MOMI (September 1999) and the relocation of NFT to the West End in 2001. The new building is scheduled to open around 2005. Check local newspapers and listings for exact information regarding temporary locations and interim activities.

6 | Tate Modern

architects: HERZOG (Jaques) & DE MEURON (Pierre), 2000
25 Sumner Street, SE1
020-7887-8000
www.tate.org.uk
Sun–Thurs, 10–6; Fri–Sat, 10–8
admission: free, special exhibitions—variable
tube: Southwark

Shuttle buses and boats link the Tate Modern with the Tate Britain.

The Tate Modern has been the centerpiece and foremost catalyst of redevelopment in the Bankside area. Promoted as a symbol of London in the 21st century, it aims to become a powerful magnet for bringing tourists to this side of the Thames after it opens in May 12, 2000.

Though the riverfront area of the borough of Southwark was largely left in an abandoned, oppressive state of ruin after being heavily bombed during World War II, its colorful past remained alive. History and legend mark it as a swarming den of iniquity from the medieval era to Shakespeare's time. Lying outside the walls—and propriety laws—of the City of London, it was a minefield of raucous theaters, inns, taverns, animal-baiting arenas, brothels and gambling hangouts. Nightly brawls, prison roundups and public executions were common.

Herzog & de Meuron, Tate Modern; Norman Foster, Millennium Bridge

The postwar creation of a national arts center—the South Bank complex—aimed to signify the renewal of London as a modern, culturally engaged city. But this reconstruction effort was restricted to a few buildings clustered around Waterloo Bridge. Not until Millennium fever and its lottery riches struck Britain in the 1990s did the whole south waterfront receive long overdue attention. Fortuitously, a most conspicuous building in this landscape—Bankside Power Station—and the Tate Gallery joined forces to bring focus to the redevelopment plans. Designed in 1947, completed in 1963 and decommissioned in 1981, the oil-fired power station is prominently situated facing the Thames directly across from St. Paul's Cathedral. Its new next-door neighbor is Shakespeare's Globe Theatre, a replica of the original building, which opened for performances in June 1996.

The process of converting the power station into a museum began with an international design competition in 1995. From 148 entries, the proposal by the Swiss architects Herzog & de Meuron was chosen. Their plan retains the brick outer shell and soaring chimney but opens up the interior space to natural light. Most dramatic are two floors encased in glass running atop the entire building above the section housing galleries. This rooftop zone (referred to as the "lightbeam" or "lightbox") with its panoramic views of London will feature a public space containing an upscale restaurant.

Visitors enter from the west end, walking down a ramp that descends into a grand reception area, formerly the turbine hall. Nothing prepares you for the mind-boggling scale of the space. It extends the full length and height of the original building: 500 x 155 ft (155 x 35 m). Envisioned as a "covered street," the cavernous space with a pitched skylight running down its center leads visitors to the museum's constituent parts. These include three floors of collection and special exhibition galleries plus two floors housing an education center, auditorium, film and seminar rooms, book- and gift shops, and a café-brasserie with an outdoor terrace.

Most important, a significant selection of the Tate's collection from 1900 to the present will finally be on view. Previously crowded into a smattering of galleries at the Tate at Millbank or kept in storage, modern and contemporary art will now enjoy the attention it deserves. With strong holdings of cubist, surrealist, abstract expressionist, minimalist and conceptual art, and key objects by Brancusi, Matisse, Picasso, Duchamp, Dalí, Giacometti, Moore, Hepworth, Dubuffet, Pollock, Rothko, Bacon, Warhol, Hockney, Richard Long, Sarah Lucas, Damien Hirst and others, visitors will get a good overview. Moreover, the installation of the collection in itself will be eye-opening. Diverging from the inveterate chronological or "ism" orientation, the art will be arranged in thematic groupings that cut across movements and disciplines and fuse the historic with the contemporary, painting and sculpture with film, video and photography. Satellite displays of relevant documents or popular culture artifacts will add contextual material while raising awareness of how slippery the dividing line between "art" and everything else became during the 20th century. Within the themes, there will also be various monographic exhibits and In Focus explorations centered on individual works of art.

A new agreement between the Tate and the photographic department of the Victoria and Albert Museum facilitates loan exchanges on a regular basis. Indeed, the inaugural exhibition at Bankside takes advantage of the extraordinary V&A collection by including vintage prints from Henri Cartier-Bresson, Man Ray and other masters of the 1920s and 1930s. Another agreement with the Froehlich Foundation in Stuttgart (in effect since 1996) gives the Tate access to an incredible collection of 320 major works by nine German and 10 American contemporary artists. For its opening, the museum has selected benchmark objects by Nauman, Warhol, Beuys and Flavin.

As with most major museums, special (temporary) exhibitions are a dominant aspect of the program. The Tate enjoys a worldwide reputation for the high caliber and broad scope of the exhibits it presents and the quality of accompanying catalogues. During the initial year, the museum will use level 4—the special exhibition galleries—to show some of the large-scale installation works it owns but has rarely displayed due to a lack of space. These include film, video and sculpture projects by artists such as Matthew Barney, Rebecca Horn, Cornelia Parker and Bill Viola.

A new "projects series" will present the latest developments by commissioning work for particular locations in the building. Though not exactly part of this series but quite exciting in its own right is the unique opening exhibition devoted to Herzog & de Meuron. For this, the architects will design ten stations to be situated throughout the museum. These will reveal unusual aspects of the building, both old and new, indicate interesting views and convey ideas and creative processes involved in the amazing renovation. The stations draws on models, plans, photographs and videos.

The Tate Modern will also commission large-scale projects (one each year for the next five years) for Turbine Hall as part of the Unilever Series. The first work by Louise Bourgeois—an inspiring octogenarian who repeatedly comes up with something scintillating and utterly imaginative—will be unveiled in May 2000 when the museum opens.

Since 1998 the Tate Modern has been organizing temporary art and outreach projects in the area around its new building. These have included *Performing Buildings*, projections onto the exterior walls of the Power Station of art films by Gordon Matta-Clark, Robert Smithson, Andy Warhol and others; *The Wedding Project*, a public celebration staged in Borough Market by Anna Best; *Bankside Browser*, a computer database and open archive exhibit of work by 250 Southwark artists; *Turbulent*, a double-projection film exploring gender, cultural and religious issues by the Iranian artist Shirin Neshat (installed in a City church); and *Beach-coming on London's Foreshore*, an archaeological-like dig in the Thames at Tate Bankside and Millbank by Mark Dion. This initiative will continue after the museum opens its doors to the public.

7 | Millennium Bridge

architect—Norman FOSTER; artist—Anthony CARO; engineers—ARUP, 1999–2000
Thames River

This pedestrian bridge, scheduled to open in April 2000, connects old and new landmarks: St. Paul's Cathedral and the Tate Modern. Designed to be as unobtrusive as possible, the crossing appears as a "thin blade of stainless steel" by day and a "sliver of light" by night. Even if you have no reason to take the five-minute walk across the river, the wonderful views of the city alone are worth the trip. Should you need added incentive, stroll down the enhanced riverside walk along the South Bank. You can go in either direction on what is now a seamless path from Westminster Bridge to London Bridge and beyond. It's especially enjoyable at sunset.

8 | Jerwood Gallery

171 Union St, SE1 0LN
020-7654-0171 f: 7654-0172
www.jerwoodspace.co.uk
curator@jerwoodspace.co.uk
daily, 10–6
admission: free
tube: Borough, Southwark

Located just south of the railroad between the Ewer St underpass and Great Guilford St.

Previously an old bike shop, the gallery building has been handsomely converted into three interconnected rooms of modest size with great light, a small sculpture court and stylish café. Just behind, in a renovated Victorian school, are five rehearsal studios for dance and theater companies. The whole complex, open since the fall of 1998, is supported by the Jerwood Foundation.

Focusing on work by young artists, the exhibition space often gives unknown talents their first professional experience. The program features individual artist presentations or thematic group shows. A popular favorite is the Jerwood Painting Prize—an annual exhibition of the 10 finalists for a £30,000 ($48,000) award. Prunella Clough won in 1999; Madeleine Strindberg in 1998; and Gary Hume in 1997.

Recent exhibitions: *Glenn Brown, Jason Coburn, Jacqueline Donachel Alison Gill, dumbpop, Formerly (Mark Cannon, Ana Prada, DJ Simpson), Natural Dependency, Sarah Jones.*

9 | Southwark Underground

architect: Richard McCORMAC, 1999
With architectural finesse, McCormac designed this Underground station (part of the Jubilee Line extension) so daylight shines down into the interior. Light effects are enhanced by rays bouncing off a curving blue glass wall created by the artist Alex BELESCHENKO.

Bermondsey– South London

1 | Delfina

50 Bermondsey St, SE1 3UD
020-7357-6600 f: 7357-0250
admin@delfina.org.uk
Mon–Fri, 10–5; Sat–Sun, 2–5
admission: free
tube: London Bridge

This alternative space, located in a renovated chocolate factory in a warehouse area undergoing rapid gentrifica-

Susan Hiller, *PSI Girls*, 1999

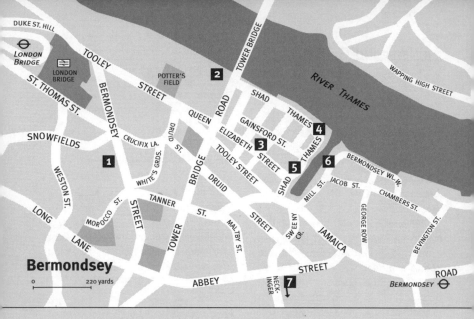

tion, is a popular artist hangout. In fact, the large front area is a restaurant-café. It's a very informal place where people are friendly and gregarious. The gallery occupies its own space, also large and unpretentious, all the way in back through the double doors. The exhibition program is incredibly varied with no apparent cohesiveness in the kind of art shown—except that it's all new work by some of the most adventurous, one-of-a-kind artists. Young or midcareer, internationally recognized or just starting to get widespread exposure, the artists take advantage of the freedom offered at Delfina to present formidable projects. Don't think twice about visiting here; put it on your list of must-see places.

Recent exhibitions: *Abstract Art (Eric Bainbridge, Simon Bill, Ian Dawson, Keith Farquhar, DJ Simpson, Gary Webb), Eric Bainbridge, Ellen Cantor, Martin Creed/Ceal Floyer/John Frankland, Wim Delvoye, Anya Gallaccio, Ludger Gerdes, Susan Hiller, Manuel Ocampo,* *Pia Stadtbäumer, Keith Tyson, Mark Wallinger, Elizabeth Wright.*

Defina is actually a charitable trust established in 1988 by Delfina Entrecanales, a lively septuagenarian from Spain with a very generous soul. She wanted to support artists so they could develop new work and, especially in the case of foreign artists, get the chance to experience the London scene. In addition to free studio space (above the restaurant and gallery) and living accommodations (for foreigners), the 18 artists-in-residence can use the site facilities—darkrooms, kilns, workshops and photographic equipment—and enjoy subsidized lunches.

Greater London Authority Headquarters

2

architect: Norman FOSTER, 2001
riverfront west of Tower Bridge, SE1
tube: London Bridge, Tower Hill
The newly formed position Mayor of

London necessitated an impressive new building and Norman Foster designed just that. It's a unique, elliptically-shaped structure located prominently on the edge of the Thames alongside London Bridge. Rising 10 stories high, the GLA will house offices for the mayor and Assembly Secretariat on the upper floors, public services on the lower floors, a flexible, open space ideal for exhibitions or banquets on the top floor (Foster calls this "London's Living Room") and a spectacular public terrace on the roof.

The building, scheduled to be completed by 2002, sits between a new plaza opening onto the waterfront and Potter's Field Park. It is part of a mixed-use development that includes offices, a hotel, shops and restaurants. There will be enhanced landscaping in the area.

3 | The Circle

architects: CZWG, 1987–90
Queen Elizabeth St, SE1
tube: London Bridge, Tower Hill

You'll undoubtedly encounter flocks of tourists around Tower Bridge but can quickly escape by turning down Queen Elizabeth Street. As you walk ahead, curious buildings sheathed in cobalt glazed bricks with "owl-ear" rooflines come into view. These are actually paired structures on each side of the street sharing a common entrance. All curve around a circular forecourt formed from the widening of the street. A large bronze horse standing on a pedestal in the middle of the street and other quirky features—like the alignment of balconies running diagonally across six stories of each facade and the white slanted mullions on all the windows—add eccentricity to the design. When the street and facades straighten out, some of the oddities remain but lose their oomph. The roofline is now a gently undulating rhythm; the stepped pattern of the balconies is shorter,

CZWG, The Circle

hence less emphatic; and above all, the bricks are just commonplace—a type known as yellow London stock. (They're actually a dull beige and always very weathered-looking.)

Though it's not too clear from the exterior, this complex of buildings is a mixed-use development composed of 302 flats, 8 office suites, 12 shops, 1 restaurant and a swimming pool/health club.

4 | Design Museum

architects: Conran ROCHE, 1989–90
22 Shad Thames, SE1 2YD
020-7403-6933 f: 7378-6540
daily, 11:30–6
admission: £5.25/4
tube: London Bridge, Tower Hill

Prior to becoming a derelict zone, the old Victorian buildings in this neighborhood, known as Butlers Wharf, were warehouses occupied by flour, corn and rice merchants and then used to store spices. When Conran Roche revitalized and gentrified the area, the buildings were transformed into luxury apartments, specialty shops, gourmet restaurants, middle-income flats, student housing and offices. Roche also spruced up the waterfront with a wide promenade and redeveloped the charming cast-iron and timber bridges over narrow streets and canals.

The Design Museum, a brainchild of Stephen Bayley and Terence Conran, aimed not only to call attention to mass-production consumer goods (like the ones Conran created and sold in his Conran Shop and Habitat Stores) but also to give focus and enrichment to the neighborhood. Although previously a warehouse, the building now has a 1930s, International Style appearance: white undecorated surfaces, stark geometric form, horizontal window bands and a flat roof. Basically, it's an uninspired clone despite enhancement from a stepped-back facade and terrace café overlooking the Thames.

The museum collection on the second floor is nicely installed in a double-height, skylit space with marble and oak floors. Displays range from kitchen wares to motorcycles, luggage to cameras. There's something for everyone, and visitors generally have a fun time. Unlike the conventional museum, here you're actually invited to touch and try some objects—like the various models in "chair alley." The main drawback is the character of the selections: it's not very adventurous and lacks historical breadth.

Special exhibitions (located on the first floor) tend to be more fascinating than the collection display. Objects are placed in contexts other than aesthetics, and in-depth treatment of a particular subject or designer enlarges the scope of design activity. Recent exhibitions: *Bosch—Industrial Design, Design Now—Austria, Design—Process—Progress—*

Practice, Charles and Ray Eames, Modern Britain (1929–1939), On the Road—The Art of Engineering in the Car Age, Vernon Panton, Ferdinand Porsche, The Real David Mellor.

Rounding out the facilities in the museum are a library and well-stocked gift shop. There is also a theater or lecture hall in an attached building fronting on Maguire Street, though it seems museum programs for this space have been cut considerably.

5 | David Mellor Building

24 Shad Thames, SE1
architect: Michael HOPKINS,
1987–91
tube: London Bridge, Tower Hill

This finely crafted building was created for David Mellor, England's esteemed designer of kitchen utensils, and now is owned by the Conran enterprise. Serving as the London headquarters for Mellor, it includes a ground-floor showroom whose front window-wall is set back to accommodate a covered walkway; three floors of workshops and offices in the middle; a top-floor residence with balconies, roof terrace, harbor views and privacy; and a side tower attaching an enclosed staircase to the main structure.

The simple rectangular form and concrete frame belie extraordinary detailing (some of which was made by Mellor himself) that sets the design apart from the norm. Most extraordinary is the lead paneling covering the exterior side walls.

6 | China Wharf

architects: CZWG, 1987–89
29 Mill St, SE1
tube: London Bridge, Tower Hill

On the one hand, this building establishes links with the industrial architecture of its neighbors. This is most evident in the side adjacent to Reeds Wharf, which is sheathed in London stock bricks and punctuated by align-ments of curve-topped, multipaned windows. On the other hand, the build-ing blatantly stands out as new con-struction of the zany, postmodern vari-ety. The street facade exemplifies this by means of a scalloped, white stucco wall with the bottom hollows painted bright red and windows positioned inside the scooped-out sections so they face the sun. The river facade goes even further by having its front dominated by a strangely shaped red concrete frame with arches that vaguely recall a pagoda (except here the arches point down-ward instead of upward).

Squeezed between two renovated warehouses, China Wharf was added to fill a gap and create visual continuity. Offices occupy the first two floors, and 17 apartments, laid out so each has a river view, fill the upper five floors.

Gavin Turk exhibition, 1998

7 | South London Gallery

65 Peckham Rd, SE5 8UH
020-7703-9799 f: 7252-4730
www.southlondonart.com
mail@southlondonart.com
Tues–Wed, Fri, 11–6; Thurs, 11–7;
Sat–Sun, 2–6; closed Mon
admission: free
tube: Oval then bus 36; Elephant &
Castle then bus 171, 12, P3

Don't be put off by its far-afield loca-tion. South London Gallery is one of London's best contemporary art venues. Having existed as a community art cen-ter for years, it moved into the high-profile sphere in the mid-1990s by orga-nizing shows of Gilbert and George and Tracey Emin. Since then it has consis-tently presented new work by major and emerging contemporary figures or influential work from the past that has rarely, or not recently, been seen in Britain. Each undertaking fills a gap rather than rehashing familiar territory or advancing the latest, hottest band-wagon. A remarkable exhibit (fall of

1998) of the young British artist Gavin Turk, for example, brought together a full range of his challenging creations for the first time.

Occasional theme projects are partic-ularly geared to promote a dialogue about relevant social issues. For exam-ple, *Non Place Urban Realm* (summer of 1999) explored urban renewal by look-ing at art and cultural practices made visible in the work of three artists—Marcelo Expósito from Spain, Marc Pataut from France and Paul O'Neill from Ireland. A rigorous program of forum discussions with speakers from diverse backgrounds accompanied the show. Such events—as well as perfor-mances, music evenings and exhibition catalogues—are standard fare.

Located in an old Victorian building, the gallery occupies a huge, high-ceilinged room with lots of space for display. In addition, it sponsors off-site projects and commissions public art. *Route 12:36*, for instance, is an ongoing series launched by Blast Theory and Grennan & Sperandio who put art on the advertising panels in city buses with the added ingredient of engaging pas-sengers in both the process and the product. The second work in the series was a website by Faisal Abdu'Allah.

Recent exhibitions: *Drive-by—New Art from LA, The Elders—Brother Everald Brown & Stanley Greaves, Lucio Fontana, Intimate House—Live Art, Jorge Molder, New Contemporaries 99, Non Place Urban Realm, Mimmo Paladino, Marc Quinn, Julian Schnabel, Sean Scully, Site Construction, Sound Factory, Gavin Turk, Vanished! (Brian Catling and Tony Grisoni), Stephen Willats.*

Isle of Dogs–Millennium Dome

Since the early 19th century, east London was an industrial area that turned the Thames into a working river and shaped the marshlands into an amazing circuit of docks bustling with commerce and life. Then, in the 1960s, activity came to a halt. Largely as a result of strikes and the arrival of container ships (which needed deep waterways), the harbor shut down. Almost overnight it became an abandoned wasteland, remaining so until the Thatcher government established the London Docklands Development Corporation (LDDC) in 1981. The regeneration efforts that followed and are still going on have been controversial at nearly every stage. Some have been successful but most have been plagued by financial woes, business fiascoes, bad (or nonexistent) planning decisions, leasing difficulties, opportunistic chaos, a lack of adequate and timely infrastructure (especially public transportation) and boring corporate architecture.

A word about the word "dock." When associated with the Docklands, dock almost always refers to the *waterway* designed for the reception of ships rather than the platform to which ships are loaded, unloaded or attached.

Canary Wharf Development, phase 1

master planners: SKIDMORE, OWINGS & MERRILL (SOM), 1987–99
architects: GENSLER, KOETTER KIM, KOHN PEDERSON FOX, PEI COBB FREED, Cesar PELLI, SOM, TROUGHTON McASLAN

The most conspicuous and largest single development is Canary Wharf on the Isle of Dogs. It is called Canary Wharf since many of the imports to the docks in question were from the Canary Islands. And the name Isle of Dogs refers to the royal dogs once kenneled on the property—which some consider to be a peninsula and not an island—so they wouldn't disturb the residents and guests at the royal palace in Greenwich (formerly the playground of kings and queens).

The master plan created by SOM for the first phase of development concentrated on mega-office buildings with very little public space inside and very formal, rather antiseptic space outside. The architecture is massive and austere. Corner towers, pediments, columns, decorative window frames, covered arcades and stone cladding establish a historical aura. But unlike the disjunctive conglomerates that typify postmodernist borrowings, here calm order prevails and historicism infuses the build-

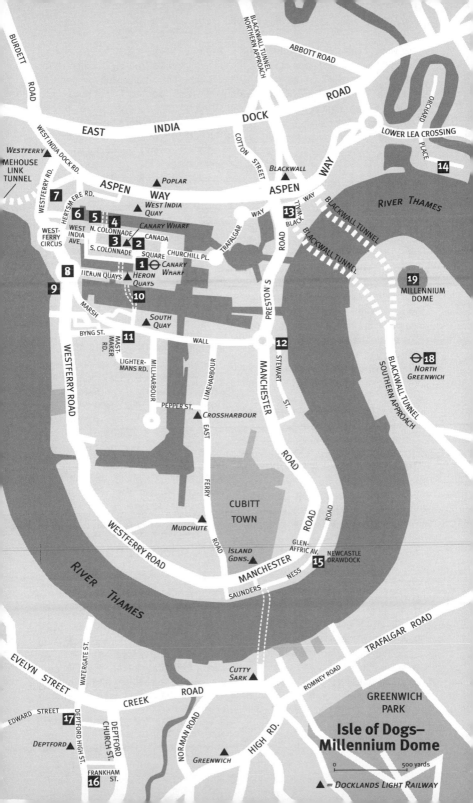

Isle of Dogs–Millennium Dome

0   500 yards

▲ = DOCKLANDS LIGHT RAILWAY

ings with classical magnitude and secure stability—albeit on a level of generic blandness. It was important to present an image with widespread appeal. Nothing radical, nothing that might offend potential occupants. The restrained ambience even included computer-controlled water jets in the Cabot Square fountain so passersby wouldn't get wet because of changing wind currents. This in a city where rain dominates the weather!

Despite promotion as a multiuse development, Canary Wharf initially paid virtually no attention to cultural amenities, park or leisure facilities. Moreover, only limited space was devoted to retail businesses, and the original complex included just one apartment building. New housing did proliferate on the Isle of Dogs, though not in Canary Wharf and not according to any overall plan. Indeed, the residential zone that is emerging along lower Westferry Road leaves a lot to be desired, as does the total separation of work and shops from housing.

After a rocky beginning, when the initial investors (Olympia & York) hit bottom and Britain was struggling through hard economic times, the Canary Wharf development grew fast and furiously. By the late 90s, almost every inch of available land in the northern end of the isle was sprouting yet another giant office building. Three of these, all located on Canada Square, are towers—not just high buildings but the three tallest buildings in the UK. Virtually all these buildings are occupied by banks and financial institutions, thus following the initial idea of turning Canary Wharf into an outpost of the City of London.

Without question, the dominance of a conservative, corporate aesthetic in the buildings and the regimented character of the setting make it feel like a picture-perfect metropolis—a clone from The *Truman Show* replete with

Disney's spanking-clean, control-freak ideals. And yet the environment has a certain allure because of the pervasive waterways. Some of the newer construction projects are also (finally) adding overdue amenities and spice to the setting: an entertainment complex, hotel with casino, additional shops and green space.

It would have been nice if imaginative artists had been involved in the planning or in the creation of virtuoso works of public art, but this wasn't the case. You will see some token art strewn about the landscape, either commissioned by the LDDC or by individual developers, who sadly were not required to include a percentage for art in their construction budgets. Most all the work is, however, quite mundane, not the stuff that pushes boundaries and stands apart. What a lost opportunity!

For your visit to the Isle of Dogs, go one way on the tube's Jubilee Line extension, and the other on the Docklands Light Railway (DLR) so you can experience these new transportation systems and see their architecturally designed stations. Be sure to save time for a walk along the Thames Path, a delightful riverside promenade where you'll get wonderful views of the near and distant cityscape.

Canary Wharf
1 Undergorund

architect: Norman FOSTER, 1994–99

Seeking to minimize the visible and physical presence of this Underground station, Foster designed the three entrances as domed bubbles integrated into the sloping grass banks of a public park and recreation area. The steel-and-glass entrance canopies also admit daylight into the station, which is entirely underground, constructed within a drained dock. The ticket hall below, entered by 20 escalators, is a cavernous, unencumbered space containing shops and services. The size of this station (as long as the Canary Wharf Tower is high) is geared to handle more passengers than Heathrow. This gives you a sense of how many offices with commuting workers are planned for the Canary Wharf development.

Be sure to take a gander at the magnificent space here, even if you don't take the Underground.

2 | Canary Wharf Tower

architect: Cesar PELLI, 1989–91
1 Canada Sq, E14
DLR or tube: Canary Wharf

You can walk from Cabot Place East through a passageway into the tower, but you won't get beyond the reception desk in the lobby. The tower with its many high-profile corporations and financial institutions is off-limits to the public. (Past IRA bombings in London have made it necessary to tighten security restrictions.) In any event, the interior is far less interesting than the concept of the structure and its presence in the landscape.

It's the tallest skyscraper in Britain (880 ft; 244 m high) and the first ever to be clad in stainless steel. Despite the use of a modern-day, unconventional material, the building is archetypal. Pelli (he's the architect who did the tower over MoMA in NY) described it as "a square prism with pyramidal top in the traditional form of the obelisk." Rigorously minimal, it has a somber window grid repeated on all 50 stories and all four sides. Only when the metallic surface reflects sunlight is the symmetry disturbed.

The tower is fully equipped to accommodate the latest computer technology, and its floor plan, able to be configured as a large open space of double height, can be used as a trading floor. If you like statistics, it's amusing to know that the tower has 3,960 windows, 4,388 steps, and it will take you just 40 seconds to get from the lobby to the top in the elevators!

Norman Foster, Canary Wharf Underground

3 | DLR Station, Retail and Conference Center

architect: Cesar PELLI, 1989–91
Cabot Pl, E14
DLR or tube: Canary Wharf

Located between the main outdoor plaza and the landmark office tower, Cabot Place is the focal public space within Canary Wharf. It's actually two buildings (Cabot East and West) framing the DLR station. In addition to serving as a kind of thoroughfare, it's an indoor mall with shops and restaurants. Since this is the only such facility in Canary Wharf and on the isle (as of 1999), it's almost always extremely crowded. In one respect, it answers practical needs by having a supermarket, dry-cleaning shop and various take-out eateries. But it's also designed for pleasure with a glass-domed, marble atrium providing a bottoms-up view of the adjacent tower and an assortment of upscale boutiques. Above the underground and ground-floor mall, Cabot

West fills another function by providing a conference and banquet center composed of an auditorium with 1,000 seats, reception and meeting rooms.

The most impressive part of the architecture is the DLR station or, more specifically, the sweeping glass roof shaped as a parabola which covers the tracks and platforms. Its graceful curve not only adds height and openness to the station but also acts as a strong counterpoint to the bulky stone buildings visible all around.

4 | Bruce McLean

Sculptured railings
Wren Landing, E14
DLR or tube: Canary Wharf

If you walk north from Cabot Square toward the floating footbridge, these black steel railings serve as a guard barrier for the terraces and stairs on Wren Landing. They compress layers of scribblelike lines, drawn images of hands and flat planes in circular and rectilinear shapes. Effusively decorative, they offer a sharp contrast to the nearby architecture, recalling instead the energetic swirls of Art Nouveau and the stylized designs of Charles Rennie Mackintosh and the Glasgow School.

5 | West India Quay Footbridge

architects: FUTURE SYSTEMS, 1996
DLR: West India Quay

This simple bridge with its lightweight, slightly arched, slender form, flashy color (yellow-green) and nontechnological structure is quite an oddity in the Canary Wharf environment. Using an age-old, archetypal method of construction, it floats a narrow path on pontoons (four pairs). Structural revival aside, the walkway is made of steel and aluminum and has integral lighting on the handrails and decks. As you cross between Wren Landing and West India Quay, you'll also notice how a tapering in the middle emphasizes perspectival views and exaggerates length.

6 | William Pye

Archimedes, 1997
West India Docks, E14
DLR: West India Quay

Look left (west) from the footbridge, and you'll see two highly polished stainless-steel forms anchored in the water at the end of the dock. One is a cone shape set upright and the other is a curlicue positioned on a slant. The imagery pays tribute to Archimedes, the ancient Greek inventor and mathemati-

Future Systems, West India Quay Footbridge

Richard Wentworth, *Globe*

cian (with special expertise in geometry). Among his great achievements were formulations related to the measurement of a circle and the area and volume of curved surfaces. One of his major creations was a screw device—now called Archimedes' screw—used to pump water. Pye's sculpture is actually water-powered, though often the gushing-water components are not functioning for some reason.

7 | Richard Wentworth

Globe
Cannon Workshops Wall,
Westferry Rd, E14
DLR: Westferry
tube: Canary Wharf

If you descend Westferry Road going north, the sidewalk soon gets squeezed between the street and a very long, slightly curving, blackened yellow (London stock) brick wall. A row of 17 clocks near the top of the wall is an artwork by Richard Wentworth. Each clock runs according to the present time in a different place in the world (noted on the clock faces). In addition, the align-

ment suggests a path encircling the earth's sphere beginning and ending with Alaska. (The Alaskan clocks have only their inward halves visible with their outward halves painted black and hanging off the ends of the wall.)

According to the artist: "Canary Wharf's proximity to the Meridian is the basis for *Globe* . . . . Geographical good fortune is the source of London's success, and in their previous form the West India Docks were central to it. Two hundred years later it is international time zones which dictate the ebb and flow of life and business at Canary Wharf. *Globe*... reveal[s] a sample of these times and places simultaneously, re-employing the generous nineteenth-century tradition of displaying time publicly."

8 | Pierre Vivant

Traffic Light Tree, 1995–98
Heron Quays Roundabout, E14
DLR: Heron Quays
tube: Canary Wharf

Playing with the idea that trees are usually removed to make way for directional signals and road markers, Pierre

Vivant has created a tree image composed of traffic lights. Placed in the middle of a traffic circle beside two live trees, it comically makes this point to all drivers and passengers who whiz by on their way into Canary Wharf, a very denatured setting. With its 18 green branches made up of 65 units randomly flashing the familiar red-amber-green lights, arrows and walking or stationary figures, the tree vividly captures attention and bemusedly mocks the very notion of traffic control.

9 | Cascades

architects: CZWG, 1986–88
2–4 Westferry Rd, E14
DLR: Heron Quays
tube: Canary Wharf

Do not overlook this imaginative building if you're anywhere near the Isle of Dogs. It redefines the image and character of high-rise housing without relying on new technology or fancy add-ons.

Located on the riverfront just below (but not part of) the Canary Wharf development, it was among the first structures to be completed within the isle's regeneration plan. Instead of ignoring the past, the architects created an exterior of yellow London stock bricks with bands of dark blue engineering brick and white features as a reference to the ships' bridges and factories that formerly dominated the area. They also borrowed portholes, turrets and an industrial chute image. Indeed, it is the chute that is the cleverest design element. It's actually a fire-escape staircase running down the side of the building enclosed in a shedlike covering with private terraces belonging to a stepped cascade of penthouses on either side. And what could be more appropriate than having the cascade end in a swimming pool at the bottom!

Basketlike enclosures for patios and little rounded balconies that further articulate the facades give residents spectacular views. At its height, the building has 20 stories and contains one-, two- and three-bedroom apartments, a health club, conference rooms and some retail shops.

South Quay
10 | Footbridge

architect—Chris WILKINSON; engineer—Jan BOBROWSKI, 1995–97
DLR: Heron Quays
tube: Canary Wharf

Like the pontoon bridge on the north side of Cabot Square, this cable-stay footbridge reveals an avant-garde spirit that is missing in the architecture at Canary Wharf. Its eccentric S-curve winds across the dock between Heron Quays and South Quay giving one of the best views of the conglomerate of new buildings. With its two high steel masts angled out over the water, its oak planks set diagonally on the deck and its sinuous path emphasized by a phosphorescent light along the handrail, it

CZWG, Cascades

offers in a walk across an amazing spatial experience.

Since tall boats still use the docks, the bridge had to be designed to enable their passage. A structure of two identical halves, one static and the other capable of pivoting open, provides for this.

11 | Eilís O'Connell

Vowel of Earth Dreaming Its Roots, 1994–98
Marsh Wall at Mastmaker Rd, E14
DLR: South Quay

Taking account of the location—a plaza alongside a busy street overlooked by the elevated tracks of the DLR—O'Connell sought to treat the site as a refuge from its speed-oriented surroundings. Therefore, instead of a complex object, he created an ensemble of primary elements: a tall cone surrounded by clusters of cubes (which can be used as seats) and a series of arcs delineated in stone within the gravel surface of the ground. Making reference to the former existence of the land here as a marsh, he used carboniferous limestone, a lumpy gray material embedded with shell fragments, for the cone. The

title derives from a verse in *Kinship* by the Irish poet and Nobel laureate, Seamus Heaney.

Storm-Water
12 | Pumping Station

architect: John OUTRAM, 1986–88
Stewart St, E14
DLR: South Quay

At the juncture of March Wall and Manchester Road there's a path leading to Stewart Street. The Pumping Station, which moves storm water from the isle into the Thames, is just ahead on the left (east). It's the polychrome, pagoda-like building behind the dark brick wall. Attracting immediate attention are the eccentrically shaped, brightly colored "capitals" atop thick brick columns, the stark white attenuated pediment with a big fan, hanging half beneath the roof's overhang, as its centerpiece. What a weird and wonderful design! Hardly what you'd expect to find in an industrial, infrastructure building.

In fact, Outram purposefully hid the pumping machinery underground and flamboyantly decorated the exterior to camouflage the station and enhance

John Outram, Storm-Water Pumping Station

the environment. So successful was he in devising eye-catching architectural embellishments, you hardly notice how massive the building is, nor that it's windowless and essentially a box shape with a heavy concrete substructure, completely outfitted to be bomb-proof and terrorist-resistant.

Nothing is what it seems. The portholes are fake. The columns don't support the pediment but instead hide stairs and ducts. The strange, turbojet-engine-looking fan with slow-turning blades, on the contrary, actually functions to evacuate gases from the interior. And the decorations, which seem quite arbitrary, follow a carefully formulated schema. They symbolize the landscape from which the storm water flows: the slate blue bricks represent the river, the big columns signify tree trunks and the red and yellow stripes denote the mountainside.

Be sure to walk all around the Pumping Station, not only to see the full program of imagery and architecture but also to get a terrific view of the Millennium Dome directly across the Thames. If you want a break from "site-seeing," you can meander down the riverside path and have a picnic or relax at one of the lookout spots with benches.

Reuters
13 Services Centre

architect: Richard ROGERS,
1987–89
Blackwall Yard, Gaselee St, E14
DLR: Blackwell

This building is off-limits to the public but you can get a good view of the architecture near the entrance to the fenced-in property. To get there, take Preston's Road; turn right onto St. Lawrence Street; make a quick left onto Gaselee Street and continue until it curves into Blackwall Way. In the midst of the desolate acreage to the right you'll see an isolated, large black-glass cube. This is the Docklands home of Reuters, the information, news and business giant.

Following his renowned flair for exposing the service components, Rogers places the stairwells in glazed towers external to the facades. He also creates a vast roof plant by extending the steel framework of the cubic shape upward but leaving it in an exposed state. Typically, he adds brightly colored elements to enliven the industrial design. Here these are blue and green equipment containers and small yellow roof cranes.

This building is rather restrained for Rogers, especially when compared with his ultra-high-tech design for Lloyd's of London (see p. 112-13). In fact, it's not so much the architecture but the eerie image of this black safeguarded structure juxtaposed with the white curving tower of a nearby nuclear energy plant that rattles the mind.

14 Jem Finer

Longplayer, 1/1/2000–12/31/2999
Trinity Buoy Wharf Lighthouse
64 Orchard Pl, E14 0JW
020-7336-6803
www.longplayer.org
Sat–Sun, 11–dusk throughout 2000
admission: free
DLR: East India Dock

Turn right when you exit the DLR station, bear right at the traffic circle onto Orchard Pl and keep following the signs. (10-minute walk)

Through an exploration of generative forms of music rooted in the fields of artificial life and complexity, Jem Finer has developed a system resulting in an ever-evolving piece of music. This composition will play continuously for 1000 years beginning on January 1, 2000. It will be launched at various listening posts throughout the UK and elsewhere. In London, Artangel (the sponsoring organization) has set up a post in an unused lighthouse on Trinity Buoy Wharf, where you can hear *Longplayer* during the millennial year 2000. If you're visiting the Millennium Dome across the Thames, listen for echoes of *Longplayer* in the dome's rest zone.

15 | Grenville Davey

One and Four Thirds, 1997
Newcastle Drawdock,
Glenaffric Rd, E14
DLR: Island Gardens

The riverside path goes by this sculpture project, which is situated close to the Greenwich Foot Tunnel, in and around a small plaza at Newcastle Drawdock's public slipway. Realizing that the site offers telling views of Greenwich (its historic, new and deteriorated cityscape) while also providing a community recreation and gathering area, Davey created an inventive array of five sculptures to be used as seating or play objects. Also in the plaza are old black-and-white striped cannon bollards, a paved rainwater pool and large stone blocks positioned to mark off the location of a chapel destroyed in the blitz.

One, a giant circular form (inspired by the image of a button) set on a narrow base, is the primary object in the series. Made of galvanized steel with a ring of oak seat panels on top, it has an industrial character related to the region. Though not immediately evident, the four sculpture-benches derive their shape directly from *One*. Each is a mold of a one-third slice of the whole disk flipped upside down. The seat panels are appropriately repositioned and legs are added to raise each of the *Four Thirds* to a comfortable height for sitting.

Unfortunately, the humor in Davey's ensemble gets lost in the overly austere, uninviting design of the plaza. It is also nearly impossible to comprehend the clever relationship of parts to whole because the sculptures are widely spread out—three in the plaza proper and two on an elevated lookout across the slipway.

DEPTFORD, a growing artists' haven, lies cross the Thames (Greenwich Reach) in an area now more accessible, owing to the DLR, and appealing because of its proximity to Goldsmiths Art School. As in the East End and Hoxton neighborhoods, the prevalence of artists has led to exhibitions in empty warehouses. They also take place in makeshift galleries within the artists' studio complexes (Artists in Perpetuity Trust, ACME Studios, Lewisham Arthouse, Faircham Trading Estate). To find out about these shows, keep an eye out for posters or announcements, which usually are placed in popular art spaces.

16 | Hales Gallery

70 Deptford High St, SE8 4RT
020-8694-1194 f: 8692-0471
hales@btinternet.com
Mon–Sat, 9–5
DLR: Deptford Bridge
train: New Cross

Attached to a café and next to a street market, this high-energy gallery gives meaning to the idea of community and keeps alive the original notion of an alternative art space. The setting is not eye-catching or chic yet Hales has become a meeting place for artists living in southeast London. Quite pragmatically, the gallery uses profits from the café to fund exhibitions. It can therefore afford to give artists a rare degree of creative freedom and support. Its commitment to young developing artists is not limited to those in London, as evidenced by the recent exhibition *Cache: Art from the Top of Ireland*. Often there are installations in the basement. Artists: Sarah Beddington, Andrew Bick, Jonathan Callan, Clare

Carter, Judith Dean, Leo de Goede, Claude Heath, James Hyde, Rachel Lowe, Martin McGinn, Tomeko Takahashi.

17 Museum of Installation (MOI)

175 Deptford High St, SE8 3NU
020-8692-8778 f: 8692-8122
www.moi.dircon.co.uk
moi@dircon.co.uk
Tues–Fri, 12–5; Sat, 2–5;
closed Mon
DLR: Deptford Bridge

During the 1990s, installation work proliferated and became the trendy, dominate mode of creative expression. Mainstream artists and young rebels alike jumped on the bandwagon developing sensate spaces, cluttered assemblages of common objects, technologically complex productions and everything in between.

MOI was founded as a gallery so that upstart and little-known artists might have the opportunity to create and show installation projects. Recent exhibitions: *Day for Night, Thomas Eller, Wolf Kahlen, Mischa Kuball, Louise Sudell, Test Sites ECM 323—Sound Installations, Mark Themann.*

18 North Greenwich Underground

architects: ALSOP and STORMER, 1999

Like the new Canary Wharf Station for the Underground extension of the Jubilee Line, this one is built to accommodate huge numbers of people. During 2000, it will particularly serve visitors to the Millennium Dome. Indeed, its massive sense of space is in keeping with the grand scale of the dome. The decorative aspect of the cobalt blue glass walls and tiles is, however, quite different.

19 Millennium Dome

architect: Richard ROGERS, 1999
Greenwich , SE10
www.dome2000.uk
admission: £20,
reductions for special categories,
families and groups
tube: North Greenwich

In 1884 Greenwich was designated the Prime Meridian of the World. That is to say, it's the location of the imaginary dividing line between the Eastern and Western hemispheres; longitude zero; the place from which time is calculated. Elevating its importance as the "home of time," the British government

Richard Rogers, Millennium Dome

deemed Greenwich the perfect site for celebrating the millennium. Plans soon centered on the construction of a Millennium Dome that would itself be a glorious 21st-century image as well as an international showcase for British design and ingenuity—not to mention a big tourist attraction.

Richard Rogers, a leading force in high-tech architecture, became the mastermind behind the dome's design: a cable-net structure of gargantuan proportions supported by a circle of 12 yellow steel masts and covered with a gleaming white Teflon-coated glass-fiber roof. Although the technology is quite distinctive, the idea of suspending a roof over a vast area or city was actually envisioned in the mid-20th century by Buckminster Fuller.

If you can conceptualize in terms of numbers, just imagine the dome's colossal scale: each mast is over 330 feet (100 m) high and weighs 105 tons; the interior covers 20 acres of ground space; and the roof is about 1/5 mile (320 m) in diameter and 165 feet (50 m) high. If you're better at thinking in terms of imagery, consider that the roof is strong enough to support a jumbo jet, and the Great Pyramid of Egypt or Eiffel Tower lying on its side would easily fit within the dome. For those who prefer a liquid measure for comparison, the dome could contain 3.8 billion pints of beer!

Inside, a sunken performance arena, visible from all over, sprawls across the center. Sound, light and music shows with plenty of high-tech wizardry and live entertainers present multimedia spectacles here on a nearly continuous schedule. Surrounding this space are 14 theme zones examining aspects of mind, body, spirit, work, learning, environment, dreams, communication, leisure, atmosphere and Britain. A gigantic, seated androgynous figure is a featured object. You enter its cathedral-like body through the heel, wind around numerous experience and information centers in the leg and torso to end at an observation deck in the head. Many exhibits on display within are interactive with a futuristic component brought to life in virtual reality displays.

The vanguard architect Zaha HADID designed the Mind Zone, a hanging maze-like structure which includes compelling works of art by Helen Chadwick, Richard Deacon, Ron Mueck and Gavin Turk. This zone, which explores sense and perception through mind games, visual tricks and optical illusions (there are even morphing machines that let you change your gender and race), is one of the highlights of the dome in terms of its content and design. The Rest Zone, a flotation tank produced by Richard Rogers, is also interesting as an architectural structure.

Although most grand proposals provoke critical reactions, the Millennium Dome has faced an onslaught of controversy at virtually every stage of development. Never-ending complaints are raised against the cost—over £750 million ($1.25 billion)—and massive scale of the project—especially since it's only a temporary extravaganza. On the plus side, the dome has revived a derelict area and been the catalyst for an overdue upgrading of public transportation and infrastructure in the eastern sector of London.

The dome is only scheduled to be open for one year beginning with the inaugural hoopla on December 31, 1999. After its closing, the structure will go up for sale.

East End

This is a poor, warehouse-filled, industrial and working-class area of London, still grim and desolate here and there, with rapidly spreading pockets of gentrification. Interspersed are artists' studios, galleries and exhibition spaces.

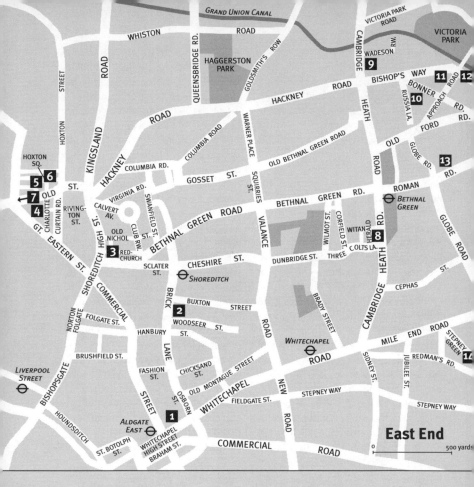

1. Whitechapel Art Gallery
2. Atlantis
3. Modern Art Inc.
4. The Agency
5. The Lux—Centre for Film, Video + New Media; LEA Gallery (1st floor)
6. White Cube 2
7. Victoria Miro Gallery
8. Maureen Paley Interim Art
9. Anthony Wilkinson Gallery
10. The Showroom
11. The Approach
12. Chisenhale Gallery
13. Camerawork
14. Matt's Gallery

Many of these are low-budget operations in decrepit-looking buildings on seedy, deserted streets. However, some of the big name dealers from central London have begun to move to the area, turning spacious warehouses into upscale galleries. Regardless of appearances, you can count on viewing a diverse range of experimental, imaginative work, some of it brimming with potential, some of it kitschy and awful.

Keep an eye out for announcements about special exhibitions in studios or abandoned buildings. For example, in the fall of 1998, Jake and Dinos Chapman held a public showing in their work-abode on Fashion Street.

If you visit the area on Sunday morning (6–1), you can also meander through a classic street market at the northern end of Brick Lane. You'll find stalls selling every variety of fresh and packaged food, clothing, household goods, collectibles, discount books and junk related to the local immigrant populations and old-world British culture. It's a great complement to the art you'll see in the East End exhibition spaces.

Whitechapel
1 Art Gallery

📠 80 Whitechapel High St, E1 7QX
020-7522-7888 f: 7377-1685
📧 press@dial.pipex.com
Tues, Thurs–Sun, 11–5;
Wed, 11–8; closed Mon
admission: £4/2.50 (variable),
free Tues
tube: Aldgate East

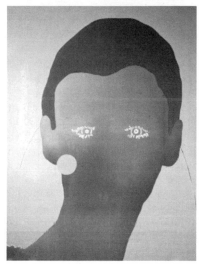

Gary Hume, *Cerith*, 1997

Conveniently located adjacent to an Underground stop, Whitechapel Art Gallery is on a bustling commercial street, housed in a distinctive stone building with square corner towers and a massive arched doorway positioned off-center. The building, specifically designed for the art center in 1897–99, was refurbished and expanded in 1984. It now includes light and airy exhibition spaces on two floors, an auditorium, bookstore and café.

If you need a good reason to go to London's East End, this is it. Whitechapel has a well-deserved reputation as a premier space for showing cutting-edge art and superb exhibitions. Rather than jumping on bandwagons to be trendy, the gallery continuously displays leadership by presenting challenging work, even if it's not popular or easy to digest. Thematic shows, which often set forth unusual relationships among objects from different eras and diverse media, are especially engaging. You'll also see art from outside the Western mainstream.

The gallery, whose history dates back to the 1880s, was never a collecting institution. Initially, its intention was to bring world-class art to the East End

and to show the work of local residents. A concentration on modern art increasingly developed, and bold moves, like the showing of Picasso's *Guernica* in 1939, put Whitechapel on the international map. Since the 1950s, the clear focus has been on art with an experimental edge. More specifically, the current aim is "to show work that advances both the artistic debate and our understanding of the world" whether by "up-and-coming artists, widely recognized contemporary figures or artists from the early 20th century whose work remains relevant." Both one-person and thematic projects are part of the schedule, which also features lectures, films and a range of educational programs.

Recent exhibitions: *Aligiero e Boetti, Tony Cragg, Peter Doig, Examining Pictures—Exhibiting Paintings, Lucian Freud, Gary Hume, Fernand Léger, Live in Your Head, Henri Michaux, Cathy de Monchaux, Speed, Francisco Toledo, Rosemarie Trockel, Bill Viola, Aubrey Williams, Terry Winters, 000ZeroZeroZero* (British-Asian cultural provocateurs).

2 | Atlantis

146 Brick Lane, E1 6RU
020-7377-8855
tube: Aldgate East, Shoreditch
Located between Woodseer and Buxton Sts in the Old Truman Brewery.

Atlantis is mainly a supplier of art materials though exhibitions and art projects take place on its premises from time to time. The large space on the top floor is an extremely attractive location for all sorts of installations. Check the current press listings to see if anything is scheduled here; if so, don't miss it. Recent shows include the screening of *Feature Film* by Douglas Gordon, and the presentation of *13 Different Keys*, with work by Deborah Bull, Gill Clarke and Siobhan Davies.

3 | Modern Art Inc.

73 Redchurch St, E2 7DJ
020-7739-2081 f: 7729-2017
www.art-online.org/modernartinc
modernart@easynet.co.uk
Thurs–Sun, 11–6; closed Mon–Wed
tube: Old Street, Liverpool Street

This well-connected East End gallery arrived on the scene in 1999 and has been assertively establishing itself as a London and international presence. The focus is on young artists and new talent. If word on the street is a gauge of quality and character, this gallery will be around for a long time.

Artists: Simon Bill, Ian Dawson, Peter Geschwind, Joanna Kirk, Maria Lindberg, Tim Noble & Sue Webster, James White & Tim Steward, Richard Woods.

4 | The Agency

35–40 Charlotte Rd, EC2A 3DH
tel/fax: 020-7613-2080
theagencyltd@agency-
gallery.demon.co.uk
Tues–Fri, 11–6; Sat, 11–4;
closed Mon
tube: Old Street, Liverpool Street

The Agency is renowned around London as the premier center for extravaganzas like *Fete Worse Than Death*. It thrives on being outside the mainstream and open to all sorts of artsy, edgy projects and productions. Exhibitions include the screening of Paul McCarthy's ribald films and new work by Faisal Abdu'Allah, Joshua Campston, Edwin David, Mary Beth Edelson, Kazuo Katase, Ken Lum, Seamus Nicolson, Mabel Palacin, Ross Sinclair, Stephen Willats, Peter Zimmerman.

The Lux–Centre for Film, Video & 5 | New Media

2–4 Hoxton Sq, N1 6NU
020-7684-0101 f: 7684-1111
www.lux.org.uk
gallery@lux.org.uk
tube: Old Street

You'll find artists' studios at every turn in the area around Hoxton Square. And the art spans the gamut from fine arts to furniture, books, film, architecture, textiles, media and graphics design. The Lux, though only open since 1997, has become a pivotal center for the neighborhood as well as an internationally known hub for activities involved with moving images. It houses the Lux Cinema on the ground floor and the London Film Makers' Co-op, London Electronic Arts and LEA Gallery on upper levels. Equipped with state-of-the-art facilities for film, video or multimedia production and offering in-house services associated with distribution, funding, exhibiting, training and education, the Lux is a haven for both newcomers and professionals.

When you're in the cinema lobby, be sure to look down to check out the video monitors sunk into the floor. The theater here functions like a cinémathèque showing retrospectives of a director, film star or producer and thematic programs dealing with a particular genre or subject.

The biennial festival, *Pandaemonium 1998—London's Festival of Moving Images* (September), exemplified the energy of the center. It featured a fantastic program of new work in a variety of forms at a multitude of venues across London. Combining open submissions, curated programs, commissions and collaborations, the festival made the term "avant-garde" come alive. It provided an of-the-moment, unique, diverse snapshot of the most potent artistic practices by some of the most exciting international talents.

5 | LEA Gallery

2-4 Hoxton Sq (1st floor), N1 6N U
020-7684-2785 f: 7684-1111
www.lea.org.uk
info@lea.org.uk
Wed–Fri, 12–7; Sat–Sun, 12–6;
closed Mon–Tues
admission: free

Access to LEA is by an elevator and staircase entered from a glazed hallway (not well marked) between the theater lobby (right) and the Blue Note (a club next door).

The LEA gallery (associated with London Electronics Arts and often called the Lux Gallery) is one of the best places in the world to see truly inventive, compelling works in the realm of creative video and electronic media art. Its rich program of exhibitions includes single and multiple projections as well as installations. Several works by the same or different artists, some of whom are familiar because of their sculptures or paintings, are on view at any given time.

A particularly riveting presentation that was both visually and conceptually engaging was *Within* (1998) by Dryden Goodwin. It enclosed viewers inside a tight space surrounded by four monitors suspended from the ceiling and slanted inward. Standing in the middle and turning to grasp the various sequences, you'd see figures posed in casual acts, but the images would alternately move in and out of focus, be shown from shifting camera angles and be captured in prolonged freeze-frames. You'd also hear three sound movements revolving in different combinations with the images.

Other recent exhibitions: *Animation (Mat Collishaw, Tim Hutchinson, Tim Macmillan, Kay Shepherd), Susan Collins—Suspect Devices, Drugs, Erotic Italia, Gary Hume—Night Time Window Projections, John Maybury, Pulse, SODA (Lucy Kimbell, Julian Saunderson, Fiddian Warman, Neal White), Anne Tallentire, Vegas, Nick Waplington.*

In addition to its on-site exhibitions, LEA organizes programs for various London venues (including the Tate, Serpentine, Whitechapel) and publishes *Coil*, a journal for the moving image (£5).

6 | White Cube 2

48 Hoxton Sq, N1
tube: Old Street

White Cube 2, an outpost of the White Cube gallery on Duke Street, moves into its spacious new quarters in April 2000. The inaugural exhibition features world-renowned artists who are among the gallery stars: Jake & Dinos Chapman, Tracey Emin, Antony Gormley, Gary Hume, Sam Taylor-Wood, Gavin Turk. (For more information about White Cube, see p. 38.)

7 | Victoria Miro Gallery

16–18 Wharf Rd, N1
tube: Old Street

Walk east on Old St from Hoxton Sq; turn right onto City Rd and continue as it curves westward; turn right onto Wharf Rd, a bit after the intersection with Sherpardess Walk and Bath St.

In June 2000 the Victoria Miro (see p. 26) will move into this renovated Victorian furniture factory, where the gallery will quadruple its exhibition space.

Paul Noble, *Welcome to Nobpark*, 1998

Maureen Paley
8 Interim Art

⬜ 21 Herald St, E2 6JT
020-7729-4112 f: 7729-4113
Thurs–Sun, 11–6; closed Mon–Wed
tube: Bethnal Green

Located just off Cambridge Heath Rd on the corner of Witan St.

For years Maureen Paley ran her gallery out of the tiniest of houses on a little street crossed by elevated railroad tracks in a fringe poverty area. As her exhibitions gained prestige, she slowly expanded into an annex and finally, in September 1999, moved all operations into the annex—a converted factory on Herald Street. Widely recognized as a hot spot for emerging talents, many fresh from art school, the gallery is already profiting from its spacious, conveniently located, new setting.

Paley has been deeply committed to promoting young Brits, especially those who create unorthodox work and experiment with blending thematic, image and media categories. Photography with a biting edge is favored. For example, in his first one-person show (spring of 1998), Paul Noble covered the gallery walls with an eccentric photofrieze, disjunctively overhung by framed drawings which likewise depicted scenes of a sublimely odd forest (called *Nobpark*) populated by cutouts of grinning animals and marked by the presence of a tent.

Artists: Kaye Donachie, Mark Francis, Ewan Gibbs, Sarah Jones, Karen Knorr, Paul Noble, David Rayson, Paul Seawright, Hannah Starkey, David Thorpe, Wolfgang Tillmans, Gillian Wearing, Paul Winstanley.

Anthony Wilkinson
9 Gallery

⬜ 242 Cambridge Heath Rd, E2 9DA
020-8980-2662 f: 8980-0028
wilk@ndirect.co.uk
Thurs–Sat, 11–6; Sun, 12–6;
closed Mon–Wed
tube: Bethnal Green

The art shown at this well-regarded gallery spans the range from ethereal, minimalist and seductive compositions to funky, witty vernacular imagery; from painting and mixed-media to photography and video. If you had to pick a dominant thread, it would probably be color: the brightly toned grounds in Christopher Bucklow's negative-image photographs or the rich color fields in the tantalizing paintings of Edward Chell and Simon Callery. But then color is overshadowed by absurdity plain and simple in Glen Baxter's work and tinged with commentary in Jessica Voorsanger's art.

The main thing, it's all strong, refreshing stuff. Most of the artists are British and they clearly love to experiment, investigate new possibilities and keep upping the ante by pursuing variants.

Artists: Glen Baxter, Christopher Bucklow, Simon Callery, Edward Chell, Angela de la Cruz, Dominic Denis, Peter Ellis, Matthew Higgs, Nicky Hirst, Olav Christopher Jenssen, Dhruva Mistry, Silke Schatz, George Shaw, Mike Silva, Bob & Roberta Smith, Johnny Spencer, Jessica Voorsanger.

10 | The Showroom

44 Bonner Rd, E2 9JS
020-8983-4115 f: 8981-4112
theshowroom@mail.excite.com
Wed–Sun, 1–6; closed Mon–Tues
tube: Bethnal Green

This is one of London's alternative spaces, valued for its support of ambitious, maverick projects and artist residencies. The Showroom has a notable record for commissioning works that have become springboards for artists in the early years of their development. The gallery also presents new work by established artists from the UK and abroad, especially those who focus on an overlap between visual and live art.

Typifying its program was the intriguing exhibition developed by Andrea and Philippe Bradshaw in the fall of 1999. For this, Philippe painted a re-creation of Ingres's *Turkish Bath* in anodized metal chain while living in a homemade lean-to in the gallery, and Andrea enhanced an otherwise private area by planting it with a romantic garden.

Recent projects by: Claire Barclay, Pierre Bismuth, Francis Cape, Freddy Contreras, desperate optimists, Ceal Floyer, Alan Kane, Phillip Lai, Jim Lambie, Rachel Lowe, Christina Mackie, Stephen Murphy, Florence Paradeis, Adrian Schiess, Smith/Stewart, Gordana Stanisic, Fergal Stapleton, Simon Starling, Sam Taylor-Wood, Rebecca Warren, Gerard Williams, Elizabeth Wright, Oliver Zwink.

11 | The Approach

The Approach Tavern, 1st floor
47 Approach Rd, E2 9LY
tel/fax: 020-8983-3878
Thurs–Sun, 12–6; closed Mon–Wed
tube: Bethnal Green

You'll probably question the address since Approach Road is a nice residential street with a school on the corner, and #47 is a neighborhood pub. This is indeed the place, and the gallery, an alternative space, is in a simple room on the 1st floor. Take advantage of the location not only by stopping for something to eat or drink but by inquiring of the bartenders and patrons about the exhibitions. Chances are you'll get a totally unaffected critique of current and past projects as well as a telling commentary on contemporary art.

Open since February 1997, the Approach gives evidence of the enterprising character of the East End community. Most exhibitions are curated by writers and artists, and virtually all shows feature young Londoners. Exhibitions: *Liz Arnold, Daniel Coombs, Enrico David, Ana Genovés, Idlewild, It's a Curse—It's a Burden, Emma Kay, Look of Love, Michael Raedecker, Emma Simpson, Jane Simpson, Kerry Stewart, Martin Westwood.*

12 | Chisenhale Gallery

64 Chisenhale Rd, E3 5QZ
020-8981-4518 f: 8980-7169
www.chisenhale.org.uk
mail@chisenhale.org.uk
Wed–Sun, 1–6; closed Mon–Tues
tube: Bethnal Green, Mile End

From the look of the exterior—a dilapidated brick factory—you may be tempted to turn away and skip a visit here. True, the building doesn't look much like a serious art gallery, and you may well encounter a gang of grungy youth (unsavory hustlers? art students?) at the front door. Not to worry. Inside, it's a classic alternative (nonprofit, independent) space whose large, unobstructed hall, Sheetrock walls and concrete floor are perfect for all sorts of exhibitions. In fact, Chisenhale consistently pushes the envelope by commissioning work from uncompromising artists and presenting exhibitions that stretch the concept and context of art. Regardless of what's on display, you should absolutely visit this respected, influential gallery.

Chisenhale's history of supporting bold projects includes Rachel Whiteread's *Ghost!* (1990)—her famous cast of an entire room; Cornelia Parker's exploded and reconstituted shed; and installation video projects by the likes of Jane & Louise Wilson, Sam Taylor-Wood and Gillian Wearing. Many such commissions and debut solo shows, awarded at a crucial stage of an early career, launched artists into orbits of national and international attention. The gallery also organizes exhibitions of up-and-coming international artists (e.g., Pipilotti Rist, Wolfgang Tillmans), often giving them their first major exposure in the UK.

Recent exhibitions: *Juan Davila, Lili Dujourie, Exit—Art & Cinema at the End of the Century, Simon Faithfull, Thomas Hirschhorn, Norman Hogg, Jasper Joffe, Michael Landy, Hilary Lloyd, Sarah Lucas, Lisa Milroy, Sigalit Landau & Saskia Olde Wolbers, Tim Nobel & Sue Webster, Path, Root, Marijke Steedman, Nick Stewart, Simon Wood.*

13 | Camerawork

121 Roman Rd, E2 0QN
020-8980-6256 f: 8983-4714
www.camerawork.net
info@camerawork.net
Thurs–Sat, 1–6; closed Mon–Wed
tube: Bethnal Green

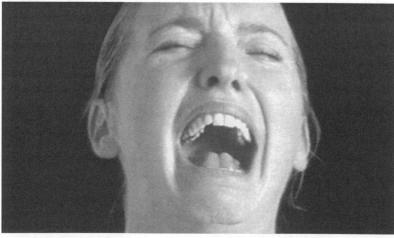

Sam Taylor-Wood, *Hysteria*, 1997

Camerawork combines a gallery with darkroom facilities. It has existed for over 20 years as a place for creating, showing and discussing photography. Using its exhibition program as a point of departure, it has particularly sought to explore the role of photography in popular culture, documentary work and conceptual art. Recent exhibitions: *Baffle, Fiona Christ, Pals and Chums, Postcards on Photography, Scheufler & Heiss, Tail Out—Experimental Film & Video.*

15 | Matt's Gallery

42–44 Copperfield Rd, E3 4RR
020-8983-1771 f: 8983-1435
Wed–Sun, 12–6; closed Mon–Tues
tube: Mile End

Don't panic because you can't find a gallery sign: it doesn't exist. Just head for #42–44 in the midst of the string of industrial buildings bordering the southwest side of Mile End Park near the stadium.

The gallery was named after a dog—Matt E. Mulsion—and operates on the premise of carte blanche freedom. This means giving an artist all the time and resources necessary to develop ideas or experiment with methods and media while producing work specifically for the gallery space. As practiced at Matt's, the open approach has resulted in an incredible record of outstanding projects. Among them are Richard Wilson's oil piece, 20:50 (now installed at the Saatchi Gallery), and innovative work by Tony Bevan, Willie Doherty and Jimmy Durham. The gallery also publishes catalogues and artist's books.

In 1992 Matt's moved to its present location—large, airy premises with several flexible spaces—and in 1993 it changed from being a commercial gallery into a nonprofit organization. The basic direction has remained the same. Though Matt's customarily works with artists who are young and little known, it also supports established artists wanting to explore new paths or create unique projects.

Artists: Tony Bevan, Brian Catling, Melanie Counsell, Juan Cruz, Xenia Dieroff, Willie Doherty, Sean Dower, Graham Fagen, John Frankland, Nat Goodden, Lucy Gunning, Melanie Jackson, Jaroslaw Kozlowski, Ian McKeever, Mike Nelson, Kate Smith, Matthew Tickle, David Troostwyk.

City of London

1 | Barbican Centre

Silk St, EC2Y 8DS
020-7638-8891 f: 7920-9648
www.barbican.org.uk
tube: Moorgate, Barbican

The Barbican Centre, London home to the Royal Shakespeare Company, London Symphony and British Chamber Orchestras, was constructed in 1982 as a multifaceted, municipal cultural complex. The building is a maze of terraces, walkways, staircases and elevators connecting two theaters, a concert hall, three art exhibition galleries, three cinemas, conference suites, two convention halls, shops, a lending library, tropical conservatory, restaurants, bars, cafés and the Guild Hall School of Music and Drama.

With luck you will find the main entrance and be able to follow the signage to desired components and ultimately wind your way through the contorted path to the exit. Sadly, the Barbican building isn't very welcoming, and its heavy, dark gray concrete does little to alleviate the bleakness of the surrounding area—a residential zone composed of high-density towers and slab buildings with a geometrically shaped "lake" in the middle. This area suffered heavy bombing during World War II and was developed into a self-

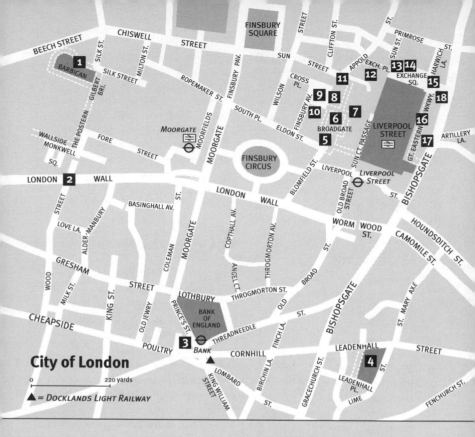

City of London

0   220 yards

▲ = DOCKLANDS LIGHT RAILWAY

1. Barbican Centre
2. Alban Gate
3. One Poultry Street
4. Lloyd's of London
5. Richard Serra (public art)
6. Broadgate Circle
7. Barry Flanagan (public art)
8. Jacques Lipchitz (public art)
9. One Finsburg Avenue
10. George Segal (public art)
11. Stephen Cox (public art)
12. Howard Hodgkin (mural)
13. Xavier Corberó (public art)
14. Exchange House and Exchange Square
15. Fernando Botero (public art)
16. Lincoln Seligman (public art)
17. Bishopsgate; Jim Dine, Craig-Martin (public art)
18. Bruce McLean (public art)

contained housing project thereafter. Justifiably, the architecture and plan have been extensively criticized.

In addition to art exhibitions (see below), classical music and Renaissance theater, the Barbican presents a wide range of spectacular events: jazz concerts, a Beckett festival, Bangladesh music and dance, poetry readings, folk music, etc.

Barbican Art
1 | Gallery (level 3)

020-7382-7105 f: 7628-9364
Mon, Thurs–Sat, 10–6:45; Tues 10–5:45; Wed 10–7:45;
Sun, 12–6:45
admission: £6/4; Mon–Fri after 5, £4

This is the main exhibition space for art in the Barbican Centre and a major venue in London for important temporary exhibitions, some of which deal with vanguard contemporary art.

Regrettably, the layout with its over-hanging balcony and central atrium puts a serious constraint not only on the type of art that can be displayed but also on installation creativity.

The bookstore carries mainly survey picture books, texts related to exhibitions, posters and postcards.

Recent exhibitions: *African Photography, Art of the Harley, David Bailey, Joseph Beuys—Multiples, Cuban Art, James Ensor, Magnum—Photographs 1989–99, Malevich's Vision of the Russian Avant-Garde, Native Nations—Journeys in American Photography, Picasso and Photography, Andy Warhol.*

Barbican Concourse and Foyer Galleries
1 (ground floor)

 020-7638-4141 f: 7382-7252
Concourse: Mon–Sat, 10–7:30;
Sun, 12–7:30
Foyer: Mon–Sat, 9 am–10 pm;
Sun, 12–10
admission: free

Exhibitions in the Concourse Gallery are more low-key and often related to crafts. Recent exhibitions: *American Bookworks, Contemporary American Basketry, Contemporary Print Fair, Elliott Erwitt, London Artists' Bookfair, US Video.*

2 Alban Gate

architect: Terry FARRELL, 1987–92
125 London Wall (at Wood St), EC2
tube: Moorgate

The London Wall area, like the Barbican, required near total redevelopment because it was so extensively devastated in World War II. Reconstruction created a highway bordered by office towers raised up on podia and connected by bridges. The results left much to be desired, so much so that several buildings were redesigned or replaced within a few decades.

Alban Gate (previously the site of Lee House) is the largest, second-generation project. Composed of two 20-story blocks, it straddles the London Wall roadway with an arch, an image recalling city entrances of yore. (London Wall—built c. A.D. 200—did, in fact, enclose the original town of Londinium in Roman times.) The linked high-rises, set skewed to each other, have facades with alternating rose-toned granite and reflective-glass segments, exposed structural beams, projecting and recessed parts. Farrell thus aimed to reduce the massiveness of the whole and to avert the archetypal regularity of modern office buildings. Overwhelming scale is also assuaged by topping each tower with a curved roofline. These curves are actually the ends of glazed vaults covering interior atria—a ubiquitous element in tall buildings designed in the 1990s.

3 One Poultry Street

 architects: James STIRLING and
Michael WILFORD, 1986–97
1 Poultry St, EC2
tube: Bank

Tightly positioned on a wedge-shaped corner in the midst of a neighborhood crowded with the country's major banks, this office building stands out even as it bears witness to—albeit in a postmodern spirit of parody—the stately, massive, thick-walled, classical and bland facades in the vicinity. Capriciously, it agglomerates their diverse architectural features into a zanny, unorthodox structure. Striped, curved, flat, V-shaped, projecting, recessive, glazed and solid surfaces abound, punctuated by circular, square, arched, horizontal and vertical shapes.

As lively as the building appears when viewed from the street, you will undoubtedly be taken aback when you walk through one of the lateral passageways into a wide drum—a circula-

Stirling & Wilford, One Poultry Street

tion hub with shops on the ground and lower levels—whose center is an open triangular courtyard. Shiny blue-tiled walls with square inset windows painted with flashy pink, yellow and blue borders exaggerate the theatricality of this inner space. Corner sections, sheathed in the same stripes of muted rose-toned granite and sandstone as on the street facade and topped by eccentric turrets and canopies, add further pizzazz. Invisible from below are the roof gardens and restaurants, a nice accouterment for an office building in a crowded urban setting.

While most architecturally significant buildings are designed for a specific client-occupant, #1 Poultry Street was created as speculative rental property for a forward-thinking developer—Lord Peter Palumbo, owner of homes by Le Corbusier (Paris), Mies van der Rohe (Chicago) and Frank Lloyd Wright (near Pittsburgh). The bold design survived an endless stream of planning battles, but unfortunately, its architect, James Stirling, did not live to see the vigor of his creation, especially as compared with the cold, industrial style of so many contemporaneous constructions in London. (Stirling died in 1992.)

4 | Lloyd's of London

architect: Richard ROGERS, 1978–86
107 Leadenhall St, EC3
tube: Bank

With extreme panache, Lloyd's, one of Britain's stalwart institutions, boldly departed from its own style and that of conservative London when it commissioned a radical new headquarters on the site of its former offices—a pompous structure erected in 1925. You're either going to like this building or hate it. No one who sees it remains neutral, and pundits have had a field day poking fun at it. Having been a prime source of the unbridled attacks made by Prince Charles in 1988 against modern architecture, it still arouses impassioned commentary and heated controversy.

Anyone familiar with the Pompidou Center in Paris, also designed by Rogers, will recognize a commonality in the placement of service and support elements—elevators, fire stairs, bathrooms, pipes, ducts, girders—on the outside. Here, these are allied with six independent towers whose stacked box and cylindrical modules of shiny stainless steel look like overgrown Donald Judd sculptures or high-tech versions of Brancusi's *Endless Column*. The details of the facade have been described as "magnificently obsessive," but sadly the effect is more claustrophobic than exhilarating since the building is so tightly bounded by neighboring structures and streets that it has little room in which to breathe or display its profiles. The long, dark shadows cast by its looming height increase the harsh, cold appearance.

By moving the service zones to the exterior, Rogers gave the interior an open plan. At Lloyd's this centers on a vast, undivided area for the underwriters—The Room. Covering the entire ground floor and the first three mezzanine levels, it lies at the base of a cathedral-like, 12-story atrium topped by a glazed barrel vault. Additional floors of offices, resting on huge concrete columns, fan out from the atrium, and four levels below ground contain restaurants and services.

Although security and privacy restrictions won't permit you to go inside, you can get an impression by peering through the glass-walled vestibule at the Lime Street entrance. On the one hand, the atrium is a majestic space with a zigzag stream of escalators at the far end, and in the middle, a stately colonnaded rostrum containing the Lutine Bell. (The bell was recovered from the shipwreck of the HMS *Lutine* in 1799 and has been a fixture in Lloyd's since 1857. The bell is rung to announce the arrival of news related to a risk insured at Lloyd's.) On the other hand, the atrium is a windowless, depersonalized office space—a sea of 98 desks, all made of the same highly polished wood and all occupied by men and women dressed in dark suits who seem to stare relentlessly at their desktop computer screens. Rather than a workplace designed for the future, it appears like a surreal update and upgrade of the anonymity-plagued, mass-production factories of the past.

If you haven't responded favorably to Lloyd's from a daytime visit, try to view it at night from across the Thames. Gleaming under blue floodlights and showing its irregular silhouette to great advantage, it stands out emphatically within a skyline populated by too many monolithic gray buildings.

Richard Rogers, Lloyd's of London

Broadgate Development

architects: ARUP and SKIDMORE OWINGS & MERRILL, 1984–91
Liverpool St/Bishopgate, EC2
tube: Liverpool Street

This massive development project surrounding Liverpool Street Station responded to the newly deregulated financial activities in Britain and the new age of international electronic communications. It greatly expanded City of London operations by providing enlarged, flexible office space and well-equipped trading floors. Although the plan included some retail and leisure facilities and sets buildings in a nicely landscaped environment, traversed by pedestrian streets and dotted here and there by sculptures, it is predominantly a Monday-to-Friday business zone, devoid of housing and non-worktime value. Employee comfort was a big consideration and the whole development was designed with this in mind. But on weekends, when none of the 25,000+ occupant-commuters are around, you can't even buy a cup of tea, and the vast area is a ghost town. If you want to get a good visual sense of the setting itself without the people-hustle, weekends are a good time to visit. Beware, however, that Saturdays and Sundays bring out the skateboard fanatics who use Broadgate as a practice field. The sonic reverberations in the empty plazas can be excruciating, and the crash landings that inevitably occur inches from your body are nerve-racking to say the least.

Arup Associates designed the first phases, 1984–88, which roughly cover the southwest section bordered by Liverpool, Eldon, Finsbury and Sun streets. The buildings here are of modest height, sheathed in red granite and glass, enhanced with high-tech elements and typically centered on a glazed-roof atrium. For the most part, the architecture is unspectacular, widely criticized for the monotonous repetition of grid patterning. Grids, often looking like ice-cube trays, are omnipresent. They appear in small, medium and large sizes; in granite and in metal; situated like a framework around windows; as lattices for hanging vines; and as sun-screens in front of window walls. At least the buildings are not arranged in a grid layout! Instead, they are informally placed around two linked squares, one a simple space, the other a terrain for public entertainment.

SOM completed the Broadgate project, 1988–91, by developing the land between Appold Street on the west and Bishopsgate on the east. Also included is a section over the tracks to the north of Liverpool Street Station. The buildings follow the same model as in the earlier phases except here scale has become monumental, and vegetation—a vitalizing counterpoint to the hard stone surfaces and rigid, geometric forms—has practically been eliminated. There is one very formal, terraced plaza meant for leisure activity but it's not very inviting nor designed for casual relaxation. (Its greenery is a flat, rectangular plot of perfectly cut grass.)

In all there are 14 buildings in the Broadgate complex and fewer than 20 artworks. Most all the art is autonomous, object sculpture, despite the fact that the most engaging, innovative public art created during the 1980s and early 1990s was developed in a site-specific mode, often by artists working collaboratively on integral designs with architects and landscapists.

The following discussion, which highlights the major buildings and art within Broadgate, takes a roughly clockwise path around the complex, beginning near the southwest corner of Liverpool Street Station.

5 | Richard Serra

Fulcrum, 1987
Octagon Arcade, Eldon St entrance
to Broadgate

Located in a congenial passageway lined with nonauthoritarian buildings, this severe, brutalist sculpture stands out. Its overwhelming scale and the formidable sense that its seemingly precarious structure, composed of five crude Cor-ten steel plates, leaning against one another, may collapse is hardly inviting. Nevertheless, the three doorwaylike openings formed by the leaning plates draw you into the center space. Once inside the dark interior, your attention readily turns upward to the opening between the plates. Viewing the incredible, pentagonally shaped patch of sky and light high above unexpectedly shifts the mood, imbuing the minimalist industrial work with a mystical aura. This is a classic sculpture of Richard Serra, the revered American artist who emerged in the mid-1960s.

Richard Serra, *Fulcrum*, 1987

6 | Broadgate Circle

architects: ARUP
Broadgate, EC2

This superbly designed circular arena set within a large, square plaza is Broadgate's hub for outdoor public activities. During the winter months it becomes an ice-skating rink, and in summer it hosts lunchtime performances of soul, rock, jazz and classical music as well as other entertainment or cultural events. On a nice day, you might well find a throng of tie-and-jacket gentry, shirtsleeved twenty-somethings, jean-bedecked teens and bemused old-timers casually standing about, sitting on stairs and benches or at restaurant tables throughout the plaza.

The amazing thing about the Broadgate arena and its surrounding amphitheater-like structure is that it completely hides four million square feet of shopping arcades, pubs and restaurants within and beneath its shell.

All you see on the outside are terraced, colonnaded walls covered with incredible cascades of verdant plants. A screen-enclosed extension of a restaurant on one sector of the bottom terrace hints at an occupied interior, and close inspection of the covered walkway on the ground level reveals shop windows inside. By totally shielding this commercial sector and keeping all related signage out of sight, the arena harmonizes with the other anonymous facades of Broadgate. And yet, its enclosing walls serve as a barrier separating it from the offices, and the prevalence of natural greenery on its surfaces offers a strong contrast to the man-made, rigorously rectilinear shapes of and on the surrounding buildings.

Do spend time meandering around and through this unusual construction, even if you're not an architecture aficionado.

7 | Barry Flanagan

Leaping Hare on Crescent and Bell, 1988
in front of 10 and 12 Broadgate

Located on the east side of the center plaza, this whimsical bronze sculpture features the signature image of the popular British artist Barry Flanagan. True to character, the long-eared, spirited rabbit with the somewhat anthropomorphic body displays utter freedom and joyous abandon. Here it is seen flying through the air atop a crescent which rests on the ground beside a large bell. The nonsensical nursery rhyme—Hey diddle diddle, the cat and the fiddle, the cow jumped over the moon—comes to mind, albeit in a discombobulated, personalized state.

Barry Flanagan, *Leaping Hare on Crescent and Bell*, 1988

8 | Jacques Lipchitz

Bellerophon Taming Pegasus
in front of the Pavilion, 3
Broadgate

Lipchitz's polished bronze sculpture set high on a pedestal holds its own in front of a smallish towerlike building totally clad in rose granite, except for full-height, dark glass walls over the entrance tunnel. The work is a figurative composition representing fulfillment of Bellerophon's wish to fly riding the winged horse Pegasus. According to the Greek myth, the god succeeds in taming the beloved animal, then happily rides her, sometimes using her ability to fly for accomplishing heroic feats. But eventually, in a foolhardy attempt to reach Mount Olympus, the heavenly realm of immortality, he is hurled off the horse's back and falls back to earth.

9 | One Finsburg Avenue

architects: ARUP, 1982–84
1 Finsbury Avenue, EC2

Walk behind the Pavilion and cross the tree-laden plaza—Finsbury Avenue Square—on your right. You might want to linger on one of the stone-block seats and take in the setting.

The building at the end of Finsbury Avenue, among the first created at Broadgate, became the British archetype for a new breed of developer-financed, speculative office structures. In contrast to the ubiquitous monolithic tower with a service core in the middle and windows all facing outward, here offices are grouped around a sunlit courtyard that functions as a communal center. Covered by a steel-and-glass roof displaying high-tech engineering skill and creativity, the atrium gives the architecture a futuristic edge. Similarly, the scaffoldlike framework with industrial sunscreens and diagonal rods that fronts the exterior adds some zap to the mundane glazed facade.

10 | George Segal

Rush Hour
in front of 1 Finsbury Ave,
Finsbury Ave Sq

Positioned on a walkway leading away from an office building, Segal's dark bronze sculpture depicting six life-size figures—men and women all wearing trench coats and walking in a cluster as they might at the end of a workday. With their heads and eyes downcast, they seem saddened or pensive, though their determined gait adds a physical, enlivening quotient to their appearance. True to form, Segal captures a moment of everyday life in his sculpture.

11 | Stephen Cox

Ganapathi and Devi, 1988
traffic circle, corner of Appold and Sun Sts

This sculpture, composed of two large stone blocks, is located on the western perimeter of Broadgate, in the middle of a traffic circle bordered by trees and shrubs. Though retaining their massive, abstract form, Stephen Cox—a British sculptor rooted in classicism—has shaped the stones to suggest Devi, the great Indian Hindu goddess, and her son Ganapathi, the elephant-headed god.

12 | Howard Hodgkin

Wave
Broadgate Club, 1 Exchange Pl

If it's a weekend, you may wonder about the constant stream of people going in and out of this building. Follow them into the tiny elevator in the tiny lobby and get out at the top. You'll exit directly into a plush gym and health club. The front area is scattered with comfortable chairs and there's a bar and restaurant off to the side. Don't worry, you won't stand out like an alien in street clothes! Head toward the reception desk and explain that you'd like to take a look at Hodgkin's *Wave*. Hopefully, they'll point you in the direction of the pool at the back of the lobby.

The painting is actually an extraordinary tile wall running the length of the pool. Composed of rich, seductive shades of blue, welling up and down in sweeping rhythms scaled for a body the size of Moby Dick's, the image provides a curious backdrop for swimmers gliding across the still water in a rectangular pool marked by lane-dividing, straight lines.

13 | Xavier Corberó

The Broad Family
West Terr, intersection of Exchange Pl and Exchange Sq

What a delight to come upon *The Broad Family*—mother and father watching their child play ball with her dog. Though devoid of naturalistic details—except for the little girl's tiny shoes—subtle modulations within the flat, tactile, irregularly shaped carved forms animate and characterize the figures. As is typical of Corberó, a Barcelona artist, imagery remains suggestive so as to evoke narratives and memories. It probably wasn't purposeful, but this witty sculpture depicting a leisure moment in the Broadgate setting is a marvelous counterpoint to George Segal's solemn group of office workers.

14 | Exchange House and Exchange Square

architects: SKIDMORE OWINGS & MERRILL
Broadgate, EC2

The 10-story office building, spanning the tracks emerging from Liverpool Street Station, largely derives its structure from bridge technology. Its steel framework, comprising a gridded box and four parabolic arches, rests entirely on eight concrete piers. Because the ground floors exist as an open void, except for a glazed lobby in the middle, the supports and suspension system become part of the design. As with 1 Broadgate, the framework (inset with metal sunscreens) is totally exposed and overtly displayed as the facade. Moreover, the black steel curve dominates, asserting a marked contrast to the polished rose-toned granite and rectilinear articulation on most Broadgate buildings. The curve also echoes the sweeping wrought-iron arches of the vaulted train shed whose open back is directly across Exchange Plaza.

Taking advantage of the commanding view inside the shed, the architects

Skidmore Owings & Merrill, Exchange House

created a grand plaza across its width. Designed for performances and recreation, it has a bank of stepped seating between an upper and lower terrace as well as a stage area, flat expanse of grass and small water garden. Unfortunately, it's all quite formal and vapid, especially during the non-summer months when there are no outdoor activities filling the space. What a lost opportunity not to have commissioned some artists with inventive imaginations and a sense of humanism and humor to enliven the setting. Although the Broadgate complex is free of cars, urban chaos and advertising clutter, its controlled, staid environment with its ultra-orchestrated, bureaucratic veneer suffers from a lack of spontaneity and exuberant energy.

15 | Fernando Botero

Broadgate Venus, 1989
Exchange Sq, in front of Bishopsgate

Excessively rotund and curvaceous, the monumental Broadgate Venus with her upturned, reclining body epitomizes the sculpture style that has brought international renown to Botero, an artist from Colombia. His figures are invariably bold and volumetric with sensuousity exaggerated by highly polished, exceedingly smooth surfaces. Stillness and an aura of classical beauty also predominate as recurring features.

16 | Lincoln Seligman

Alchemy, 1991
Great Eastern Walk, Bishopsgate

Behind the Botero, follow the signs to the entrance door for the Great Eastern Walk, a covered passage squeezed between the railroad shed and the equally long Bishopsgate Building. This two-story high, light-filled walkway is a clever solution to the problem of pedestrian circulation in a tight space. The upper level of the side bordering the station combines windows with open-air voids. In contrast, a granite wall pierced by low-lying, deeply inset arch windows demarcates the lower level. The repetitive patterning accentuates the orthogonal pull down the full length of the seemingly endless corridor.

When you reach the end of the Great Eastern Walk, facing you is a painting by Lincoln Seligman of three large stone blocks leaning against one another.

Though not a great composition, if you turn around and look back down the corridor, you'll see a related, more interesting, site-specific work by this same British artist known for creating surreal public murals. By painting the midstory cross beams of the 300-yard-long passageway with a color sequence progressing from soft-toned blue-greens to brown-reds to orange-yellows, he evokes the alchemical transformation of base matter into gold. Considering that most people walking through this corridor are preoccupied with the country's financial business, the theme is not so far fetched.

17 | Bishopsgate

architects: SKIDMORE OWINGS & MERRILL, 1987–91
155 Bishopsgate, EC2

This huge office building with an arcade extending its entire length was one of the last constructions in the original Broadgate plan. Repeating materials used elsewhere—green-tinted glass, green steel, rose and gray granite—makes the structure blend into its setting even while its bulk makes it stand out. The use of marble and gold at the main entrance and the addition of corner turrets and light fixtures with the image of a bishop's head do little to enhance what is ultimately an uninspiring design.

17 | Jim Dine

The Modern Day Venus
entrance hall, 155 Bishopsgate

Two enormous sculptures representing a contemporary version of the classical goddess of beauty are perfectly positioned on the side walls facing the main entrance door of Bishopsgate. These bronze casts by the American artist Jim Dine, who emerged as a member of American Pop art in the 1960s, welcome visitors into the ersatz grandeur of the building's lobby.

17 | Martin Craig-Martin

Globe and Umbrella: Window "Drawing" in Mirror Glass
entrance lobby, 175 Bishopsgate

Craig-Martin's sculpture would probably capture attention even if it weren't located at the foot of a main escalator in a window facing the ever-crowded arcade in Bishopsgate. Somewhat like the chance meeting of an umbrella and sewing machine on a dissection table, an image that served as inspiration to the surrealists, the artist here presents the odd pairing of a mirrored globe and an umbrella. Viewed contextually however, you can consider the umbrella as a likely referent to London—clearly, it's the most ubiquitous, indispensable object about town—and interpret the juxtaposition as representing micro and macro positions in the universe. The fact that the mirrored globe is an incredible matrix of reflections from its surroundings and vice versa further suggests the degree to which positions are relative, interchangeable and exponential.

18 | Bruce McLean

Untitled
in front of 199 Bishopsgate

Located at the northeast corner of Bishopsgate, this brightly colored sculpture—a lively conglomerate of linear forms and gestural rhythms—greets people as they enter the arcade or pass into the center of Broadgate. Unfortunately, since the architecture of Bishopsgate is itself color-toned and riven with linear details, the sculpture tends to disappear into the environment. It becomes nearly impossible to perceive the spatial intertwines and points of punctuation. Because the object is also rather tame, lacking the expressive fervor and comic bravura that characterize McLean's best work, it gives little evidence as to why he is an esteemed member of Britain's older generation of contemporary artists.

Clerkenwell– King's Cross

Laure Genillard Gallery

1

⌂ 82–84 Clerkenwell Rd (1st floor), EC1M 5RJ
020-7490-8853 f: 7490-8854
laure@x-stream.co.uk
Tues–Sat, 11–6; closed Mon
tube: Barbican, Farringdon

This gallery makes the most of a compact space by installing art in its two rooms and on extraneous available walls. The work shown is by young, promising artists who are exploring personal visions and new techniques. The gallery is partial to conceptually based art focused on more enigmatic, penetrating images than the ribald, explosive kind favored by the YBA. The figures of Lindsay Seers, for example, traffic in unexpected alterations of body form and a stark, gripping intensity that creeps under your skin. If you

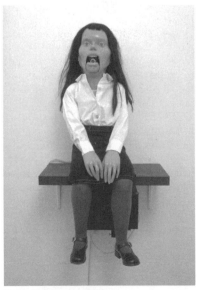

Lindsay Seers, *Candy*, 1999

prefer landscapes, paintings by Stepanek & Maslin push nature to a haunting extreme. Though the majority of artists shown are British, there is also an international strain from the Continent and Australasia.

Often there are shows that feature artists not represented by the gallery who have had little exposure in London. Recent examples include: *Alighiero e Boetti, Kill Yr Idols*, This Season (*Jim Iserman, Graham Little, Gary Simmons*). Artists: Douglas Allsop, Julian Dashper, Sylvie Fleury, Lesley Foxcroft, Giuseppe Gabellone, Dean Hughes, John Nixon, Lindsay Seers, Elisa Sighicelli, Alice Stepanek & Steven Maslin, Simon Tegala, Gladstone Thompson, Padraig Timoney, Günter Umberg.

Andrew Mummery Gallery

2

⌂ 33 Great Sutton St, EC1V 0DX
tel/fax: 020-7251-6265
www.amummery.com
MummeryA@aol.com
Tues–Sat, 11–6; closed Mon
tube: Barbican, Farringdon

Located off the corner of St. John's St, a block behind Clerkenwell Rd. Once inside #33, you go down a dark staircase, which seems like a fire exit, into a grungy hallway leading to the gallery door.

The bare, large space, devoid of designer-renovated chicness and still laden with an old-building, basement aura, is a throwback to upstart galleries of the 1970s and 1980s. If you're unfamiliar with this setting, don't be turned off. Despite the setting and the hang-loose ambience, the gallery offers a distinctive take on contemporary art.

The focus here is on painting, especially paintings revealing or expressing aspects of the painting process itself. Though this may sound a bit retrograde, the gallery represents artists like Alexis Harding, who offer a postminimalist

Clerkenwell–
King's Cross

0   500 yards

1. Laure Genillard Gallery
2. Andrew Mummery Gallery
3. Cabinet Gallery
4. Sadler's Wells
5. Cubitt Gallery
6. British Library

version of grid-structured compositions and monochromatic color fields with seductive, energized surfaces.

Most of the artists are recent art school graduates, just beginning their careers, so you probably won't recognize any of the names. Typically, work by one artist occupies the main area of the gallery, and an installation or special group of objects by another artist is in a space in the back called the project room. If you have time and an interest in contemporary painting, ask to see a few works from the storage racks. Artists: Philip Akkerman, Michael Bach, Maria Chevska, Richard Forster, Ori Gersht, John Goto, Alexis Harding, Peter Harris, Tim Hemington, Hans-Jorg Holubitschka, Louise Hopkins, Chila Kumari Burman, Ingo Meller, Carol Rhodes, Stuart Taylor, Graeme Todd, Laura Viale.

3 | Cabinet Gallery

20a Northburgh St, EC1V OEA
020-7253-5377 f: 7608-2414
Wed–Sat, 12–6; closed Mon–Tues
tube: Barbican, Farringdon

Cabinet relocated here (spring of 1999) from a tenement flat in Brixton, where it earned a reputation for showing maverick art by subversive artists in group and solo shows or performance spectacles. The move hasn't changed a thing. You'll still encounter a playfully philistine attitude and be able to see counter-culture expressions in work that is often enticing despite itself. Recent exhibitions: *Gillian Carnegie, Martin Creed, Jeremy*

Alexis Harding, *Untitled*, 1998

121

Deller, Jason Fox, Karl Holmquist, Gareth Jones, Lovecraft, Owada, Rob Pruitt, James Pyman, Sunday, Lily van der Stokker, Village Disco (Elizabeth Peyton, John Williams, Jeremy Deller, John Maclean), Would Have Had.

4 | Sadler's Wells

redevelopment: RENTON HOWARD WOOL LEVIN, 1997–98
Rosebery Avenue, EC1R 4TN
020-7863-8074
www.sadlers-wells.com
Mon–Fri, 6–11; Sat, 2–11 (performance days only)
tube: Angel

Located at the top end of Rosebery Ave in the borough of Islington on a site known since Roman times for its medicinal springs and assorted waterworks.

The enlarged, totally renovated Sadler's Wells—London's premier dance venue, renowned for its classical and contemporary programs of talent from around the globe—features a vast foyer designed to accommodate projects commissioned from artists. Indeed, three grand-scale works by Gary Hume launched the space when the theater reopened in October 1998. Following this, the space was enlivened with sculptures by the acclaimed German Stephan Balkenhol, expressionist face paintings by the Londoner Tony Bevan, blackboard drawings by the rising British star Tacita Dean, and an installation formed from eccentric materials by Anya Gallaccio. Not only are the foyer's high ceiling and backdrop wall rising through three levels conducive to various forms of art, but the glass frontage makes the art visible to passersby on the street as well as patrons inside. Recent exhibitions: Duncan MacAskill, Lisa Milroy.

Although the building is quite modest, intentionally plain so as not to overwhelm the surrounding residential neighborhood, a huge polyvision screen set behind the glazed entrance wall flashes images and messages into the environment. If all goes according to plan, the "floating image" screen will eventually intersperse original creations by artists with theater-related projections. The idea is to make innovative art part of the experience of a visit to Sadler's Wells. In line with this goal, the theater commissioned a collaborative work by the artist Vong Phaophanit, the architect Ushida Findlay and the landscapist Robert Rummey for the garden court.

The architectural renovation, enabled by lottery money, entailed the virtual destruction of the entire former theater, except for the core of the auditorium. In contrast to its cramped predecessor, the new state-of-the-art theater has a large and versatile stage, space for a 90-person orchestra, 134 dressing rooms, four rehearsal rooms, a lecture hall, gym and fitness facilities and the aforementioned lobby and café. Stretching from corner to corner of the block, the building even overhangs the sidewalks to maximize space. The exterior of brick and glass, modulated by overlapping grids (a trait common to many 1990s buildings) has a warehouse character that is decidedly nonelitist and nonpretentious.

5 | Cubitt Gallery

2-4 Caledonia St, N1 9DZ
020-7278-8226
gallery@cubittltd.demon.co.uk
Thurs–Sun, 11–6; closed Mon–Wed
tube: Kings Cross

Located on the east side of King's Cross train station, one block up from Pentonville Rd.

In 1991 about 38 artists occupying studios in this and two nearby buildings joined together in an umbrella organization that administers the studios and runs this gallery. The artists don't show their own work but instead invite guest curators and outside artists to participate in exhibitions, talks and events. Collaborations and installation projects are particularly encouraged. Because there is a continual turnover of member artists, new talent, ideas and energy prevail and artists gain valuable experience in gallery operations.

A bulletin board outside the building on the east end posts announcements of artist projects and special events in the area. This is a good place to check if you want to see the work of young, emerging artists who may not yet be associated with galleries.

6 | British Library

architect: Colin St. John WILSON, 1998

96 Euston Rd, NW1 2DB
020-7412-7000
www.bl.uk
Mon, Wed–Fri, 9:30–6; Tues, 9:30–8; Sat, 9:30–5; Sun, 11–5
admission: free
tube: King's Cross/St. Pancras

Located on the west side of St. Pancras train station.

After more than three decades, endless delays, several location changes, ridiculous political interventions, horrendous cost overruns, a stream of scandals and vituperative royal tirades, the British Library—its 12 million books, 200 miles of underground shelving and 11 reading rooms—finally opened in 1998. The reception was at best lukewarm. Press and public alike lamented the banal, boring structure that looked more like a warehouse than a majestic building for a revered institution. Alas, its brand of modernism wasn't eccentric, and, worse still, it wasn't monumental. Prince Charles's harangue, made at the height of his architectural crusade in 1988, reverberated among the naysayers: the design suggests "a dim collection of brick sheds groping for some symbolic significance.... [It resembles] an academy for secret police."

You enter the premises through a brick gatehouse, at the corner of Euston Road and Ossulston Street, and find yourself in a rather inhospitable, barren plaza. The flat expanse, paved in a grid of brick and travertine, is devoid of places to sit, meet with others or read a book, except for a nominal area—which also includes the only greenery on the site—tucked away along one side. The sole object on display is a bronze statue, *Isaac Newton after William Blake*, by Eduardo PAOLOZZI. It shows Newton, his vigorous, muscle-toned body crouching over a pair of dividers with which he is plotting the immensity of the universe. Paolozzi contends his figure is not imbued with the antinature, antiscience implications of Blake's satirical portrayal but instead conveys "an exciting unity of two British geniuses. Together they present to us nature and science, poetry, art, architecture, all welded, interconnected, interdependent." Despite this revision, the Newton-Blake composite (also possessing the facial likeness of Paolozzi) still shows the noble search of an exalted mastermind in terms of a classicized, solitary figure who is totally consumed with finding a definitive truth or expression of absolute beauty. Moreover, the sculpture is placed in a formidable, out-of-reach position high atop a 12-foot plinth. It thus reiterates and glorifies outdated, if not alienating, values that have been widely denounced by scholars in almost all fields during the past several decades. Is such an image (or a traditional figurative sculpture for that matter) a meaningful, appropriate artwork for a national library built at the end of the 20th century?

Even as you are led diagonally across the plaza toward the corner with the clock tower and a few flagpoles, it's not clear that the dark area beneath is the main entrance. A similar lack of definition occurs with the conference center

Bill Woodrow, *Sitting on History*, 1995

(located on the right side of the plaza) whose entry doors are hidden within the depths of a covered walkway. Some aspects of the architecture are equally ambiguous on the interior, where staircases, ramps and escalators seemingly terminate at dead ends, and planar walls mark off invisible or inaccessible territories. To be sure, the cavernous, skylit lobby is a grand space, but so icy cool and austere that it has little grandeur or comfortableness. (In the words of one critic, the atrium has "all the charm of an airline terminal.")

Sadly, the two artworks commissioned for the lobby do little to affect the aura. Situated off to the far right front is a bronze sculpture of an open book, which doubles as a bench attached to a ball and chain. *Sitting on History* (1995) by Bill WOODROW is a clever, witty image, but it is lost as a single, relatively small object set on the floor of an overwhelming space. Moreover, its dark tone and hard surface reiterate the severity of the surroundings. The second work, hanging on a wall to the left side of the lobby, is a huge tapestry based on the landscape painting *If Not, Not* (1975–76) by R. B. KITAJ. In his characteristic mode, the artist has conflated fragments of literary and historical references. Here, the strange landscape of disparate imagery was inspired by T. S. Eliot's *The Wasteland* and the Holocaust.

If you climb the center stairs and walk straight back, you'll find yourself unexpectedly confronting floor-to-ceiling shelves of old leather-bound books contained within a glass-walled enclosure. This is the King's Library donated to the nation by George IV in 1823. You can sit and gaze at the collection and its beautiful installation from an adjacent café. However, the lighting is so low to protect the precious books that the ambience verges on a movie set for an Agatha Christie murder mystery. Alternatively, you can walk farther back to the restaurant, or, if you have a library pass, you can peruse the various reading rooms on this level and the upper three floors. In terms of seeing these areas, don't be disappointed if you can't get a pass (this is not a public library open to the hoi polloi but a restricted, elite institution). There's nothing of the magnificence of the former reading room in the old library (see British Museum, p. 50), just bland halls filled with benign cubicles and desks.

Its new building notwithstanding, the British Library is world renowned because of its incredible collection of rare books, illuminated manuscripts and historic documents. In the John Ritblat Gallery (off the left side of the lobby), you'll find an extraordinary, elegantly installed exhibit, *Treasures of the British Library*, where you can see a selection of these. On display are handwritten or folio gems by Shakespeare, the Brontës, Beethoven and the Beatles; the Lindisfarne Gospels, Diamond Sutra, the Gutenberg Bible, Leonardo's notebooks, Galileo's telescope, the Magna Carta, a suffragette scrapbook and much, much more. Should you want to learn the history of reading and writing, visit the Pearson Gallery of Living Worlds, located alongside the Ritblat Gallery. There are also a philatelic exhibition room and temporary exhibition galleries, which sometimes are devoted to modern culture and its arts.

Free concerts take place in the lobby, auditorium or Conference Centre (usually on Fridays, 12–2). Films, readings, lectures and dramatic performances are also part of the public program.

South Coast

Goodwood

Sculpture at Goodwood

West Sussex, PO18 0QP
01243-538449 f: 531853
www.sculpture.org.uk
w@sculpture.org.uk
Mar–Nov: Thurs–Sat, 10:30–4:30
admission: £10/6

Train from London (Victoria) to Barnham, 1 hr 40 min; from Southampton, 1 hr. There's no public transportation from Barnham to Goodwood. It's about a 10-min taxi ride costing approximately £8–10.

Overlooking the Roman city of Chichester and its 11th-century cathedral, with views of the Channel coast, Goodwood is a great place to take in the English countryside while seeing contemporary art. Since 1994, this 20-acre estate with rolling hills, wooded groves and grand vistas has served as a sculpture environment displaying about 40 works by young and established British artists. The objects are carefully placed to be discovered and seen individually in the nearly untouched, open-air landscape.

In an unusual arrangement, the Goodwood Foundation commissions (or as they term it, enables) around 15 sculptures a year, which it owns in partnership with the artist. Goodwood covers the casting and fabrication costs and encourages artists to realize works that might otherwise be beyond their financial reach. Some are new projects and others implement preexisting designs. The works are displayed for one or more seasons until they are sold, at which time Goodwood is repaid its investment plus a small percentage. The remaining proceeds go to the artist. The money

Goodwood receives from the sales replenishes the kitty, providing funds for the commission of new work. Financial support for the production of sculpture and a continual reconstitution of the display are therefore built into the program. Since artists give the foundation a drawing and model or maquette related to the piece they have made for Goodwood, a collection—albeit not of outdoor sculpture—develops. It both documents the program and over time will provide a general overview of contemporary British sculpture.

Though you will see a broad selection, Goodwood conveys a rather conservative view of British art and a staid orientation to sculpture. Most all the work is object-oriented, showing little awareness of the site-specific, land art, conceptual or commentary tendencies that have preoccupied artists over the past several decades. Considering the

Daniel Buren, *With Arcades, Three Colors*, 1994

challenging, vanguard creativity of such contemporary British sculptors as Mona Hatoum, Michael Landy, Richard Long, Rachel Whiteread and Gavin Turk, the presentation is especially wanting. Perhaps Goodwood will expand its orientation in the near future. In any event, visits here give a rare opportunity to see large-scale sculpture in a natural environment, and that alone is refreshing.

Goodwood's program also includes publications and Saturday talks by artists whose work is on display. Recent commissions: Edward Allington, Zadok Ben-David, Hamish Black, Peter Burke, Lynn Chadwick, Stephen Cox, Tony Cragg, George Cutts, John Davies, Mark Firth, Laura Ford, William Furlong, Bruce Gernand, John Gibbons, Steven Gregory, Charles Hadcock, Nicola Hicks, Jon Isherwood, Allen Jones, David King, Phillip King, Peter Logan, David Mach, Dhruva Mistry, Cathy de Monchaux, David Nash, Paul Neagu, Eilís O'Connell, Zora Pavlova, Victoria Rance, Peter Randall-Page, William Pye, Andrew Sabin, Michael Sandle, Sophie Smallhorn, Keir Smith, Wendy Taylor, Almuth Tebbenhof, William Tucker, Jim Unsworth, Bill Woodrow.

*Note. There are no eating facilities or picnic areas on the grounds though these are available nearby.

Keir Smith, *Stephano*, 1997

Southampton

Train from London (Waterloo), 1 1/2 hr.

Southampton City Art Gallery

Civic Centre, Commercial Rd,
SO14 7LP
023-8063-2601 f: 8083-2153
Tues–Sat, 10–5; Sun, 1–4;
closed Mon
www.southampton.gov.uk/leisure/art
artgallery@southampton.gov.uk
admission: free

Southampton, a commercial port city badly damaged in World War II, has little to recommend it as a place to spend much time. However, the City Art Gallery is one of the few British museums outside London with a decent contemporary art collection. If you enjoy the richly decorative paintings of Burne-Jones and the Pre-Raphaelites, you'll have two good reasons to visit Southampton.

The main hall at the top of the grand staircase serves as the display space for the most recent art. Its vast scale ridden with arches makes it a difficult environment in which to show art. The museum was smart to buy the installation work *With Arcades, Three Colors* (1994) by Daniel BUREN (an esteemed French artist), created specifically for the hall's ceiling as part of a temporary exhibition. By enlivening the setting with stripes of rich red, gray and emerald green which follow contours in the architecture, Buren gives the hall a new identity and ambience. Simultaneously, he transforms perceptions of the space and calls attention to its rhythmic lines.

The collection is exclusively British art —a nice mix of figurative, abstract and conceptually based works of sculpture, painting, photography and mixed-media. Though the objects are sometimes not the classic images associated with a particular artist, they are superb choices. Many works are accompanied by small informational cards (picture and text) that visitors are free to take with them. (A great educational tool!) Artists represented include: Gillian Ayres, Helen Chadwick, Tony Cragg, Peter Davies, Barry Flanagan, Hamish Fulton, Gilbert & George, Antony Gormley, Allen Jones, Abigail Lane, Richard Long, Fiona Rae, Boyd Webb, Rachel Whiteread.

In addition to the main hall, other galleries show contemporary art. One grouping focuses on popular culture (it includes non-British work), another on expressionist abstraction and a third on minimalist painting. If you're not familiar with British artists like Alan Charlton, Patrick Heron, John Hoyland, Callum Innes, Zebedee Jones, Peter Joseph, Moses Lee and John Walker, the display is an excellent resource. Don't miss *Wessex Flint Line*, an exceptional sculpture by Richard Long (1987), installed in the Baring Room.

Contemporary art also figures in the museum's temporary exhibition schedule and the shows are worth seeing. *Accelerator* (1998), for example, explored the issue of transience in popular culture as exemplified internationally in work by a broad spectrum of young artists.

John Hansard Gallery

University of Southampton,
Highfield, SO17 1BJ
023-8059-2158 f: 8059-4192
hansard@soton.ac.uk
Tues–Fri, 11–5; Sat, 11–4;
closed Mon
admission: free

Train to Southampton Parkway/Central, then bus 7. The university is north of the Common (a huge city park), and the Hansard Gallery is in the northwest section of the campus, off University Rd, behind the Turner Sims Concert Hall.

The Hansard Gallery—located in a mundane, one-story, 60ish building—

presents a mixed bag of contemporary British art. Some exhibitions deal with topical issues and engaging work and others are somewhat safe and a bit after-the-fact. You won't see ground-breaking or radical art here, but you will get a good take on facets of current activity in the art world. The gallery offers a strong program of artist talks, seminars and conferences either related to its exhibitions or focused on provocative issues.

Should you want an art magazine, the selection in the shop is better than you'll find anywhere in the region. There's also an abundance of posters and postcards, but few notable art books or catalogues.

Recent exhibitions: *Art in Ruins, Martin Creed, Gerard Hemsworth, Lie of the Land, The Masque, Postcards on Photographs, Sublime—Darkness and Light, John Wood & Paul Harrison.*

Thames Valley

Henley-On-Thames

Depending on your temperament, you either visit or avoid Henley in early July during the annual regatta. To British royals, Henley ranks with Ascot and Wimbledon as a high-society event; to those infatuated with boating and the sport of crew racing, it's a world-class competition. The town itself is charming and the surrounding landscape, idyllic. Train from London (Paddington), 1 1/4 hr.

Henley Royal Regatta Headquarters

architect: Terry FARRELL, 1985

The classical aspects of this riverfront building may at first suggest an impressive heritage, but its bright colors and whimsical exaggerations firmly establish its contemporary identity as a postmodern structure. Not surprising, since its architect, Terry Farrell, is one of Britain's leading exponents of this hybrid mode of borrow-and-distort design. (See Vauxhall Cross and TV-am in London.)

The building has a simple templelike form, although the scale of the pediment (the triangular end of the low-pitched roof) is grossly enlarged to equal that of the exceedingly compressed base. On the side facing the river, an elaborate window ensemble with balconies and a focal arched form extends its dark shape up to the roof's peak and down across the stone foundation (containing a boathouse) to the water's edge. Although Farrell has not used cheap, industrial materials—a common characteristic of postmodern architecture—he has boldly painted the stucco and wood, thereby camouflaging and transforming their appearance.

On the interior, offices, a large hall and committee room compactly occupy the ground floor, and the upper level houses a small apartment. Not an inch of space is wasted, and it's all cleverly laid out and divided according to specific functions.

River and Rowing Museum

architect: David CHIPPERFIELD, 1994–97
Meadow Rd
www.rrm.co.uk
museum@rrm.co.uk
Apr–Oct: Mon–Sat, 10–5;
Sun, 11–5. Nov–Mar: Mon–Sat,
10–4; Sun, 11–4
admission: £4.95/3.75

Located on the south side of the town bridge in Mill Meadows, at the end of the Mill Mead car park. Follow the green finger signs.

Borrowing astutely from the architecture of local boathouses and wooden barns and then assimilating traditional elements with modernist forms, David Chipperfield created a light and airy building that works well with the riverside setting. Window walls on the lower level and open terraces establish a dialogue with the surrounding landscape; beautifully crafted oak cladding on the upper level produces an elegant rustic tone; and tall pitched roofs sheathed in stainless steel with a narrow skylight running the length of the blunted peak add a contemporary pulse.

The museum's mission is to display examples of rowing boats and tell the history of the sport and the township of Henley-on-Thames. It's not inherently a thrilling subject but it's what you'd expect in place totally obsessed with a single activity.

Oxford

Like Cambridge, Oxford is a lively university town in a picturesque country setting. Streams of students endlessly hustle through the narrow streets on bicycle and on foot, sometimes relaxing by punting (poling a shallow-bottomed boat) on the Thames. The "campus" spreads out on all sides of the city center, comprising 40 different colleges, each with their own cluster of buildings, and numerous associated structures dating from the 11th century to the present. Train from London (Paddington Station), 1 hr.

Museum of Modern Art

30 Pembroke Street, OX1 1BP
0186-572-2733 f: 572-2573
Tues–Wed, Fri–Sun, 11–6;
Thurs, 11–9; closed Mon
admission: £2.50/1.50; free Wed,
11–1, and Thurs, 6–9

Located in the center of Oxford, one block down from Queen St just off the corner of St. Ebb's.

Given its reputation of having one of England's best programs of contemporary art, it's surprising to find the Oxford Museum of Modern Art housed in an unassuming street-front structure—a renovated 1880s brewery. To clarify some pervasive confusions, the museum is an independent entity, affiliated with neither the university nor the city of Oxford. It bears the designation "museum," but since it doesn't have a collection, it's really an exhibition space, not a museum.

Don't be putoff by the environment of the ground-floor galleries. Unfortunately, they retain a cellarlike character from their former existence as beer storage rooms. The low ceilings and windowless brick walls are a bit claustrophobic and

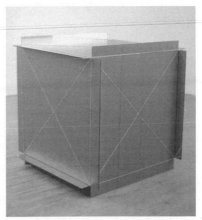

Michelangelo Pistoletto, *Cubic Meter of Infinity (Minus Objects)*,1996

not very accommodating of art. But the main galleries on the top floor, which have high ceilings and skylights, are spacious, flexible and great environments for showing most any type of creative work. Adding to the whole is the ever-crowded café in the basement—a popular neighborhood and student eatery—and a small bookshop in the lobby. There's an easy, casual ambience throughout that is notably different from the austere, intimidating setting of many museums.

Exhibitions vary from the historical or thematic to one-person shows of vanguard leaders and unfamiliar artists, be they at the beginning, middle or mature point in their careers. For example, the 1998–99 season included the conceptual, performance work dating from the late 1950s by a little-known artist-activist, Gustav Metzger; photographs by a hot new star from New York, Anna Gaskell; a compelling video installation about place and perception by Ireland's Willie Doherty; and an exhibition exploring Alfred Hitchcock's influence on contemporary art. Unlike most art institutions, Oxford MOMA organizes all its own shows (some then circulate) and accompanies them with free brochures, information rooms, artist talks, lectures and small catalogues.

Other recent exhibitions: *Audible Light, Contemporary Art from Scandinavia, Mona Hatoum, Gary Hill, Jiri Kolar, Sarah Morris, Matt Mullican, John Murphy, Yoko Ono, Michelangelo Pistoletto, Edward Rusha, Julião Sarmento, Mitja Tusek, Weegee.*

Blackwell's Art Bookshop

27 Broad St, OX1 2AS
0186-579-2792 f: 579-4143
www.blackwell.co.uk/bookshops
oxford@blackwellsbookshops.co.uk
Mon, Wed–Sat, 9–6; Tues, 9:30–6;
Sun, 11–5

Blackwell's is a huge book emporium with separate stores for different subject areas. The shop specializing in art includes a broad span of publications on painting, sculpture, architecture, theory, interior design, photography, crafts and design. It also has an extensive selection of posters and cards. You won't find small press books or museum catalogues here, but the stock is rich in monographs and histories of particular periods and styles.

Ashmolean Museum

Beaumont St (corner of St. Giles), OX1 2PH
0186-527-8000 f: 527-8018
www.ashmol.ox.ac.uk
Tues–Sat, 10–5; Sun, 2–5;
closed Mon. May–July: Wed, 10–8
admission: free

The Ashmolean is a world-renowned museum with an encyclopedic collection covering ancient, Asian and Western art. Its treasures include major paintings from the modern era but nothing after 1950.

Florey Building

architect: James STIRLING, 1968–71
St. Clements St, Queen's College

Take High St east. Just past the Botanic Gardens (on your right), you'll cross the river and come to a large traffic circle. Take the left fork onto St. Clements St. Turn left just ahead into an unmarked delivery road. When the road curves to the right, the Florey Building is on the left.

James Stirling is an architect revered for his imaginative organization and articulation of the component elements of a building. He deconstructs and recombines the forms and formal language espoused by such modernist masters as Le Corbusier to create structures with sharp visual contrasts and strangely fragmented geometric shapes. This orientation is strongly manifest in the Florey Building, though the whole doesn't really click and the quirky parts seem mannered and lifeless. By way of explanation, critics have related the design to the prevailing mood of rampant cynicism, one terming it "a masterpiece of the neurotic late-'60s longing for more heroic times."

Florey is a residential hall situated on a slope going down to the River Cherwell. To get a sense of the building's oddities, you must walk all around it. Only then can you appreciate how dramatically Stirling shifts gears, unexpectedly differentiating sections and creating autonomous perspectives.

In front, discrete elevator towers and giant stiltlike concrete supports angling out from the base of the main structure, which slants forward as it rises, are the dominant forms. Ground-floor public rooms, set underneath the buttress legs, appear strangely detached, and bends in the facade that swing the building around keep its overall shape a mystery.

In back, the building takes on a horseshoe-like shape—it's actually 5/8 of an octagon—surrounding a courtyard, defined with an irregular perimeter and containing a ground-level, tightly enclosed breakfast room topped by an eccentric exhaust stack. In marked contrast to the red tile on the front facade, the back is sheathed in glass, offering views of the river landscape.

Swindon

Train from London (Paddington), 1 hr; from Oxford, 35 min.

Renault Distribution Centre

 architect: Norman FOSTER, 1980-82
Whitehill Way and Rivermead Dr
Follow signs to West Swindon; pass the Link Centre on the right and turn right at the next traffic circle past the de Vere Hotel on the left; follow the signs to the Meads; go straight ahead, it's on the left.
Access to the interior is limited.

Swindon is probably not on your tourist itinerary, but if you're in the region or can include it as a side trip you'll get to see a uniquely constructed, captivating work of architecture by Norman Foster. Unlike the chic museums and glazed office buildings that have largely established his reputation, this is a rare factory-type project. Structural prowess, shaped by technological innovation, plus design and engineering ingenuity have been paramount in all Foster's projects. But here structure itself is emphatically laid bare as the form, frame and visual dynamic of the building.

The mandate was to create a distinctive entity that would a) encompass a warehouse, distribution center, regional offices, showroom, training school, workshops and staff restaurant; and b) upgrade Renault's image in Britain. In response, Foster accommodated all activities within a single huge shed structured by a frame conspicuously painted bright yellow and extended outside the exterior walls so that its complex design and technology are vividly exposed. The frame comprises a long span of steel arches and complex assemblies of radiating tension cables

Norman Foster, Renault Distribution Centre

and beams—they resemble umbrellas—suspended from hollow steel masts.

The modular system evident in the frame also characterizes the grid of 42 square bays that define the shed. A corrugated-steel roof, punctured by glass skylight panels in the center of each bay, lies overhead, and screen walls surround the building except in the front, where glass encloses the vast showroom. A grand canopy, which spreads across the showroom's facade, further reveals and foregrounds the structural system.

Despite the building's massive size, a sense of buoyancy prevails. As if to emphasize this achievement, the showroom humorously displays the skeletons of four car bodies floating in space.

Milton Keynes

This is England's infamous "new town," begun in 1968 and still flourishing economically, socially and as the butt of an endless stream of jokes, many based on its developer-constructed box housing and atypical layout in an American-style grid. The community boasts a new university and bustling downtown shopping plaza, recently expanded to include a cineplex, food center and a piazza-like boulevard with outdoor cafés and restaurants. Train from London (Euston), 35 min; bus from Oxford, 1 hr.

Milton Keynes Gallery

900 Midsummer Blvd, MK9 3QA
0190-867-6900 f: 855-8308
www.mkgc.co.uk
mkgallery@mkgc.co.uk
Tues–Sat, 12–5; Sun, 1–5

Located downtown, east of the cineplex and food center and west of Campbell Park.

Profiting from a sizable National Lottery Grant (1995), Milton Keynes built an ambitious new theater and gallery complex. The high-ceilinged exhibition space is amenable to all sorts of art, including adventurous installation projects. Judging from the first season's schedule, the gallery will be presenting a nice variety of work, largely by established artists. The inaugural show in the fall of 1999 featured a new series—*The Rudimentary Pictures*—by the popular ever-transgressive duo, Gilbert & George. Other exhibitions: *Patrick Caulfield, Mark Francis, Richard Hamilton, Printers Inc.*

East Anglia

Cambridge

A visit to historic Cambridge with its stately buildings, courtyards, perfectly trimmed lawns, medieval streets, lively shopping passageways, meadows, gardens and riverbanks is a delight. You'll see fine examples of architecture from all periods, including the current era. Sadly, the university and city have shown little inclination to embrace modern or contemporary art.

The best way to see Cambridge is on foot, so hope for good weather or bring a big umbrella and hefty pair of rubber boots. Train from London (King's Cross), 1 hr.

1 | Queen's Building

architect: Michael HOPKINS, 1993–95
Emmanuel College,
University of Cambridge St

Ask the porter at the entrance to Emmanuel College on St. Andrew's Street how to zigzag through the courtyards to reach Queen's Building. In general, it's off to the left behind the main quadrangles just inside the gates along Emmanuel St.

Hopkins respected the venerated setting of the university by wrapping his building in a bland, ahistorical exterior of yellow-toned limestone. Though

blending into the surroundings, its oval shape, wood-paneled arcade (all around the ground floor), mullionless dark windows (especially the irregularly placed ones on the first floor) and spiral firestairs enclosed in a separate glass-brick tower are distinctive but hardly radical.

By Cambridge standards, this college building is quite small, seeming more like an afterthought hemmed into a remnant of land than a serious project. This oddity is magnified by the lack of a defined entrance. The interior, which houses common rooms and a 170-seat multipurpose auditorium on the upper two floors, continues the use of wood with exposed stainless steel adding touches of 1990s design, albeit refined and formalized. A critic's description of the building as "a beautifully crafted casket" is not far off the mark.

2 | Cambridge Arts Cinema

Market Passage, CB2 3PF
0122-357-2929
daily, variable time schedule

Located between Market and Green Sts.

If you're a cineast, this is a haven. There are four screenings daily plus matinees and late shows on the weekends. Comparable to the best cinémathèques, the film selection ranges from classics to premiers including shorts, silent, animation and experimental films. Retrospectives of visiting filmmakers, the Cambridge Film Festival, guest appearances, discussions and debates add spice to the program.

3 | Kettle's Yard Gallery

Castle St, CB3 0AQ
0122-335-2124 f: 332-4377
www.kettlesyard.co.uk
kettles-yard-gen@lists.cam.ac.uk
Tues–Sat, 12:30–5:30;
Sun, 2–5:30; closed Mon
admission: free

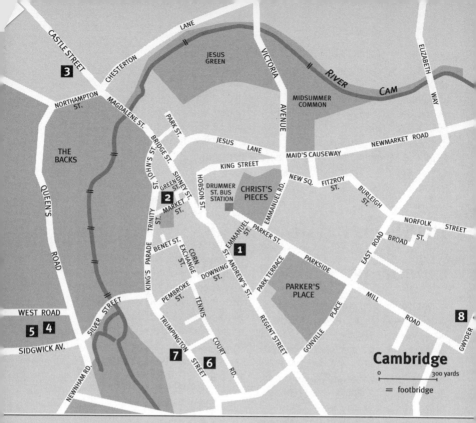

1. Queen's Building
2. Cambridge Arts Cinema
3. Kettle's Yard Gallery
4. Cambridge Law Faculty
5. Cambridge History Faculty
6. Judge Institute of Management Studies
7. Fitzwilliam Museum
8. Cambridge Darkroom Gallery

Go north on St. Andrew's, Sidney, Bridge and Magdalene Sts to Castle. It's all the same street but keeps changing its name. When the shops start thinning out after you cross Northampton St, you'll pass some large street-front windows (left side of the street) with views into the gallery. To enter, walk down the side path to the back courtyard.

Kettle's Yard Gallery is a very low-key, no-hype exhibition space. The shows, spread out in several ample rooms, present work by relatively unknown British artists who are good but not the movers and shakers at the forefront of the avant-garde. Recent exhibitions: *The Art of a Lifetime, Stephen Chambers, Prunella Clough, Juan Cruz, Daniel Edwards, '45–99, David Griffiths, David Kindersley, Bob Law, Kenneth Martin, Noise, Physical Evidence, Diet Sayler, Richard Wentworth.*

The private house sharing the court-yard is also part of Kettle's Yard. Formerly the residence of Jim Ede, a curator at the Tate Gallery, it now displays his collection of 20th-century British art, furniture, ceramics, textiles and other decorative arts. Included are some middling works by Henry Moore, Barbara Hepworth, Ben Nicholson and Henry Gaudier Brzeska. (Tues–Sat, 1:30–4:30; summer, Sun, 2–4:30)

Cambridge
4 Law Faculty

architect: Norman FOSTER, 1998
University of Cambridge

Located west of the River Cam across Queen's Rd between West Rd and Sidgwick Ave.

Situated in the midst of a campus green, the Cambridge Law Faculty offers very different impressions from each approach. On the south, there's a long expanse of wall clad with stone and opaque glass. In contrast, the north shows a sweeping, concave wall of glass that curves over the building as its roof. Yet another perspective is available at the main entrance, where you get virtually no sense of the great volume and reach of the building.

Foster's renowned sensitivity to space and light, which give his buildings an airy feel, is immediately palpable when you enter the grand lobby. White staircases and floor planes float in an open realm devoid of enclosing perimeter walls. Clearly a feat of engineering ingenuity and skill made it possible to use only five structural columns of reinforced concrete and a framework of tubular steel (painted white).

Norman Foster, Cambridge Law Faculty

around and see that the whole is a complex integration of several different geometric sequences. The building comprises seminar rooms and offices housed in two seven-story wings; a library reading room occupying a great fan-shaped, tent-roofed space set within the quadrant formed by the right-angled positioning of the wings; library stacks bordering and forming a base below the reading room; and basement lecture halls.

Without question, the reading room with its glazed roof structured in tapering layers of vertical and pitched planes that extend up to the apex of the wing's juncture is a striking image. But attention has also been given to subtle articulations that decrease the blockiness of large forms. For example, the facade on the north side of the towers is a cascade of three unequally sized attenuated steps. The facade, moreover, is sheathed in a wall of tall narrow-paned glass. (The glass walls on both the north and south sides of the towers actually line corridors.)

Cambridge
5 History Faculty

architect: James STIRLING, 1964-67
University of Cambridge

Located next to the Cambridge Law Faculty at the north end of the Sidgwick Ave campus.

If you're interested in architecture, this building—a cult object for design students—is now considered a classic, the best-known work of James Stirling, third winner (1981) of the prestigious Pritzger Prize.

A first glance from any perspective reveals dynamic juxtapositions. Amazingly, this impression is sustained as you walk

James Stirling, Cambridge History Faculty

Judge Institute of
6 | Management Studies

renovation: John OUTRAM with
Fitzroy ROBINSON, 1996
Trumpington St, University of
Cambridge

Remodeling a 19th-century hospital into an academic building obviously ignited the wit and decorative passions of John Outram. Expanding on the existing wealth of architectural forms, he increased the size and number of columns and floating walkways; exaggerated line and shape details; added patterning; and colored the whole in tones of turquoise, sky blue, green, orange, yellow, rust and cream. If you think the exterior is a bit excessive, walk into the lobby to really experience ornamental excess—combined with zigzagging space effects right out of Escher or Piranesi. The lobby, or Gallery, serves as a link between two other buildings, the Ark and Castle.

As with most of his projects, Outram freely borrows from history and then relates everything to a concocted, indiscernible narrative. Devising a fantasy vocabulary to match eccentric fabrication techniques, he explained that in this case the concrete-and-crushed-brick mix, "blitzcrete," was sliced to reveal a nougat quality, and the molding process, "doodlecrete," resulted in cylindrical beams with an engraved scroll pattern in a contrasting color.

Craziness notwithstanding, Outram designed his building to be energy-efficient and low-maintenance. Here, for instance, the massive columns in the lobby are hollow, filled with services that are thus fully integrated into the structural fabric of the building and cleverly positioned for easy access.

7 | Fitzwilliam Museum

Trumpington St, University of
Cambridge, CB2 1RB
0122-333-2900 f: 333-2923
www.fitzwilliam.cam.ac.uk
Tues–Sat, 10–5; Sun, 2:15–5;
closed Mon

The Fitzwilliam has one of the world's great encyclopedic museum collections including ancient treasures and masterpieces by Titian, Rubens, Hals, Gainsborough, Constable, Monet, Degas, Cézanne and Picasso. The representation of art from the 20th century is slim and narrowly focused on a few mainstream developments. The display, located in the Adeane Gallery, rotates so only one aspect is visible at any time. For example, during most of 1998, the installation featured an exhibition of American color-field painting by Helen Frankenthaler, Kenneth Noland, Jules Olitski and Larry Poons. Sadly, the museum barely owns anything of more recent vintage.

8 Cambridge Darkroom Gallery

Dales Brewery, Gwydir St, CB1 2LJ
0122-356-6725 f: 331-2188
cambridge.darkroom@dial.pipex.com
Tues–Sun, 12–5; closed Mon
admission: free

Gwydir St is off Mill Rd, and the gallery is back from the street, accessed by a driveway.

Cambridge Darkroom Gallery combines a lively exhibition program (1st floor) and public darkroom and digital-imaging facilities (ground floor). Defining photography quite loosely, shows include art created by all sorts of image-making processes including lens-based, mixed-media, video, film and performance work. You're bound to see challenging, rigorously conceptual art here, some by young talents who are still finding their own paths and some by established, more sophisticated artists. Recent exhibitions: *Disrupting the Scene (Fionna Banner, Pierre Bismuth, Fionna Crisp, Tacita Dean), Falling Angels, Alison Marchant, Masque, Postcards on Photographs, Louise Short, Thomson & Craighead.*

Duxford

American Air Museum

architect: Norman FOSTER, 1995–97
Duxford, CB2 4QR
0122-383-5000
daily: summer (Mar 15–Oct 24),
10–6; winter, 10–4
admission: £7/4.70

Duxford, 8 mi south of Cambridge, is accessible by Stagecoach Cambus.

If you balk at the idea of visiting a military museum, think of it exclusively in terms of seeing one of the most praised, award-winning exemplars of contemporary architecture and one of the best works by the widely esteemed Norman Foster. (It won the Stirling Prize for the outstanding completed building in the UK or Europe in 1998.) True to form, Foster created a simple, elegant structure whose gargantuan size is magically mitigated by the awesome sense of light and space captured within.

Duxford, a city that played a vital role in World War II, is now the center for historic aviation. The American Air Museum (constituted as part of London's Imperial War Museum) is a tribute to American air power as well as a memorial to the thousands of US airmen who died in World War II, especially those who flew from British bases. The display comprises 21 combat aircraft dating from World War I to the Gulf War and related imagery. By far, the dominant object and centerpiece is a B52 Stratofortress bomber. In fact, Foster's whole design was geared to the mega-dimensions of the B52.

With its broad curving roof, the building appropriately evokes the image of a hangar even as it integrates seamlessly into the flat, surrounding landscape. You enter through a tunnel-like passage, emerging in the middle of the vast interior facing the nose of a B52. It,

Norman Foster, American Air Museum

like all the other aircraft, is suspended from the roof as if in flight. To say the effect is spellbinding is to underestimate the power of the installation and the space. What's more, there's the realization that the virtuoso single-span, pre-cast concrete roof is also engineered to hold up an unfathomable tonnage!

At the end of the museum, where the roof accommodates the 52 1/2-foot-high (16 m) tail fin of the B52, a glazed wall abruptly slices off the building's curvature. It is the only dramatic feature in a building that effectively serves as a neutral backdrop for its contents. The glass facade also floods the interior with natural light and gives contextualizing views of the airfield and runways beyond.

Ipswich

Train from London (Liverpool Street), 1 1/4 hr; from Cambridge, 1 1/4 hr.

Willis Corroon Headquarters (previously Willis Faber & Dumas)

architect: Norman FOSTER, 1973–75
Friars St (curves into Princes St and Franciscan Way)

If you're a Foster fanatic or an architecture buff, or if you happen to be exploring the rural landscape of Constable country, this building is worth a look. You won't have any trouble finding it since it's the only one in the historic town of Ipswich with a spread-out, curvaceous shape sheathed in dark, frameless, solar-tinted glass. (Some people call it the Big Black Piano.) It would even stand out in a big city where curtain-wall office buildings—many born from this model (the majority, bad clones)—are commonplace.

During the day, the facade is like a mirror reflecting the surroundings. At night, when the exterior is transparent and spotlights shine inward, the building's shape, structure and interior are vividly manifest. The three-story height respects the scale of the old cityscape, and the undulating form—which flows to the edge of the site, virtually following the medieval street pattern—uses the full land area. Design notwithstanding, the engineering skill enabling the totally suspended glass wall was a notable achievement several decades ago and is still striking. (The top panels hang by a single bolt from the roof, and all others are attached to each other by a system of clamps.)

Not only does the glass curtain create fluidity between the people working in the building and the outside world, but the layout of the interior as an open plan does the same. Floors float atop structural columns and a central atrium serves as a common focal point and circulation area. (Escalators located here are an integral part of the building's accessibility and openness.)

The architect aimed to make the work environment more pleasant (this is an insurance company) within the office realm—the 2nd and 3rd floors—in addition to including leisure areas within the building. An Olympic-size swimming pool occupies a large space on the ground level, and a restaurant and garden fill the roof.

Norwich

Fairy-tale images abound in this picturesque medieval city whose winding streets encircle a 12th-century hilltop castle or lead to a majestic cathedral and grandiose open-air market steeped in an old-world flavor. In contrast, the University of East Anglia—located three miles west of the town center on the banks of the River Yare—is an explicitly 20th-century creation. Norwich's idyllic aura still prevails in the setting of rolling meadows and sylvan pathways, but solid stone and red-brick structures, turrets and spires have been totally forsaken in favor of concrete, glass and steel architecture, reductive primary forms and pure surfaces. Train from London (Liverpool Street), 1 3/4 hr; from Cambridge, 1 1/4 hr.

Sainsbury Centre for Visual Arts

architect: Norman FOSTER, 1978 and 1991
University of East Anglia, NR4 7TJ
01603-593199 f: 259401
Tues–Sun, 11–5; closed Mon
admission: £2/1
Buses 25, 26, 27, 35 from the city center to the Constable Terrace stop.

The Sainsbury Centre combines galleries displaying the Sainsbury Collection and special exhibitions, a study collection (installed for public viewing in open storage facilities), the University of East Anglia Collection of Abstract and Constructivist Art and Design (exhibited in the West Mezzanine), the School of World Art Studies and Museology, conservation laboratories, a conference room, restaurant, café and museum shop. The various activity areas are fluid and bounded neither conceptually nor architecturally. For example, tables and comfortable chairs are interspersed with art objects, encouraging discussion and a relaxed, extended viewing experience; and the two mezzanine galleries frame the library, faculty offices and classrooms. To facilitate movement between the center and other campus buildings, there is also an elevated walkway.

In its design, the center epitomizes high-tech modernism at its most extreme: a gargantuan metal-paneled white box with plate-glass end walls and a single, clear-span interior lined (walls and ceiling) with motorized louvers operated automatically by a sophisticated system of external and internal light sensors. (When the structure was in its original guise, sheathed in shiny, ribbed-aluminum panels—which proved to be problematic and had to be replaced—its image was far more radical.) To diversify the rectilinear form, Foster articulates the interior with one-story partitions topped by terraces, grilles, catwalks, triangular towers and a trussed, tubular-steel frame. Micro-design features notwithstanding, the overwhelming scale remains a constant, depersonalizing force. Indeed, it, the use of industrial materials and even the sound quality within the space recall the ambience of an airport terminal. (Without question, Forster was influenced by the groundbreaking architecture of the Pompidou Center in Paris, designed by his former partner

Richard Rogers in collaboration with Renzo Piano.)

Fortunately, the decision to expand the building in the late 1980s did not entail enlarging the box. Instead, for the Crescent Wing, Foster added space below ground, creatively taking advantage of the site's slope enhanced by picture-perfect views of a lake and the valley beyond. Except for a glass-enclosed side ramp that slowly disappears beneath the grass lawn and a curving sweep of slanted windows, virtually buried in the greenery, the Crescent Wing is invisible from the outside. And unlike the main structure, the interior here is divided into separate, differentiated sections.

The Robert and Lisa Sainsbury Collection, which served as the catalyst for developing the center, comprises modern Western art with fine and applied arts from Africa, Oceania, the Americas, Asia, Egypt, medieval Europe and the ancient Mediterranean. Included are some major objects by Francis Bacon, Alberto Giacometti and Henry Moore and many secondary holdings useful for teaching and study. Twentieth-century art is quite limited and focused on figurative compositions. In addition, there is no vanguard contemporary work to speak of.

In contrast to the conventional museum installation, here the display intermixes objects from various eras and cultures based on shared formal traits. Some of the resulting juxtapositions and comparisons are intriguing though they often skew or neglect an understanding of context and content. Within the special exhibitions, located downstairs in the Crescent Wing, these issues are better balanced and skillfully presented.

Overall, the Sainsbury Collection and the gallery programs are conservative, academic and somewhat New-Age spiritual. (If you are familiar with the Menil Collection in Houston, this one seems like a poor cousin and low-grade clone.) Though the center formerly put on exhibitions of contemporary art, these pretty much stopped in the mid-1990s when Sir and Lady Sainsbury lost interest and curtailed funding. The direction of the future program remains to be seen. Recent exhibitions: *Architecture for the Millennium, Be Moved...Journeys of Body & Mind, Yuri Kuper, Light, Henry Moore—Friendships and Influences, The Pleasures of Peace—Craft, Art & Design in Britain (1940s-70s), Spain is Different—Post Pop and the New Image in Spain.*

Norwich Gallery

Norwich School of Art and Design
St. George's St, NR3 1BB
01603-610561 f: 615728
www.nsad.ac.uk/gallery/index.htm
nor.gal@nsad.ac.uk
Mon–Sat, 10–5
admission: free

If you're in Norwich and want to see art with a youthful, energetic dynamic and experimental impulse, visit the Norwich Gallery, not the Sainsbury Centre. It's situated in the very center of the historic part of the city, though it stands quite apart from the puritanical attitudes that hold sway among the local population. The ambience in the meandering space of the gallery is very casual. You'll probably see people sitting on the floor or standing around engaged in serious or fun-filled discussions. Don't pass up the chance to join in and ask questions about the art—or most anything else

Yorkshire Region

This region of Britain, centered around Leeds has pockets of lively art activity.

You'll find extensive listings and articles about what's happening in Yorkshire's free monthly magazine, *Artscene*.

Nottingham

This is Robin Hood country, once the home to high sheriffs who guarded the royal land holdings encompassing Sherwood Forest and High Peak. Though it's rarely mentioned— certainly not in connection with the region's legendary past, now glorified and romanticized in the city's hilltop castle— Nottingham was originally named Snottingham by Danish settlers. The name was changed by the Normans who supplanted the Danes and couldn't pronounce the sn sound. (This is a bit of useless trivia that may some in handy during a lull in an art-world conversation.) Train from London (St. Pancras), 1 3/4 hr.

Inland Revenue Headquarters

architect: Michael HOPKINS, 1992-94
Wilford St

Located near the train station, alongside the canal and the route going up to the castle.

This civil service complex, largely filled with tax inspectors, includes six three- and four-story brick structures designed to blend with the masonry of nearby Victorian warehouses. Except for the corner towers—sheltering spiral staircases and formed of glass brick with flattened, umbrella-like tops—the office buildings appear rather commonplace. Oddly, this seems not so much a result of extensive prefabrication (nearly every structural segment and component part arrived ready-made and was assembled on the spot) but owing to a conservative design dominated by excessive repetition.

Unexpectedly, the focus of the complex is a large tented structure (the Amenities Building) housing a sports hall, nursery, restaurant, bar and other recreational activities. Its fabric roof, hung from four masts and tension cables, dramatically contrasts with the surrounding architecture, so much so that it looks like an afterthought or a freakish offspring being kept hidden so it can't be viewed by the outside world.

Angel Row Gallery

Central Library Building
3 Angel Row, NG1 6HP
0115-947-6334
Mon–Tues, Thurs–Sat, 11–6;
Wed, 11–7
admission: free

The gallery is on the first floor, accessed through a separate, street-front staircase to the left of the library entrance door.

Based on its setting in a library crowded with seniors and school kids and located in the middle of the city's old shopping district, you might expect this to be a provincial art center. Its program, weighted toward ceramics, textiles and visually pleasing work, bears this out. However, the gallery also presents touring exhibitions and shows based on work in the Arts Council Collection which often include challenging objects. This was true of *Personal Effects: Sculpture and Belongings* (1999), comprising sculptures by Jordan Baseman, Dorothy Cross, Tracey Emin, Edward Lipski, Nina Saunders, Yinka Shonibare; and *Sublime Darkness and Light* (1998), with work by Matthew Hale, Shirazeh Houshiary, Joan Key, Gustav Metzer, Lucia Nogueira, Mark Wallinger. Having four spacious rooms at its disposal, the gallery can accommodate multimedia installations and video projects.

Recent exhibitions: *Automata, Bodyscape, Chart, Dark Matter, Richard Devereux, Flexible Furniture, Formed in

Glass, Kathy Prendergast, Emma Rose, Helen Sear, Textures of Memory—The Poetics of Cloth.

Sheffield

Once a thriving industrial city and major steel manufacturing center, Sheffield is in the process of redeveloping and reinventing itself. *The Full Monty* went a long way in promoting the unabashed, friendly character of the citizenry (though also focusing attention on derelict areas), and a new stadium enhanced the existing concentration of arenas and popular teams to make Sheffield a preeminent sports metropolis. There is also a lively artsy population, tangentially associated with the city's two universities. You'll find activity in this realm bubbling in performance spaces and clubs located in the area in front of the train station known as the Cultural Industries Quarter, or CIQ. Train from London (St. Pancras), 2 hr 20 min; from Nottingham, 1 hr.

Sharon Kirland, *School for Lovers*, 1998

Site Gallery

1 Brown St, S1 2BS
0114-281-2077 f: 281-2078
www.site-map.u-net.com
gallery@site-map.u-net.com
Tues, Thurs–Sat, 11–6;
Wed, 11–8; closed Mon
admission: free

Brown St branches off to the left of Sheaf Sq, the traffic circle on the hill in front of the train station.

This is a place not to miss if you're anywhere near Sheffield. It's an unpretentious enterprise in a nicely renovated small building with a superb exhibition program. Focused exclusively on photography, Site Gallery broadens the definition of the medium to encompass film and video, computer-based creation, installation, multimedia performance. Exhibitions feature cutting-edge artists who experiment with the photographic process itself or develop innovative ways of incorporating photographic images into their art. Typically the work displayed here is not only visually but also conceptually compelling due to its mode of addressing controversial or topical issues. Other photo-oriented galleries may say they have similar programs but few present the top-notch, vanguard quality that you'll consistently see at Site Gallery. Moreover, it's not a matter of big name stars and audience-directed projects.

It's a pity that the space for exhibitions is so limited: two rooms on the ground floor and another on the first floor. The gallery expands this a bit by presenting a changing after-dark program of films, videos and electronic media projections on a window wall facing the street. Work shown in the window is commissioned from both internationally known and emerging artists. Off-site projects further augment the modest space in the gallery from time to time. For example,

Branson Coates, National Centre for Popular Music

Shunted, a 1998 "exhibition" situated in the Sheffield train station, featured five diverse talents who created interactive audiovisual installations specifically attuned to the location and activities therein. The works produced by Simon Biggs, Frances Hegarty & Andrew Stones and Mark Wallinger for this project were top-notch exemplars of public art.

Artist talks, conferences and workshops accompany exhibitions. Related publications and a general selection of magazines, critical theory and photography books are available in a small shop just off the entrance lobby. Darkrooms equipped with state-of-the-art chemical and digital facilities are also available for public use or classes run by the gallery.

Recent exhibitions: Acoustic Shadows, Jonathan Allen, Breda Beban, Bernd & Hilla Becher, Sophie Calle, Nicole & Norbert Corsino, Ben Fitton, Forced Entertainments, Immediate—New Work New Media, Sharon Kirland, Marie-Jo Lafontaine, Mark Lewis, Shift Control—Audio Rom, Star Dot Star, Traffic.

National Centre for Popular Music

architect: Branson COATES, 1998
Paternoster Row, S1 2QQ
0114-296-2626 f: 249-8886
ncpm.co.uk
info@ncpm.co.uk

Located around the corner from Site Gallery, opposite the Showroom Cinema.

You will immediately be drawn toward this building once you catch a glimpse of its utterly eccentric design. Composed of four squat and shiny stainless steel drums topped by odd, spoutlike forms (sound vents), the architecture was custom-made for the National Centre for Popular Music. Each of the three-story-high, windowless sections contains a different exhibition area, and the ground floors, connected by a glass-enclosed reception lobby, are public spaces housing a café, bar, shop, etc.

The center lays claim to being the first in the world to recognize popular music as an art form and to treat the diverse types of music—be it opera, punk or hip-hop—with equivalent acceptance. Befitting the content, the exhibition areas—History and Development of Popular Music, Making Music, Soundscapes (a three-dimensional surround sound auditorium), Visiting Exhibitions—use lots of film, audio and hands-on displays. In addition, live events, seminars and music festivals are an ongoinzg part of the program.

As one of the new cultural buildings funded by the National Lottery, it remains to be seen how well it survives as an institution.

Mappin Art Gallery

Weston Park, Western Bank,
S10 2TP
0114-276-8588
Wed–Sat, 10–5; Sun, 11–5;
closed Mon–Tues
admission: free
supertram: University

Located in the same hill-top area as the University of Sheffield, the gallery fronts Western Bank and borders Mushroom Lane.

Housed in a conglomerate of mismatched structures (some quite tacky) and attached to the funky City Museum (a haven for school kids), the Mappin Art Gallery (whose collection comprises Victorian paintings), offers a very strange setting for contemporary art exhibitions. The program encompasses exhibitions that are a slightly spiced brand of provincial pabulum to vanguard touring shows and notable regional commissions. It's hard to tell from the titles which is which and usually there's a mix of several things happening at the same time. Plan to overlook the ambience—it's a very low-key, "nail and hammer" operation—but prepare to see exceptional work, including ambitious installations by unfamiliar artists.

If you hit it right, you may catch a captivating exhibition like *Admission of Identity* (1998), featuring Rineke Dijkstra, Joseph Koudelka, Wolfgang

Tillmans and a range of other photographers who take a documentary-conceptual approach. Other recent exhibitions: *Claustrophobia, Antony Gormley—Field for the British Isles, Tracey Holland, Nomenclature, Stephen Willats.*

Leeds

Although Leeds lacks a major collection of contemporary art, it is the center of art activity in the region. The Leeds College of Art and University of Leeds—whose art history, film and women studies programs have been at the forefront of critical theory—provide a continuous influx of creative energy, and art centers in the area are increasingly presenting exhibitions by internationally renowned figures. The annual film and fringe festivals, café galleries and the significant presence (and financial support) of the Henry Moore Foundation also contribute to the city's vitality. Train from Sheffield, 45 min; from London (King's Cross), 2 1/4 hr.

Henry Moore Institute

architects: Jeremy DIXON and
Edward JONES, 1993
74 The Headrow, LS1 3AA
0113-234-3158 f: 246-1481
www.henry-moore.ac.uk
hmst@henry-moore.ac.uk
Mon–Tues, Thurs–Sun, 10–5:30;
Wed, 10–9
admission: free

It seems everywhere you go in the greater Leeds area, you come across the name of Henry Moore. As a Yorkshire native and alum of the Leeds College of Art, Moore stipulated that his foundation's activity—developing "public interest, knowledge and appreciation of sculpture of all periods and nationalities, with an emphasis on contemporary work"— should be based in his home region. With unprecedented generosity, the foundation has followed his wish, supporting the Yorkshire Sculpture Park (West Bretton), Henry Moore Studio (Halifax), Henry Moore Institute, its Archive and Library (Leeds) and Henry Moore Sculpture Trust Publications, and funding artist projects, exhibitions, events, conferences, lectures, residences and research fellowships, the majority of which take place in Yorkshire and focus attention on contemporary sculpture.

Occupying a group of converted Victorian offices and warehouses in the middle of the city, the Henry Moore Institute has a striking facade. Its pure black granite surface with an off-center, tall, thin cutout for the entrance and five window cutouts on top is both simple and monumental. Equally striking is a luminous gallery (formerly an interior courtyard) with a double-height ceiling and minimalist aesthetic. A spacious, oak-paneled reception area and three additional galleries complete the ground floor layout. Offices and a library and archive specializing in sculpture are located on the upper floors. The institute is directly connected to the City Art Gallery by a glass bridge.

For the most part, exhibitions feature major objects by midcareer and established artists. Intermittently, there are also shows of emerging artists and historical sculptures. You won't find many comparable programs where the selection of artist and artwork as well as the installations are consistently superb. These are small, concentrated exhibitions centered on a defined body of work. Even when a curatorial slant shapes a project, it's never at the expense of the art nor does it create a ponderously academic presentation.

True to the Henry Moore mission, the focus is always on sculpture. Yet exhibitions sometimes question the nature of sculpture by presenting two-dimensional works concerned with concepts like space, form and environment. In this spirit, Alan Charlton's monochromatic paintings, Jeff Wall's lightbox photographs and Fred Sandback's string installations composed a three-part show titled *Here and Now* (1998–99). Catalogues, conferences, symposia, talks and seminars accompany all exhibitions.

Other recent exhibitions: *Hans Arp—Reliefs, At One Remove, James Lee Byars, Andrea Blum, Cell–Cella–Celda (Edward Allington, Vittorio Messina, Jauma Plensa, Andrew Sabin), The Color of Sculpture (1840–1910), Dom van der Laan, Naum Gabo, Gravity's Angel (Lili Dujourie, Asta Gröting, Christina Iglesias, Kirsten Ortwed), Jasper Johns—The Sculptures, Katarzyna Kobro, Robert Morris—Recent Felt Pieces and Drawings, David Nash, Laurent Pariente, Serge Spitzer, artranspennine98 (Atelier van Lieshout, Langlands & Bell, Jorge Pardo, Françoise Quardon).*

Leeds City Art Gallery

The Headrow, LS1 3AA
0113-247-8248 f: 244-9689
www.leeds.gov.uk
Mon–Tues, Thur–Sat, 10–5;
Wed, 10–8; Sun, 1–5
admission: free

If you enter the City Art Gallery via the bridge from the Henry Moore Institute, you'll arrive in a cramped area with a Study of Sculpture display. It's a mixed bag of small, mainly figurative, 19th–20th-century objects. Even if you're not particularly interested in an expressly educational exhibit, some of the works are quite refreshing. There's a witty Claes Oldenburg *Maquette for a Bottle of Notes* (1990); a curious earthenware jug covered with a landscape painting from Richard Long (1965–66); a nice plaster model by William Tucker; a curving oak floor piece by Granville Davey; and various works by Henry Moore and Barbara Hepworth.

Much of the museum is still in an overly decorated, dark Victorian state, and the dominant focus is vintage British painting and sculpture. The collection does contain a dazzling, wall-hanging bronze by Antony Gormley and a few conceptual photographs by Bernd & Hilla Becher and Boyd Webb, but on the whole the representation of contemporary art is negligible. Special exhibitions of art from recent decades or the present are likewise weak, favoring watered-down, poorly cloned versions of daring currents. This said, you should check the listings anyway since occasionally a laudable show, like Mary Kelly (1999) appears in the schedule.

Leeds Metropolitan University Gallery

Woodhouse Lane, LS1 3HE
0113-283-3130
www.lmu.ac.uk/arts
Mon–Tues, Thurs–Sat, 11–5;
Wed, 11–7
admission: free

Walk around the corner from the Henry Moore Institute onto Cookridge St; follow this for two blocks and turn left at Woodhouse Lane (a main road); you'll soon see a group of ugly concrete towers set back from the street on the left (Leeds Metropolitan University); take the entrance opposite the Dry Dock pub; it leads to a building bearing a sign for the Gallery and Studio Theatre. (10-min walk)

As is often the case with university galleries, this one is housed in a bland, institutional setting. Here at least there's a degree of spaciousness since a mezzanine adds a second level and doubles the height of the room. Despite the unfortunate ambience, the gallery offers select exhibitions of contemporary art—be it paintings or new-media installations. They're not benchmark projects but they often include formida-

ble work by young artists. For example, the 1999 exhibition dumbpop, which called attention to objects that reject the pessimism of '90s British art, featured such emerging international talents as Sarah Morris, Jean-Michel Othoniel, Philippe Parreno. Other recent exhibitions: A Christmas Pudding for Henry, Kenny Hunter, Bashir Makhoul, Slow Burn, Vessel, Alison Watt.

West Bretton

Train from London (King's Cross) to Wakefield (Westgate), 2 1/4 hr; from Leeds, 15 min; from Halifax, 15 min; from Sheffield, 30 min. Take bus 41 from Wakefield to West Bretton, 8 mi south. Taxis from the train station are also available for a fare of approximately £6. If you drive, take M1, exit at junction 38 and follow A637 for 1 mi.

Yorkshire Sculpture Park (YSP)

Bretton Hall, West Bretton
WP4 4LG
0192-483-0302 f: 483-0044
www.ysp.co.uk
ysp@globalnet.co.uk
park grounds: summer—daily,
10–6; winter—daily, 10–5
galleries: summer—daily, 10–2;
winter—daily, 11–4
admission: free, £1.50 for parking

Although the address of YSP is often listed as Wakefield because it's the encompassing domain within which the hamlet of West Bretton is situated, YSP is not located in the city of Wakefield.

Depending on the weather and season, you're likely to encounter busloads of tourists and cars filled with family members of all ages gathered around the visitor center and parking lot. Not to worry. Once you wander off into the

o Paladino, *Sud II*, 1993

tered below the parking lot contain classrooms and studios. Beyond these buildings in the undulating open range populated by grazing sheep, you'll find a dozen or so nicely sited, large bronzes by Henry MOORE. The land is actually a separate entity called Bretton Country Park, but you're welcome to roam around it and look at the sculptures. Don't be put off by the fence. Its purpose is to keep the herd in rather than to keep you out. Though the entry gates are not easy to see, it's not a good idea to jump over or squeeze through the barrier!

Since its opening in 1977, YSP has been developing a permanent collection and pursuing long- and short-term loans from artists. In addition, there are outdoor and indoor exhibitions as well as temporary projects created within the artist-in-residence program. The aim is to keep changing the selection, displaying a mix of established, midcareer and emerging artists. Sculptures on view in the park have included works by Edward Allington, Jonathan Borofsky, Emile-Antoine Bourdelle, Anthony Caro, Lynn Chadwick, Ian Cooper, Grenville Davey, Elisabeth Frink, Barbara Hepworth, Sol LeWitt, Michael Lyons, Dhruva Mistry, Igor Mitoraj, David Nash, Mimmo Paladino, Eduardo Paolozzi, Jaume Plensa, Giò Pomodoro, Donald Rankin, Michael Sandle, Richard Serra, Serge Spitzer, William Tucker, Ursula von Rydingsvard, Robert Wlérick.

200 acres of 18th-century parkland, formerly a country estate (Bretton Hall), you may find yourself quite alone. The setting includes manicured lawns, terraced gardens, two indoor gallery spaces, lakes, rolling hills, woodsy glens and trails. Should you prefer not to walk, you can use an electric buggy and tour the premises like a golf pro! It takes several hours to meander around so it's best to wear comfortable shoes and come prepared with a picnic (and an umbrella). Alternatively, you can eat in the café.

Before you leave the visitor center be sure to buy a map. Free brochures are available but they are totally inadequate since they don't give the location and identity of individual sculptures. You'll find that most of the works are unlabeled and there is no background information or interpretive signage about the art within the park.

Yorkshire Sculpture Park shares its grounds with University College Bretton Hall, a teacher training and fine arts school. Thus, the buildings you see clus-

If you're familiar with contemporary art, you're likely to be disappointed in the representation (or lack thereof) of current trends. There's little in the way of vanguard expression, and even an artist like Serra, known for his benchmark steel plates of mind-boggling scale and balance, is shown here in terms of an idiosyncratic early work. Site-specific art expressly related to the setting and sculptures with a conceptual or commentary base are barely in evidence though they have been the dominant force in innovative art during the past decades. At YSP you'll instead find a prevalent modernist orientation focused on form. There is talk of commissioning work for particular places in the park and perhaps this will yield a more dynamic selection.

If your walk around the park has concentrated on the Access Sculpture Trail or the area near the lakes, be sure to visit Bothy Garden. It's just over and east of the hillside next to the parking lot, enclosed by a brick wall. Here you'll see sculptures placed within a stylized landscape recalling the grandeur and opulence of the grounds surrounding the country houses of the British aristocracy. The structure lining the top edge, once the storage for horse-drawn carriages, now houses a shop, café and small gallery. The main Pavilion Gallery is located at the lower end of the garden in a tent-topped structure. It is used for one-person exhibitions featuring small sculptures, maquettes, drawings and preparatory sketches. This display sometimes accompanies a showing of large-scale work by the same artist, installed outside in the adjacent garden space. Recent exhibitions: *Magdalena Abakanowicz, Edward Allington, Michael Dan Arche, Kenneth Armitage, Anthony Caro, Christo, Barry Flanagan, Phillip King, Jacques Lipchitz, Richard Long, Michael Lyons, Joel Shapiro, James Turrell, Ursula von Rydingsvard, Hermione Wiltshire, Austin Wright.*

Halifax

Train from Leeds, 35 min.

Dean Clough Galleries

Dean Clough, HX3 5AX
0142-225-0250 f: 234-1148
www.deanclough.com
daily, 10–5
admission: free

From the train station take Horton St into the town center; turn right at Market St, which becomes Northgate; when the road forks go left onto Cross Hills (the right fork is North Bridge). You'll pass under a highway (Burdock Way) and then see the mills on your right. Head toward the entrance marked "True North." (15 min)

Dean Clough Mills was formerly one of the world's largest luxury carpet factories (Crossley Carpets). By the 1960s the mammoth complex, composed of 16 19th-century buildings, became obsolete. It finally closed its doors in 1982. A year later, it was purchased by Ernest Hall, an entrepreneur who set about transforming the mills into a commercial and industrial complex. His own love of music inspired the inclusion of an arts component within the redevelopment scheme. As a result, Dean Clough now houses over 100 enterprises: businesses and manufacturing establishments, a café-bar, restaurant and theater, as well as organizations associated with performance, music, writing, art, crafts, design and education. Twenty local artists also occupy low-cost or rent-free studios, and several music ensembles and theater companies are based in the mill.

A year-round schedule of jazz and classical concerts, plays and performances takes place within the Dean Clough complex. In addition, there are lectures, workshops and other public events.

In 1994 the mill established a more formal presence for the visual arts with the opening of the Dean Clough Galleries. The Design House Gallery, which houses the Design and Book Shop, is adjacent to the reception area, and the Crossley Gallery lies beyond this. Additional galleries are upstairs and works from the Dean Clough collection fill virtually all corridor walls in areas with public access. The art on display—

except for an occasional touring exhibition*—is very traditional and mediocre. Indeed, the galleries tend toward being a tourist attraction rather than a serious venue for contemporary art.

(*For example, the 1998 show of ecological land art projects by Helen M. & Newton Harrison; or the 1999 exhibit of furniture by designers working in Britain 1930-70.)

For those interested in cinema, six large oil paintings from the *GBH Series* (1984) by Derek Jarman hang alongside the Viaduct Theatre. They relate to his film *The Last of England* and presumably he suggested that *GBH* stands for "grievous bodily harm," "great British horror," "gargantuan bloody H-bomb" or any such thing.

Henry Moore Studio

Gate 1, Dean Clough, HX3 5AX
0113-246-7467 f: 246-1481
hmst@henry-moore.ac.uk
Tues–Sun, 12–5 during exhibitions;
exhibitions only occur at the
end of an artist's residency;
call for information
admission: free

The Studio is immediately on the left inside Gate 1. Though it bears the name of Henry Moore, it was never his personal work space, nor does it contain the remnants of his studio or a display of his sculpture.

A viable reason to go to Dean Clough if you're interested in venturesome contemporary art is to see one of the projects in the Henry Moore Studio.

Since 1989 the Henry Moore Sculpture Trust has operated a studio in one of the old mill buildings. It's a vast space in which internationally acclaimed artists, usually one or two a year, are invited to work. Not only do the artists enjoy the benefits of a luxury space but they also receive whatever technical expertise, equipment and assistance they need plus access to the local quarries, foundries and workshops.

The studio aims to give artists the time and facilities in which they can pursue new directions, take risks, experiment and explore ideas or procedures rather than concentrate on producing objects. They are encouraged to think big without the usual creative limitations or personal constraints. Although the projects are usually open for public viewing when the artists complete their residencies, there is no pressure to create a finished object or think in terms of an exhibition.

It's as close as one comes to the ultimate dream studio. Artists who have been in residence include: Conrad Atkinson, Christian Boltanski, Christine Borland, Angela Bulloch, Anthony Caro, Dinos & Jake Chapman, Tony Cragg, Georg Herold, Magdalena Jetelová, Jannis Kounellis, Wolfgang Laib, Richard Long, Bruce McLean, Vittorio Messina, John Newling, Guiseppe Penone, Stephen Pippin, Michelangelo Pistoletto, Jaume Plensa, Ulrich Rückriem, Andrew Sabin, Peter Shelton, Georgina Starr, James Turrell, Gillian Wearing, Lawrence Weiner, Alison Wilding.

Christian Boltanski

The Lost Workers, ongoing
basement of E mill
by appointment, 0113-246-7467

Typical of Boltanski's archive projects, this one suggestively memorializes a historic situation of local importance through an agglomeration of storage boxes, each identified with a particular individual. Here the boxes contain objects that the artist collected from people who once worked in the Crossley Carpet mills.

Bradford

This old wool-producing city (9 mi west of Leeds), is not much to write home about except that a few outstanding arts attractions are located in its midst. Train from Leeds to Bradford (Interchange), 20 min; from Halifax, 15 min.

National Museum of Photography, Film and TV

🏛 Pictureville, Prince's View BD1 1NQ
🎥 01274-202030 f: 723155
　 www.nmsi.ac.uk/nmpft
📖 Tues–Sun, 10–6; closed Mon
　 admission: free,
　 cinema—£4.20/2.90,
　 IMAX—£5.80/4

Located downtown, a 5-min walk from the train; follow the signs.

Having completed a major renovation and expansion of its six-floor main building, this popular museum now includes displays about the digital revolution and how it has dramatically changing the way we use and live with media. The historical sections, which explore the stories behind photography, television and film and the industries that use them, have also been updated. Not to be overlooked are the new interactive models and hands-on film equipment that nicely complement the collections of ephemera, early cameras, TV props and rare photographs. Moreover, special exhibitions survey new trends and the work of leading artists, and the museum's three theaters (Pictureville, Cubby Broccoli and IMAX) screen vintage films, Cinerama movies and new releases.

In terms of photography, the emphasis tends toward work allied with a documentary rather than an artsy approach. The exhibitions are refreshing, featuring both well-known and unfamiliar artists whose subject matter is provocative if not riveting and whose compositional skills are outstanding. For its displays and an occasional special exhibition, the museum makes use of the large Kodak collection it has at its disposal.

Achieving a good balance of entertainment and education is not easy when dealing with photography, film and TV, but this goal enhances all the activities and productions of the museum. Recent exhibitions: *Ian Berry, The Bradford 100, National Portraits (1970s), The Patient Planet/So Many Worlds, ReVisions—An Alternative History of Photography, Street Dreams—Contemporary Indian Studio Photography, Donovan Wylie, Young Meteors—British Photojournalism (1957–65)*.

The Zwemmer gift and souvenir shop in the lobby encompasses an excellent bookshop with all sorts of magazines, critical texts and coffee-table editions on subjects related to the mechanical production of visual imagery.

Cartwright Hall

🏛 Lister Park, BD9 4NS
　 01274-493313 f: 481045
　 Tues–Sat, 10–5; Sun, 1–5;
　 closed Mon
　 admission: free
　 bus: 661–665, exit at park gates

Located 1 mi north of central Bradford off Keighley Rd (A650).

In contrast to the bleak, rundown appearance of the city, Cartwright Hall is an elegant Baroque-styled building surrounded by landscaped grounds with classic English gardens. It's not a huge museum, nor does it have a great collection, but its holdongs encompass recent art by David Hockney, Anish Kapoor and other noteworthy figures. Temporary exhibitions also present contemporary art, including new media, video and installation work. Recent exhibitions: *Clastrophobia, Keitth Piper*.

1853 Gallery

Salts Mill, Victoria Rd
Saltaire, BD18 3LB
daily, 10–6
01274-531163 f: 531184
1853gallery@saltsmill.demon.co.uk

The village of Saltaire is 4 mi north of Bradford center; direct access by local bus and train. Train from Leeds, 10 min.

If you're interested in utopian communities or if you're passionate about David Hockney, put Saltaire on your list of places to visit.

The town appears pretty much as it did in the mid-19th century when it was developed by the textile magnate Titus Salt as a model factory community for workers. As might be expected, many of the village houses have been turned into antique shops and restaurants. The big tourist feature, however, is the monumental mill, now a giant emporium of arts, crafts, book, art supply, home furnishing, decorator, stationery and sundry other shops and galleries. Since the vast floors of the old mill have been preserved as wide open spaces, the various businesses all merge together. And goods are spread out on long tables or hung from primitive display mounts, creating a picturesque scene like a country fair or town market. Opera music playing in the background enhances the ambience and pays homage to the mill's omnipresent star attraction—David Hockney, Bradford's famous son. (The music comes from those operas for which the artist designed the sets and costumes.)

In addition to the mass-production posters, postcards, ceramics, T-shirts and souvenir merchandise emblazoned with one of Hockney's brightly colored images, you can buy original Hockney photo-collages, prints and paintings in the 1853 Gallery. Actually, there are three galleries spread over the three floors of the mill. In marked contrast to the rest of the mill, the space on the third floor, housing a permanent exhibition of Hockney's paintings, is regally outfitted with classical columns, serene light and white walls, plush couches and ornate tables, vases and an antique grand piano. If this ersatz aristocratic setting doesn't appeal to you, head down to the ever-crowded, lively Salts Diner in the rear of the second floor. Not to be outdone, it too exalts Hockney by covering its walls with enlarged laser-printed photos taken by the artist on a 35-mm camera when visiting Bradford in 1993. As the sign says, "some local snaps by David Hockney, a local artist."

Hull

Some people refer to Hull, also known as Kingston upon Hull, as the "end of the line." True, it's quite removed from a major urban center, yet it's a charming maritime city with a proud heritage as a transportation, fishing and shipping hub. Recent revitalization efforts have included the pedestrianization of the downtown area and refurbishment of docks as housing and shopping zones. It's a nice place to relax and escape from bustling cities and throngs of tourists. Train from Leeds, 1 hr; from London (King's Cross), 3 hr.

Ferens Art Gallery

Queen Victoria Sq, HU1 3RA
01482-613902 f: 613710
Mon–Sat, 10–5; Sun, 1:30–4:30
www.hullcc.gov.uk/museums/ferens
admission: free

Housed in a stately building with a new addition in back (a café and two octagonal galleries), the Ferens Art Gallery is one of the city's treasures. Indeed, it's a very community-oriented museum with programs relating to everything from

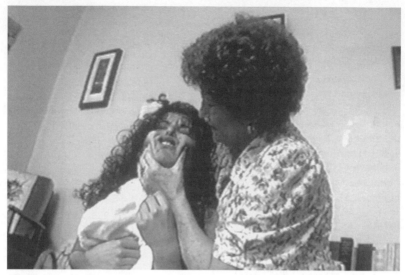

Gillian Wearing, *Sacha & Mum*, 1996

old master paintings to performance events. The modern collection and special exhibitions are quite regionally based with a propensity toward seascapes and abstraction. Intermittently, the schedule includes shows featuring more vanguard work from London, for example, *Helen Chadwick, Contemporary and Other, Liz Rideal, Spotlight on Gillian Wearing*.

Root

Root (running out of time) is the name of an international performance festival held in Hull each October. (The local term for performance art is "time-based art.") It's a popular, high-energy event comprising conferences, talks and numerous performances by preeminent and emerging artists from all over Europe and elsewhere. Venues are spread throughout the city and informal gatherings take place day and night. TOOT (totally out of tune) ROOT, the 1999 festival, highlighted audio performance.

Northumberland

The Northumberland region—also called Northumbria—stretches across the northeast sector of England up to the Scottish border. You may be tempted to omit visiting here, thinking it's just remote wilderness. Think again. The picturesque villages, castles, fortress ruins (especially Hadrian's Wall) and high coastal headlands are spectacular. Moreover, the Northern Arts Council has been aggressively working to put the region on the international art map by helping to fund landmark works of public art, new exhibition spaces and centers of contemporary art. And these aren't small, insignificant projects. Many are ambitious, internationally attuned, monumentally scaled objects and buildings.

Train from London (King's Cross) to Newcastle, 3 hr; from Leeds, 1 1/2 hr; from Hull, 2 1/2 hr.

C2C Cycle Route

Sea to Sea or Coast to Coast—C2C—is a 150-mile trail going all across the north of England from Whitehaven on the Irish Sea to Tynemouth on the North Sea. Traversing both the Lake District and Pennine mountains, the route gives an exceptional sense of the open English landscape. Sustrans (a national cycling agency) has added to the outdoor experience by commissioning artists to design the mileposts, seats, bridges, lighting, drinking fountains, ramps, earthworks and other visual and pragmatic elements along the route. It was "a way of humanizing the public space by providing focal points for meeting and resting and for commenting on the local history and context of the area."

If you're not into a grand cycle or walking trip, you can still see sculptures on an urban part of the trail running near Sunderland. (See below.)

For more information contact Sustrans, 35 King St, Bristol BS1 4D7, 0117-926-8893, (fax) 929-4173.

James Turrell

Pennine Skyspace, 2000
Kielder Forest Sculpture Park

Located at Cat Crag, a hill overlooking the northwest end of Kielder Water (reservoir). It's a slow climb of less than 2 mi (3 km) on forestry roads from Kielder Castle. Bicycles are available for rent at the castle.

This work, which is only accessible by foot, bicycle and wheelchair, may encourage you to consider incorporating an outdoor adventure within your travels. Typical of Turrell's open-air sculpture, *Skyspace* is designed so visitors can study the stars, sky, light, color and space. The work is intended as a shelter for cyclists. However, it also offers an experience often described as mystical or spiritual.

Built into an existing quarry and crag, it has the external appearance of a dry-stone wall. An arch leads into an underground chamber rimmed with stone seats. Where the roof should be there is instead a large opening that frames a pure, enigmatic and ever-changing color field, a wondrous space of indeterminate dimensions. Scheduled for completion by the summer of 2000.

Newcastle Upon Tyne

The metropolitan area centered on the city of Newcastle and extending across the geographic region linked to the Tyne and Wear rivers had a long history as an industrial center. But many of the giant businesses collapsed during the postwar period, throwing the region into decades of instability and stagnation. Efforts aimed at reviving the economy and reenergizing the social fabric are finally yielding results. Significantly, public art projects have played a big role in improving the environment and getting communities involved with decisions about their own spaces. They also have given individual neighborhoods and the region as a whole a new identity.

Considering that both sides of the waterfront were lined with derelict manufacturing plants and unsightly, air-polluting equipment up until a few years ago, the transformation is astounding. Everything you see is part of a forward-thinking decision to take back the river and regenerate the land along 30 miles of riverbank. Included within the plan was the Art on the Riverside initiative, which has been commissioning major sculptures by renowned international artists. (See below, di Suvero, Muñoz, Wilding, Langlands & Bell.)

Newcastle is a very friendly, lively place that's easy to enjoy. Though you'll initially encounter crowded, noisy traffic on the main streets and ugly storefronts in the center city, don't be put off. All you need do is turn down nearly any side street, where you'll find old buildings with hidden courtyards, narrow passages and a very different ambience. Be sure to walk down to the river to see the extensive Quayside development, comprising an attractive promenade, corporate office buildings (some in refurbished industrial architecture), housing, restaurants, bars, hotel and health club. The Riverside Walkway, extending along a considerable stretch of the Tyne at Newcastle also gives access to the Millennium Bridge, a pedestrian crossing to Gateshead and the Baltic art center.

Since some intriguing art activities in the area are temporary projects, be sure to check the current local listings to find out about them. Don't be dissuaded if an exhibition or event is outside the city center or in a location beyond Newcastle itself. The metro provides fast and convenient service throughout the immediate area, and trains do likewise for neighboring cities.

Public Art in Public Transport

The Tyne and Wear Metro system, extending from the airport through Newcastle city center and across communities on both sides of the Tyne, has 46 stations. Since 1977 artists have produced wall, floor or sculptural works for the platform and ticket areas of 15 of them. In the main, the works are pretty traditional modernist art. The enamel murals with energetic abstractions by Basil Beattie (Manors Station) and Steve McNulty (Central Station) and the sculptures with imagery borrowed from old

garden forms by Raf Fulcher (Jesmond Station) are the most appealing. To date, the conceptual-based project by Cathy de Monchaux is the only work commissioned for the Tyne and Wear Metro that relates to vanguard art practices and issues.

Hatton Gallery

The Quadrangle
University of Newcastle, NE1 7RU
0191-222-6057 f: 261-1182
www.ncl.ac.uk/hatton
hatton-gallery@ncl.ac.uk
Mon–Fri, 10–5:30; Sat, 10–4:30
admission: free
metro: Haymarket

Though somewhat provincial in its orientation, Hatton's exhibition program includes some notable touring shows and venturesome presentations of work by known and rising artists. Recent exhibitions: *Derek Jarman, Kurt Schwitters' Elterwater Merzbarn, Study and Stay, Voice Over, Ronald Max Vollmer.*

Waygood Gallery

39 Highbridge St, NE1 1EW
0191-221-1712
Wed–Sat, 11–5
metro: Monument

Walk into the back courtyard (parking lot) via the driveway between Turks Pub and Crown; head toward Riley's Snooker located on the ground floor of the left rear warehouse; climb the grungy stairwell up to the 2nd floor.

As the ambience suggests, Waygood is a low-budget, hands-on operation in the mode of the original alternative spaces that developed when a group of artists wanted to exhibit and see the latest work by colleagues in their own and other cities. Here the gallery is particularly energetic in arranging exchanges and touring exhibits showcasing work by spirited, young talents. Most exhibitions group diverse objects under a very loose, playful theme or concept. Recent exhibitions: *A Definite Thing, At the Bottom of the Garden, Friction, Run Rabbit Run, Silk Purse, Studio Bank.*

International Centre for Life

 architect: Terry Farrell, 1999–2000
Scotswood Rd, NE1 4EP
metro: Central Station

Located on the corner of Neville St and Scotswood Rd, one block up from Central Station.

This landmark Millennium project is an unusual blend of a research facility, business-conference complex and public exhibition center—all relating to the idea of genetics. As strange as it may seem, the enterprise exclusively focuses on DNA, "the secret of life itself."

Construction of the center's three components was staggered. The Bioscience Centre, comprising offices and meeting rooms, opened first in 1998. Its structure, an attractive, four-story curved building, is most visible from the street. The facade has a glass-brick section in the middle and sides sheathed in soft gray stone with narrow window bands running horizontally across. Though the shape on the street facade is emphatically curved, a contrasting right-angle configuration with a checkerboard plaza set into its center defines the back. Beyond the plaza, called Times Square, a huge expanse of space opens up. The Genetics Institute (opened summer of 1999), a premier laboratory and study complex involved with fundamental research into inherited diseases, lies to the left. Occupying the main area beyond and to the right is Helix (opens spring of 2000), a high-tech, interactive visitor center and education superlab. The aim here is to make science accessible to people of all ages and backgrounds. Following the lead of the Exploratorium in San Francisco, the exhibits directly engage visitors in discovery-oriented experience. Unlike conventional museum presentations and learning projects, they eliminate didactic, documentary and display techniques.

Byker Wall, Housing Development

architect: Ralph ERSKINE, 1969–80
metro: Byker
East from Newcastle center
on A695 to Shields Rd,
about 1 mile on right.

For anyone interested in urban development and social housing issues, a visit to Bykers is a must. This large-scale, high-density project, in which tenant participation was a vitalizing element, became famous for its nonregimented, pluralistic plan and humane environment. Sociologically, it's touted as a success story for creating a strong sense of community and dignity within mass housing. Architecturally, it's esteemed for its innovative approach to urban living and its dynamic reconstruction of an overcrowded, inadequate settlement.

The "wall" of Byker is a phenomenon onto itself. Bordering the street as it sinuously winds up and across a hilltop, the nearly uninterrupted, eight-story-high, seemingly endless facade on the outer side of the complex forms a barrier to the east and north. Though an extreme architectural design, it functions quite pragmatically to protect residents from the bitter North Sea winds and highway noise. (Because access to the city was deemed economically critical, Erskine ensured that a highway and metro were built within close proximity to the housing.) A concern with aesthetics is also evident in the construction of the wall with multicolored bricks arranged in carefully formulated abstract patterns.

The sun-oriented south side of the

wall, which slopes down the hill with views of the river, has a completely different structural and visual character. It's an irregular assemblage with a high-rise backdrop and a jumble of low-rise housing terraces traversed by winding paths, private gardens, public spaces and park areas. As intended, you get little sense of the formulaic order and homogeneity of most mass-production housing. Windows, shed-roofed balconies and wooden arcades painted in subdued tones of red, green and blue fragment and diversify the massively scaled block buildings, and the seemingly haphazard clustering of ground units adds a village ambience to the whole.

To be sure, all these features are readily apparent and warrant attention for having contributed greatly to the dialogue about social and mass housing. Nevertheless, an on-site viewing of Byker is not an exhilarating experience. Perhaps it's because the buildings

haven't worn well over time. Or maybe it's just the unbelievable size and insularity of the project. In any event, the impression of a bygone, withering community on the verge of becoming a shanty town refuses to go away.

North Shields

4.3 mi (7 km) east of Newcastle

Mark di Suvero

Tyne Anew, 1999
Royal Quay
metro: North Shields
Located on the riverside near the entrance to the new marina.

This towering sculpture—71 ft (21.5 m) tall—is the first work by Mark di Suvero to appear on British soil. Oddly, this popular American artist, who gained recognition in the 1960s with his balance-oriented, timber-and-steel conglomerates, has not yet received attention in the UK.

The work he has created for North Shields is classic di Suvero. Composed of industrial steel beams painted bright red-orange, it takes the form of a tripod supporting a pincerlike structure and enhanced by autonomous disk elements. In the words of one critic, it "resembles a cross between a shipyard crane and a Martian invader (as in *War of the Worlds*)."

Globe Gallery

97 Howard St, NE30 1NA
0191-259-2614
Tues–Sat, 10–5; Wed, 11–1
metro: North Shields

Located on the corner of Saville Rd, one block from the Beacon Shopping Centre.

This gallery is mainly involved with public art projects in the north Tyneside area. Exhibitions often include models and preparatory drawings for sculptures in process or already completed.

Mark di Suvero, *Tyne Anew*, 1999

Support for the gallery comes partly from the adjacent gift shop selling crafts by local artists.

Cathy de Monchaux

The Day before You Looked through Me, 1998
Cullercoats Metro Station

Though not in North Shields, this metro station is only two stops beyond.

Cathy de Monchaux, a London artist who was short-listed in 1998 for the Turner Prize, gives an enigmatic, disturbing twist to the theme of travel in her work at the Cullercoats Metro Station. The project features a large-scale photograph of a deserted train station with a long blood-red carpet laid out on a platform with its torn back end trailing onto the track. The suggestive ambience and extreme wide-angle view draw you into the depiction even as reflections in the glass surface confound fantasy narratives with intrusions from actuality. The image is quite compelling but the placement of the work on the side wall of a dreary, poorly lit waiting room robs it of its impact.

Gateshead

Tyne Millennium Bridge

architect: Chris WILKINSON, 1996-2000

This pedestrian and bicycle bridge provides a convenient, direct link between Newcastle and the new Baltic art center in Gateshead. The imaginative design also enhances the riverfront. In contrast to conventional drawbridges, Wilkinson's ingenious structure, a single-arch suspension bridge, flips up for ships to pass by. Described as a rotating eyeball, it is visually intriguing as a form at rest and in motion.

Baltic, Centre for Contemporary Art

renovation: Dominic WILLIAMS, 2001
Quayside
0191-478-1810 f: 478-1922
www.balticmill.com
b4b@balticmill.com
admission: free

While London is getting a whopping infusion of contemporary art energy from the new Tate Modern, the north is poised for its own gargantuan injection from the Baltic, scheduled to open in the fall of 2001. But whereas the late has been conceptualized as a 21st-century museum, Baltic sees itself as a top-of-the-line "art factory" in which artists will explore fresh ideas and develop innovative projects on-site. Exhibitions and events will largely be generated by artists working in the center's studios and workshops, though some of the galleries will present touring shows and preexisting works.

Baltic's emphasis on artist residencies and the creative process is comparable to the Henry Moore Studio in Halifax, but here the public dimension is very different. Indeed, it will be a big challenge for Baltic to balance the center's need for a full public program with artists' proclivity for private workspace and unstructured activity. Above all, Baltic will have to attract leading and cutting-edge artists, both young and established, from the UK and elsewhere, to attain its goal of becoming a world-class art center.

The building will surely help. It's a monumental edifice, originally constructed as a model flour mill in the late 1940s. Its reputation as "the pride of Tyneside" was, however, short-lived. It closed in 1980, supplanted by technically advanced factories. Despite its impressive external form, conversion of the mill into a flexible art center has required the

Baltic, Centre for Contemporary Art (pre-renovation and pre-redevelopment of waterfront)

total destruction of the interior. The new layout will include five different types of galleries. These have been described as "the white cube, the multimedia space, an intimate gallery, the close-control 'museum' gallery and the high art gallery (with daylight from above)." They will accommodate exhibitions, installations, performances, digital facilities, lectures, meetings, cinemas, workshops and artists' studios. The building will also contain a rooftop restaurant, riverside café and bookshop.

Outside, the corner towers and brick facade on the east and west will remain. Glass walls, which will replace the brick on the north and south, not only will bring daylight inside but will also manifest Baltic's desire to be accessible and open to the community. Beyond the usual educational interactions, this will entail collaborations with local industries and regional organizations.

Prior to its opening, various projects have taken place under the rubric of "B4B." Perhaps the most spectacular—and a good omen of what's to come—was Anish Kapoor's installation during the summer of 1999. Using the massive void in the interior before it was rebuilt, he devised an utterly sublime spatial and color experience. The effect was created by stretching a semitransparent deep red membrane over the majestic height of the entire interior and allowing the flow of natural light to come in through the open roof so that subtle and dramatic changes would continuously occur.

A second B4B project, *Flash*, centered on the collaboration between visual artists, contemporary composers, musicians and writers. The process involved spontaneous reactions of each participant to another's work. The results were both recorded on DVDs and performed live at venues around Europe.

Regional Music Centre

architect: Norman FOSTER, 2002
Quayside

Baltic art center and this music center spearhead the development of a new cultural quarter in Gateshead. Together with the Millennium Bridge, they also mark the regeneration of a major zone of riverside property. The selection of a celebrated architect like Norman Foster will moreover bring attention to the whole enterprise and the region.

Even more than the art center, the

music center will be a multipurpose building. As a concert hall it will feature large orchestras well as individual performers whose specialty is classical, jazz, folk or chamber music. It will also be home to the Northern Sinfonia and Folkworks and will house a new regional music school.

Current plans indicate that the building will have a dramatic, shell-like form with curved terraces fronting the river. Serving as a concourse, the main terrace will be lined with cafés, bars, shops and public amenities. The music school will be located below, and a foyer above will lead to a 1,650-seat hall, a 400-seat hall and a rehearsal hall.

Riverside Sculpture Park

Southbank, alongside Pipewellgate Rd

The Gateshead section of the Art on the Riverside program was one of the first to be developed. It currently runs from Swing Bridge west to Redheugh Bridge. The park is at the lower end of a very steep, rugged slope, wooded in places and largely overgrown with grasses. Most of the sculptures here refer directly to the previous industrial use of the land and are site-specific. Since they are well integrated into the setting and unmarked by signposts or labels, it is difficult to find and identify them. Be prepared for a treasure hunt and allow extra time.

Among the works are:

Richard HARRIS, *Bottle Bank*, 1982–86 (between High Level Bridge and Tyne Bridge). This work, whose name refers to one of the oldest Gateshead settlements, was the first to be situated in the reclaimed riverside landscape and the first big sculpture commission awarded by the Gateshead Council. In characteristic form, Harris

has created an environmental work in tune with and calling attention to the surroundings. His walk-through sculpture spans a footpath with a graduated succession of steel arches. As such, it relates to the sequence of bridges which so dominates the immediate area while also emphasizing the sweeping curve of the celebrated Tyne Bridge.

Andy GOLDSWORTHY, *Cone*, 1990 (west of High Level Bridge). Built on an old foundry site, this 13-ft-high (4 m) structure formed by layers of steel plate boldly conveys man-made, industrial strength. Yet at the same time, the irregularities in the shape and evidence of a piece-by-piece evolution suggest processes in nature. The intertwining of the two reiterates a familiar Goldsworthy theme made all the more relevant here with the added overlay of reference to reclamation or cyclical change.

Colin ROSE, *Rolling Moon*, 1988 (between High Level Bridge and Metro Bridge). Though the artist sought to symbolize the idea of the moon's relationship to rising and falling tides, the imagery of a steel ball affixed to a majestic arch is lacking in the evocative potency of the subject. The sculpture's stark form and grand scale are fortunately subdued by its location on the hillside amid trees.

Richard COLE, *Windy Nook*, 1986. Creating an amphitheater, the artist transformed an ugly slag heap from a coal mine into a work of environmental art. It's quite visible as a landmark covering a large expanse of the hillside, but so allied with the terrain and so nonobjectified that it hardly stands out as an artwork. Indeed the terraces formed by concentric, semicircular stone walls (the granite was recycled from an old Tyne bridge) are quite functional, not something just to look. They have been become popular as a destination for people taking a walk or seeking an impressive view of the river and distant hills.

Antony Gormley, *Angel of the North,* 1998

Richard DEACON, *Once Upon a Time*, 1990. To find this sculpture, locate the one surviving abutment of the demolished Redheugh Bridge (near the current Redheugh Bridge) and look up high on the wall. You (hopefully) will see an odd-looking object of painted steel with a curving form and finlike projections. As always, Deacon doesn't depict a particular or decipherable form but creates a provocative image and titles it with a cliché expression that enhances its metaphoric potential.

Antony Gormley

Angel of the North, 1998
metro to Gateshead, then bus 725, 726 to Birtley
0191-232-5325 (bus info)

Located 3 mi south of downtown Gateshead alongside the A167 highway near its intersection with A1 at the Birtley rotary.

Fact-ridden documentation reveals that *Angel of the North* was designed by Antony Gormley (Turner Prize winner, 1994); engineered with the help of modern digital technology and time-honored industrial and shipbuilding techniques; fabricated by regional steelworkers and craftspeople; and transported to the site, assembled and installed by skilled crews operating monstrous pieces of equipment. The official statistics also relate that the figure weighs 100 tons and is 65 ft (20 m) tall with a wingspan of 175 ft (54 m). Its size is thus approximately the same as a jumbo jet. Beneath the ground, the concrete-pile foundation on which the sculpture rests is 65 ft (20 m) deep and reinforced by 52 bolts each 10 ft (3 m) long. Without question, the *Angel* is a colossal, mind-boggling work of art.

The sculpture serves as a kind of signpost at the southern entry into the Tyneside region. Strategically placed, high atop a grassy hilltop in an open stretch of barren landscape, it is prominently visible to people in cars heading north on the main A1 highway. (90,000 vehicles presumably pass by every day.) You can even see it as a passenger traveling on the London-Edinburgh train. In addition to being a landmark, the sculpture was envisioned as an promotional icon bolding asserting a new identity for the area. (Auspiciously, it stands on land previously used as a coal mine.) As might be expected, local residents were initially skeptical, if not sharply critical, of such an enormous and costly art project. Many, however, now view the *Angel* with pride as a symbol of the Gateshead-Newcastle regeneration. Undeniably, the city, region and nation recognized the sculpture's potential value as an international tourist attraction and extraordinary public monument. At one fell swoop it put Gateshead on the map.

All that said, nothing really prepares you for the experience of seeing the androgynous, humanoid, faceless, rib-structured, utterly symmetrical, poised, stock-still *Angel*. Looming large over people, who only come up to its ankles, and standing upright in full command of the landscape like a majestic presence, it's a very impressive sight. Actually, the figure is more provocative than overwhelming. It's called an angel, and yet its rusted-steel, welded form, heavy materiality and straight line, firmly grounded body hardly seem angelic—at least not according to conventional visions of weightless, fluttery blond cherubs in diaphanous white robes! True, the cruciform posture adds a spiritual aura, but more than this Gormley's sculpture conveys an enigmatic, mystical sense of time and place. Somewhat like the menhirs at Stonehenge or the abstract paintings of Mark Rothko, the *Angel of the North* eludes definition even as it sustains wonderment.

Juan Muñoz, *Conversation Piece*, 1999

South Shields

Juan Muñoz

Conversation Piece, 1999
riverside at Littlehaven,
off Harbor Dr
metro: South Shields

Located at a spectacular site looking over the harbor and beyond to the open sea, this sculpture and setting inevitably arouse thoughts about time and place, existence and survival. They evoke memories and dreams, hopes and fears.

The work is composed of 22 bronze figures, each approximately 5 ft (1.5 m) high. Though the figures bear a human likeness, they lack clear designations of gender, age and individuality. With their torsos wrapped in cloth and their wobbly lower bodies shaped like stuffed bean bags, they are virtually immobilized, frozen in a particular state. They can gesture and sway back and forth but can never walk away and move onward. Scattered across the pavement, each appears alone, abandoned, imprisoned in an indeterminate, inescapable condition despite the fact that some are grouped as if in conversation and all share common physical characteristics, as though they belong to the same family, sect or community.

The sculpture is called *Conversation Piece* but an uneasy silence prevails. It's not a momentary lapse, but a Beckett-like suspension of time, an eternal waiting in which the gaps in conversation are more meaningful than anything said or done.

Here, as in most all his work, Juan Muñoz, a celebrated sculptor from Madrid, focuses on the absurdity and impossibility of getting away from particular situations and places.

Consett

Local bus from Newcastle.

Tony Cragg

Terris Novalis, 1997
Hownsgill Park

Located a short distance from the town center. This work is part of the C2C cycle route and the Consett & Sunderland Sculpture Trail.

Tony Cragg, one of England's foremost artists, focuses attention on the urban landscape by creating sculptures assembled from or representing industrially produced, man-made objects. In Consett, his sculpture consists of gigantic enlargements of two pieces of surveying equipment: a theodolite and a surveyor's level. They are exactingly depicted in stainless steel except that they possess strange animal-like feet inspired by symbolic heraldry found on shields, coats of arms, plaques and similar items associated with the land and ownership. Indeed, the imagery and title make ironic reference to the site—a plot formerly occupied by steel manufacturing and now reverted to a natural setting. Considering the dramatic upheaval to the environment, perhaps only such colossal, monster-footed mapping tools as Cragg has developed would be suitable for measuring and mapping the new land.

Sunderland

An energetic public art program and the development of arts institutions are central aspects of the city's efforts to move beyond its industrial past and reinvent its identity. Train from Newcastle, 20 min.

Northern Gallery for Contemporary Art

Fawcett St, SR1 1RE
0191-514-1235 f: 514-8444

Housed in the City Library and Arts Centre, a 2-min walk from the railway station.

A good reason to visit this gallery, regardless of what's on exhibit, is the permanent installation of *Pent-Up*, a marvelous wall of images by the hot London artist Sam Taylor-Wood. The work sets the stage for lively, provocative interchanges and unexpected relationships between viewer and artwork or among viewers.

With its varied program comprising a wide range of media, including a substantial number of craft shows, the NGCA is a significant local presence. It hasn't yet moved into the stratum of high-profile, national art centers, though you can see risky artwork by emerging artists in some shows. Recent exhibitions: *Cinema of Machines (Steve Farrer), Contemporaneous—New Art from New York, Luminous, Northern Glory—What's the Story, Woven Image.*

Alison Wilding

Ambit, 1999
Panns Bank, River Wear

Located just below the Wearmouth Bridge, a short walk from the city center. Go down Fawcett St a few blocks (it becomes Bridge St); turn right onto West Wear St at the traffic circle; cross the street and take the footpath for a very short distance to Panns Bank.

Panns Bank is the site of the former Austin shipyard, where a huge pontoon was regularly submerged and refloated to raise large ships from the water for repair. With reference to this history, and the pontoon in particular, Alison Wilding has created a floating sculpture, over 65 1/2 ft (20 m) long, whose outline describes the shape of a ship.

Constructed from 22 tubular stainless-steel sections connected by sprung links, the work is over 65 1/2 ft (20 m) long. Analogous to the current regeneration and redefinition of the North's identity, the sculpture isn't fixed in an inflexible state but moved freely about, modulating its shape without abandoning its core structure. This is particularly true after dusk when Ambit is illuminated underwater. Enveloped in a halo of light, it loses its industrial character ands appears like a glowing crown.

The work marks the eastern gateway to the C2C Cycle Route and Art Trail. According to current plans, it will remain in its present location for an initial period of two years (until Sept. 2001).

National Glass Centre

Liberty Way, SR6 OGL
0191-515-5555 fx: 515-5556
www.glasscentre.org.uk
info@ngctr.demon.co.uk
daily, 10–5

Located on the northern banks of the River Wear. Cross the Wearmouth Bridge; turn right onto Dame Dorothy St; continue to Liberty Way, just past St. Peter's Campus, University of Sunderland; turn right and you'll see the center straight ahead.

Open since 1998, the National Glass Centre celebrates glass as a wondrous material used variously in heavy industry, art, crafts and numerous commercial products. Moreover, it promotes awareness of Sunderland's preeminence as a capital of glassmaking, extending back to its early role in the creation of stained glass.

Within its vast interior, the center houses glass factories, studios, workshops, temporary and permanent exhibition spaces, a glass/craft shop and restaurant. In addition to exhibitions of art objects created from glass, artists adept in the medium were commissioned to design work expressly for the building. Among the permanent art installations are a ceiling assemblage comprising suspended sheets of colored glass, glazed walls with decorative panels, stained-glass windows and, on the roof, a grandiose kiln-formed sculpture. Of course, the building itself is constructed of glass, and it features a unique glass roof that visitors are invited to walk across.

St. Peters Riverside Sculpture Project

Roker Seafront
from £1; £3

During the six-year period from 1991 to 1997, a team of artists headed by Colin Wilbourn transformed a stretch of riverside land from Wearmouth Bridge to the mouth of the River Wear. Working actively with the community, the team developed a series of artworks shaped by the place, culture and history. The creations include several sets of steel gates, an incredible ruin carved in red sandstone, a picnic setting in stone, stained-glass panels, a jetty, sandstone stairs that look like a carpet runner leading to the water's edge, a mural and a pile of large books sculpted of stone with inlaid glass (positioned near the university). The project (part of the C2C Cycle Route and Art Trail) has become a local tourist attraction.

Langlands & Bell

Sunderland Gateway, 2001
railroad viaduct, adjacent to Queen Alexandra Bridge

Sure to become one of the region's main attractions, this project is an exemplar of creative, innovative public art. More than an object, it's a landmark that redirects attention to the environment.

Sited high atop a disused viaduct at the western entrance to the city, *Sunderland Gateway* can be seen by

Langlands & Bell, Sunderland Gateway (model)

traffic on approach roads on either side of River Wear. The sculpture's form is quite simple: a row of four arches facing in two directions across the city. Arches have long functioned as symbolic gateways into cities. Even as they do so here, they also refer to the old viaduct, a road-and-rail bridge steeped in local history, and allude to the architecture of Penshaw Monument, a Greek temple overlooking Sunderland.

What turns the sculpture's simplicity on its edge is its medium—one-way observation glass. The glass functions as a semitransparent mirror with light and weather conditions determining which side is transparent and which is reflective at any given time. Changes continuously occur from dawn to dusk. At night, floodlights positioned below the sculpture gradually fade and dissolve, shifting visibility from one side to the other. Thus, *Gateway* is both a beacon of light and a dazzling signpost reflecting and framing actual, of-the-moment, live views of Sunderland.

Not only does the sculpture provide a vivid reminder of the city's industrial past, but it also makes impressive use of advanced structural glass technology. Indeed, it's a cutting-edge design, one of the first large-scale forms to be constructed entirely of glass without a steel support.

The British team of Ben Langlands and Nikki Bell have worked together since 1978. Their sculptures explore the relationships linking people, architecture and the city. This, one of their most ambitious public artworks, is due to be finished in 2001.

Middlesbrough

Train from Sunderland, 1 hr; from Newcastle, 1 hr.

Claes Oldenburg & Coosje van Bruggen

Bottle of Notes, 1993
The Boulevard, Central Gardens
Located in the civic center, outside the town hall and to the rear of the library.

As ever, an outdoor sculpture by Oldenburg and van Bruggen evokes a chuckle and adds a lively spark to an urban setting. Inspired by Captain Cook, a native of Middlesbrough, the artists decided to use the image of a message in a bottle (made famous by the legendary story of Edgar Allan Poe). However, they cleverly transformed the image from a bottle containing a note into a bottle that is itself shaped out of the note or, more precisely, the cutout letters of the words making up the note.

The sculpture is 35 ft (10.7 m) high and set upright on a tilt "as if stuck in sand by a receding wave." Constructed of steel, it has an outer image painted white and an inner image painted blue. If you try very hard you may be able to read the text forming the outside. It's a quote from Cook's journal: "we had every advantage we could desire in observing the whole of the passage of the planet Venus over the sun's disc."

Stockton-on-Tees

Train from Middlesbrough, 15 min; from Newcastle, 1 hr.

Richard Wilson

Over Easy, 1999
ARC, Dovecot St

For the first time, Wilson's fascination with architecture and perceived space became actualized in a real building in ARC. As in his 20:50 installation at the Saatchi Gallery (p. 44), he subtly perverts a simple spatial setting to disturb comprehension of what is seen and experienced.

When plans for ARC, a large performance space incorporating the former Dovecot Art Centre, were being developed, Wilson was brought in to collaborate with the architects. He envisioned a design that would focus on the live-performance nature of the building. To this end he created a rotating disk, 26 1/4 ft (8 m) in diameter, to be installed into the facade. The only catch: the rotations occur so slowly—at the approximate speed of the minute hand of a clock—that the movement is indiscernible. And yet every time you see the building the disk is in a different position. It's one thing to find such a work in an art gallery where you're condi-

tioned to look at leisure, but it's quite another thing to integrate movement into a building you hurriedly pass by. Indeed, most passersby probably have never realized that the facade is in continuous motion!

Darlington

Train from Stockton, 45 min; from Newcastle, 30 min.

David Mach

Train, 1997

Although currently located on the outskirts of town in a grassy field alongside highway A66 behind a big Morrison's supermarket, the area is rapidly being developed and will probably soon be a populated neighborhood.

You won't have any difficulty finding this work if you just ask anyone in Darlington. *Train* is well known to the local citizenry, if not because it's a beloved object than because it caused such heated debate due to its size and funding from public monies. (Morrison's also supported its creation and local people were hired as consultants and construction assistants.) Mach represented the image—a life-size (i.e., gigantic),150-foot-long train containing two-and-one-half cars—as emerging from and being an extension of a mound of earth. As the engine moves ahead, smoke billows from the chimney and envelopes the cars behind in puffy clouds. The entire sculpture is constructed of brick—approximately 350,000 bricks.

Mach chose the subject of a train to honor the region's heritage in the development of train engines and the field of engineering.

Anthony Holloway, *Spiral Growth*

Lake District

Andy Goldsworthy

Sheepfold Sculpture, 1996–2001
For a map indicating the location of the sculptures, contact Cumbria Public Art, Birbeck House, Duke St, Penrith, CA11 7NA, 01768-899014.

The Cumbrian farmland has long been dotted with sheepfolds. Constructed in circular form with stone walls about four feet high and narrow openings, they serve as pens for gathering and counting sheep. Goldsworthy, who has featured stone walls in many of his environmental sculptures, is building, rebuilding or restoring 100 sheepfolds across Cumbria to call attention to the culture and history of the region. He will also create a permanent (stone) or ephemeral (sticks, grass, bracken, leaves, ice, snow, water) sculptures inside the sheepfolds.

If you plan a trek to see these sheepfolds, be aware that many are off in fields, not easily seen from the roads.

Grizedale Forest Park

Grizedale Sculpture Project

Grizedale Forest Park, Ambleside, LA22 0QJ
0122-986-0291 f: 986-0050
www.artcumbria.org
grizedaleart@hotmail.com
daily, year round

London (Euston) to Windermere or Ulverston (nearest stations), 3 1/2 hr. During the summer, buses run from Ambleside and Ulverston to Grizedale, 30 min. If you're traveling by car from the east, you must cross Lake Windermere by ferry (£2). To avoid the long waiting lines for the ferry in high season, go around the upper lake and enter the forest from Hawkshead, 2.5 mi to the visitor center. Parking fee: up to 3 hr, £1; over 3 hr, £2.

Although overrun with tourists on weekends and in the summer, it's not too difficult to beat the crowds and enjoy a peaceful outing. The land-scape is particularly incredible in the autumn when the forest is a panoply of blazing colors and sheep are graz-ing in green pastures.

Grizedale Sculpture Project was initi-ated by the park's director in 1977 as a forestry program. It is not a sculpture park. That's to say, all the art derives directly from and relates specifically to forest life and the Grizedale setting. All sculptures are created on site and must use materials from the environment (mostly wood or stone). Rather than approach nature as a backdrop for art objects, here sculptures are considered as part of the forest. As such, they wear out, decay and are destroyed over time. This is in sharp contrast to works displayed in sculpture parks or museums that are treated as precious commodities that must be maintained and conserved.

Artists are selected from an applica-tion process and then come to Grizedale for a two-to-three month res-idency. At least six new works are added annually. Over 200 works have been created since the project began, and you're likely to see about 80 works in any given year. They're all located on either the Ridding Wood (.5 mi) or Silurian Way (9.5 mi) trails, except for the few that have recently been placed on the new International Sculpture Trail. Since there are no labels near the works, if you want to identify and find them be sure to get a guide map at the visitor center. Be prepared for some seri-ous walking!

Grizedale is hardly a showcase for great sculpture or cutting-edge contem-porary art. You'll find a diverse mix whose surfeit of mediocre and mun-dane work includes many carved wood objects depicting animals and plants. Scattered within are some adventurous projects by unfamiliar names as well as sculptures by Andy Goldsworthy, David Mach and a few others long associated with environmental art. Overall, it seems the rule of thumb for selecting artists has little to do with ground-breaking creativity. It even falls below the status-quo standard of accessibility to the very safe, humdrum level of pop-ulist pleasure. It fact, this approach to contemporary art encourages compla-cency rather than pleasure.

Kendal

A prosperous town with quaint shops and pedestrian streets. Train from London (Euston), 3 hr.

Abbot Hall Art Gallery

Kirkland, LA9 5AL
01539-722464 f: 722492
info@abbothall.org.uk
Mar–Oct: daily, 10:30–5.
Nov–Feb: daily, 10:30–4
admission: £2.80/2.50

Located behind the Museum of Lakeland Life and Industry.

This is the last place you'd expect to find contemporary art. The building is a stately Georgian house set next to the parish church on a village green border-ing the river. The house is kept as a peri-od piece displaying a collection of tradi-tional British art, mainly portrait paint-ings. Special exhibitions are typical of provincial museums except that the pro-gram includes occasional shows of pre-sent-day artists like Frank Auerbach, Tony Bevan, Lucian Freud, Callum Innes, Bridget Riley, Richard Wentworth and Alison Wilding.

Lancashire

Manchester

From being a success story of the Industrial Revolution, with its cotton factories sustaining economic prosperity in the region, Manchester, England's second largest city, is only recently reasserting its prowess. Its 19th-century heritage is evident in the wealth of Victorian architecture but redevelopment efforts are matching this with a rash of modern buildings. Ambitious urban renewal plans were in fact redoubled after a 1996 IRA bombing wiped out the center city. It's a bustling, sprawling place where sports are the major preoccupation. Contemporary art hasn't played a big role here, and the situation probably won't change when the new exhibition spaces at the Manchester City Art Gallery and Lowry Centre are up and running. If you are in the area and have a vanguard art craving, hop a train and go to Liverpool, 45 minutes away. But don't go without seeing the spectacular bridge by Calatrava! Train from London (King's Cross, Euston), 3 1/4 hr; from Leeds, 1 hr.

Manchester City Art Gallery

Mosley St, M2 3JL
0161-236-5244
www.u-net.com/set/mcag/cag
Mon, 11–5:30; Tues–Sat, 10–5:30;
Sun, 2–5:30
admission: free
metrolink: St. Peter's Square

Closed for refurbishing and expansion until 2001 (architect: Michael HOPKINS). When reopened, a new extension containing collection and major temporary exhibition galleries will connect the two existing museum buildings.

Manchester will then be able to display more of its celebrated Pre-Raphaelite paintings and become a venue for important traveling shows.

The museum owns some 20th-century art, but its dominant resource by far is 19th-century British art. Dante Gabriel Rossetti's *Astarte Syriaca*, a portrait modeled on Jane Morris, John Everett Millais's *Autumn Leaves* and Ford Maddox Brown's *Work* are but a few of the many classics in the collection. These paintings may not be contemporary in terms of their dates, but the women are as fresh and stylish as those in many current fashion and cosmetic advertisements.

Piccadilly Gardens

architect: Tadao ANDO, 1999–
metrolink: Piccadilly

Tadao Ando, one of the outstanding contemporary architects, will be creating his first building in Britain as part of the redevelopment of Piccadilly Gardens. Located in the midst of the city center, the only large green space in the area, the gardens are currently a shabby, unappealing environment. Ando's design for a low pavilion with a curving wall—typical of his minimalist aesthetic—and complementary landscaping will spearhead a long overdue transformation of the setting.

Trinity Pedestrian Bridge

architect: Santiago CALATRAVA, 1993–95
River Irwell

Located off St. Mary's Parsonage near Bridge St; connects Manchester with Salford.

Simply and yet elegantly, the curving path of this dazzling bridge skims above the water. It's held aloft by streams of cables attached to a single, sloping, very tall mast. Though Santiago Calatrava is a revered master of bridge design, this is his first commission in the water-oriented lands of Britain. If you're not familiar with his work, don't miss the chance to get acquainted here.

Cornerhouse

70 Oxford St, M1 5NH
0161-228-7621 f: 236-7323
www.channel.org.uk/cornerhouse
exhibitions@cornerhouse.org
gallery: Tues–Sat, 11–6; Sun, 2–6;
closed Mon
admission: free
metrolink: St. Peter's Square

Located on the corner of Whitworth St West adjacent to the Oxford Road train station.

Cornerhouse is a multifunctional place comprising a gallery with three exhibition spaces; a film center with three theaters; two bookshops specializing in magazines, cards and books related to the visual arts; and a café-restaurant, bar and cappuccino bar. The ambience is low-key, typical of an artsy hangout with a university flavor.

The cinema program includes first-run, classic and foreign language films presented in thematic series or retrospectives. Festivals and special events, often featuring a director, producer or critic, enhance regular screenings, which occur three or four times daily. The span of titles is broad and goes beyond what you'd find in the local video store.

In contrast, the gallery program is rather narrowly skewed to an offbeat sector of the British art world with some fringe American art thrown in. Recent exhibitions: *Derek Boshier, Common Culture, Drive-By—Five Artists from Los Angeles, Johan Gimonprez, Peter Greenaway—Artworks (1963-98), Perry Hoberman.*

Whitworth Art Gallery

University of Manchester, Oxford Rd, M15 6ER
0161-275-7450 f: 275-7451
www.whitworth.man.ac.uk
whitworth@man.ac.uk
Mon–Sat, 10–5; Sun, 2–5
admission: free

Located 1.5 mi (2.5 km) from the city center; accessible by bus.

Housed in a stately red-brick Victorian building with a '60s-style addition in back, the Whitworth has an expanse of galleries. Displays from the permanent collection—an extensive selection of British prints, drawings and watercolors, textiles and wallpaper—occupy a large proportion of the museum. Since the collection goes up to the present, you'll see works on paper by Sean Scully, Lucian Freud, Paula Rego or other contemporary artists. The work tends toward pure abstraction or figurative imagery with little attention paid to the more conceptual, anti-aesthetic or subversive currents of the YBA and younger generations. This kind of art does appear occasionally in special exhibitions, like the 1998 show of Chris Ofili's eclectic paintings with their famous balls of elephant dung.

Hulme Arch

architect: Chris WILKINSON, 1995–97
Stretford Rd

As part of a project aimed at regenerating a failed social housing development in the Hulme neighborhood, a new roadway was built to provide a direct link into the city center, less than 1 mi away. Wilkinson, an architect with expertise in designing ingenious bridges, created an overpass roadway with a sculptural form recalling the Russian constructivist work of Gabo and Pevsner. It features a diagonally positioned high parabolic arch with oppos-

Michael Wilford, Lowry Centre

ing sets of cables supporting the deck. In addition to being a notable bridge design, the arch also serves as a gateway image for cars entering the city.

Salford

Within the Greater Manchester area, Salford was the toughest neighborhood—a gritty industrial zone. The barons of capitalism became rich from the Salford Quays, which were part of the booming port activity along the River Irwell, but the workers lived in boxy row houses covered with soot and enveloped by smoke from trains passing on tracks nearby. Not unlike the situation in London, the Manchester-Salford docklands went into decline in the 1970s and completely closed to shipping in 1982. A prime target for gentrification, they are gradually, but radically, being transformed. A three-mile stretch of Salford's waterfront has already been converted to leisure, business and residential use.

Lowry Centre

architect: Michael WILFORD, 2000
Salford Quays, Pier 8
metrolink: Salford Quays

It's taken years to get this building off the drawing boards, but it was worth the wait. (The center officially opens in the spring of 2000.) Set at the end of a pier and facing a new public plaza, the Lowry Centre is part of Salford's waterfront regeneration project. It's also one of the 11 landmark Millennium projects receiving major funding and special attention. With its 1,650-seat theater for world-class performances (dance, drama, music), 450-seat theater for community activities, a gallery displaying work by Lowry (a local artist for whom the center is named), another gallery for notable touring exhibitions, a children's gallery, study center, bar, café and restaurant—the center aims to enhance the area further by becoming a cultural mecca for the region.

Wilford's design is an eccentric but smart composite of geometric shapes with curving and straight edges, solid and transparent sides, tilted and upright orientations. The roughly triangular layout of the whole follows the shape of the plot with glass-enclosed sections overlooking the river. A stunning circular structure, housing the smaller theater, sits at the dominant apex. Though possessing the aura of monumentality that is traditional in public buildings, the Lowry also has an informal character, typical of contemporary places of culture and entertainment.

A generous, convenient foyer extends across the full width of the plaza frontage. Behind this, forming the central spine of the building, are the two theaters arranged back to back. Flanking them on either side are the art galleries, themselves bordered by a ramped promenade that continues around the building linking all activities. The Lowry Study Centre is located in its own domain within the tower.

Ironically, this chic community center is associated with the art of Lawrence Stephen Lowry (1887–1976), whose paintings depicted a sense of isolation and the dreary, depressing environment of the former industrial landscape in Salford and the surrounding area.

Irwell Sculpture Trail

Salford Quays–Bacup
016-1253-5111
016-1253-5915
www.bury.gov.uk/culture/irwell

Begun in 1997 with the ambitious plan of creating 50 projects over a five-year period, the Irwell Sculpture Trail is another initiative merging the popular British custom of walking in the countryside with contemporary art. The trail follows an established 30-mile footpath stretching from Salford Quays through Bury and up to the River Irwell's Pennine source north of Bacup. Should you not want to walk the entire distance, you can go partway and take the metrolink back, or even just take the metrolink to a station near one of the sculpture clusters. (Bury, for example is only 25 min from Manchester.) The trail is conveniently developed in sections.

The project involves 33 artist-in-residency awards; 8 international commissions; 6 community sculpture projects; and 3 graduate design competitions.

The following works are of particular note: Ulrich RUCKRIEM, Untitled, 1998

Ulrich Rückriem, Untitled, 1998

(Outwood Colliery, Ringley Road, Radcliffe). On the site of an old coal mine, Ruckriem has created a multipartite sculpture using his signature minimalist imagery and raw cut stones. A block appears at each of the two main entrances, and seven tall blocks form an evocative grouping at a spot where there was once a railroad line.

Edward ALLINGTON, *Tilted Vase*, 1998 (Market Place, Ramsbottom). Taking an impudent approach to form and imagery has always been Allington's strength. This is visible here in an nonsensical steel object that looks like an industrial mechanism or newfangled sound device, but is identified by the artist as a vase.

Liverpool

Like Manchester, Liverpool has acquired the reputation of being a bleak city. For decades it's been trying to emerge from the decline of a once-thriving shipping industry. Visually, much of the city has a pretty mundane appearance, and World War II destruction, urban decay and economic distress are quite apparent except in pockets undergoing regeneration. Nevertheless, you also feel the liveliness of a large student population and buoyant arts community. In fact, it's a pretty energetic, quirky place with a pulse all its own.

One successful revitalization project encompasses the waterfront area, where the grimy port and ugly warehouses of yesteryear are now upscale office buildings, museums, shops, restaurants and esplanades. A second is the Rope Walks Quarter, the downtown area between Bold and Duke Streets, where rejuvenation suddenly boomed in the late 1990s. Seemingly overnight, derelict factories and what were once fashionable residences and exclusive shops began to be transformed into design studios, galleries, bars, clubs, restaurants and artists' lofts.

It was a brilliant move for the Tate to locate its first outpost in Liverpool on the Albert Dock. Capitalizing on and complementing the thriving music, theater, performance scene in the city (only a part of which feeds off the Beatles legacy, a tourist industry unto itself), it has added a high-profile visual arts dynamic. The Tate's name alone would have been enough to elevate the city's cultural image, but to its credit the museum never treated the Tate in Liverpool as a second-string player. Indeed, the Tate Liverpool enjoys world-class status of its own based on its autonomous, continuous program of incredible contemporary art exhibitions.

Creating a Tate Gallery in Liverpool is a sign that Britain may really be serious about decentralizing its art resources and activities. Further evidence suggests that both within and beyond the decentralization scheme, Liverpool is becoming a major contemporary art city. It hosted the international *Video Positive* festival in 1997; it was the first British city to organize the ISEA (International Symposium of Electronic Arts) in 1998; it entered the prestigious sphere of cities presenting international biennials of contemporary art in 1999; and a vanguard new-media center (FACT—Foundation for Art and Creative Technology) will open its doors in Liverpool at the beginning of the 21st century.

All the art sites are located in the downtown area within easy walking distance from one another and from the Lime Street train station. Train from London (Euston), 2 3/4 hr; from Manchester, 45 min; from Leeds, 2 hr.

Liverpool Biennial of Contemporary Art

0151-709-7444 f: 709-7377
liverpool@biennial.u-net.com

With this event, held for the first time in the fall of 1999, the UK joined other countries in hosting a mega-exhibition of the latest worldwide happenings and talents in the visual arts. Liverpool's version comprises four parts. The big attraction is an international exhibit organized by a different curator each time. Anthony Bond (head curator of Art Gallery, New South Wales, Australia) held the position for the inaugural show, which he titled *Trace*. It included work referring to "journeys of discovery or use of materials that allow us to recall an object or event" by 50 artists from 24 countries.

Adding a strong national element, the biennial incorporates two other events. *John Moores*, a juried show focusing exclusively on painting, had long been held every two years at the Walker Art Gallery in Liverpool. It brings to the new biennial project a good track record for spotting rising stars. *New Contemporaries*, an annual exhibition of art in any media by students and recent grads from fine art colleges in the UK, likewise has an impressive history of selecting future kingpins like Damien Hirst, Chris Ofili, Gillian Wearing, Rachel Whiteread.

The fourth part of the biennial features initiatives by local, national and international artists. These enterprises vary from the unconventional to the more formalized small exhibit (e.g., *artlovers*, 1999, a show presenting work by 20 artist-couples from various countries).

A panoply of events, performances, films, activities, talks and an international conference supports the exhibitions. Indeed, all the arts organizations and artist communities in Liverpool participate in the biennial in one form or another. The exhibitions themselves are spread throughout the city in museums, galleries, churches, theaters, libraries, stores, office buildings, parking garages and on street corners.

Tate Gallery Liverpool

renovation: James STIRLING and Michael WILFORD, 1988, 1998
Albert Dock, L3 4BB
0151-709-3223 f: 709-3122
www.tate.org.uk
liverpoolinfo@tate.org.uk
Tues–Sun, 10–6; closed Mon
admission: free, special exhibitions—£3/2 or £5/2.50
metro—James Street; bus—222;
Smartbus—1, 4

Though only minutes away from the hodge-podgy swarm of stores and advertising signage in the center city, Albert Dock is another world. Nothing fancy, just uncluttered, monolithic brick warehouses surrounding a "plaza of water." Only the odd peach color of the heavy columns in the continuous arcade connecting the buildings on the ground level disrupts the otherwise austere setting. Lying behind this facade in the northwest corner of the "plaza" is an animated facade with bright blue panels trimmed in orange. As announced in bold sculptural lettering, this is the Tate Gallery. (In fact, Albert Dock is a major attraction and virtually all the shops lining the arcade relate to the tourist trade. Without strict codes, the appearance of the facades would undoubtably be different.)

The Tate renovated the warehouse in two phases. Though budget constraints necessitated this schedule, the museum took advantage of the situation by totally reassessing the first phase before proceeding with the second. Their evaluation actively engaged staff, artists and audience. What's more, the museum actually listened to comments and

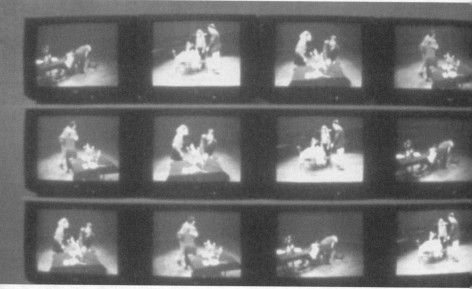

Bruce Nauman, *Violent Incident*, 1986

acted accordingly in making changes and revising plans for the second phase. The result may not be perfect but you're unlikely to find a more audience-friendly museum, where you feel that the museum has put the visitor's experience first. *You*, the interested viewer, are given priority consideration. You won't necessarily be aware of the ways this has been implemented, but your senses and intellect will probably be galvanized. Moreover, you won't feel alienated and frustrated. Check it out.

Amid the public amenities and orientation aspects of the lobby are two semicircular stone benches handsomely layered with three tonal bands. These minimalist objects of sculpture-furniture, as well as a third bench located outside, were specially designed for the entry area by Scott BURTON. They harmonize with the reductive aesthetic of the architecture even as their emphatically curving shapes contrast with the strong horizontal and vertical lines of the setting.

The exhibition program at the Tate Liverpool has thus far followed a general plan wherein the 1st floor presents modern British art from the Tate collection either in a general or subject matter (e.g., portraits, landscapes) display. The 2nd floor also shows art from the collection, but here yearlong exhibitions highlight a particularized theme or stylistic grouping. For example, *Urban* (1998–99) revealed the diversity of ways in which city life was an inspiration to artists in the 20th century. Using works by Giacomo Balla, Piet Mondrian, Jean Dubuffet, Claes Oldenburg, Ad Reinhardt, Frank Auerbach, Eduardo Paolozzi, Leon Kossof, Jeff Koons, Andreas Gursky, Tony Oursler and others, the exhibit presented art gems even as it raised awareness about historical, cultural and artistic changes over time. Other recent projects in this vein include *The Spirit of Cubism* (1998–99) and *Violent Incident* (1999–2000)—an imaginative cross section of post-1950s art in which violence was part of the creative process or depicted as the subject matter. Other collection exhibitions: *American Abstraction, Peter Blake—*

About Collage, Shirazeh Houshiary & Anish Kapoor, Modern British Art, The Other Side of Zero—Video Positive 2000.

Organizing the collection into thematic displays and regularly changing the entire installation of the collection put the Tate Liverpool in a class all its own. Typically, collection galleries in a museum are encyclopedically oriented and chronologically arranged. They also remain fairly constant over a long period of time. Since the Tate collection is spread over several museums in different parts of the country, a more focused approach makes a lot of sense and has worked well. Liverpool has benefited greatly from the arrangement since there has been so little space at the Tate in London for displaying collection treasures. It remains to be seen what will happen after 2000 when the Tate Modern (London) opens and can, for the first time, present a major showing of the collection, especially contemporary work. The collection is large enough to handle the expansion, and plans suggest that Liverpool won't become a distant satellite or subsidiary venue for watered-down exhibits from the capital. Indeed, the Tate's conceptualization of itself as a nonhierarchical whole comprising distinctive parts with independent curatorial expertise is unique.

The top floor, which has galleries with skylights and high ceilings, is where you'll find non-collection exhibitions. These are retrospectives of modern masters (*Salvador Dalí, Joan Miró*) or midcareer artists (*Tony Cragg, Richard Deacon, Paula Rego*); first museum shows for high-profile artists from a younger generation (*Willie Doherty, Mark Wallinger, Rachel Whiteread*), and group exhibits of current art (*Contemporary German and American Art from the Froehlich Collection, Heaven, Presence—Figurative Art at the End of the Century, Trace—Liverpool Biennial*).

In addition to catalogues, exhibitions are enhanced by brochures (50p); wall labels with short contextual statements and quotes; an information room with timelines and source materials; a video room; and a studio room where kids can try their hand at artmaking. You'll probably see groups of one sort or another among the visitors since the museum has a very active outreach program and advisory network involving schools, youth groups, seniors, the disabled and others.

The museum also has a residency program (MOMART Fellowship) aimed at giving young artists time to develop new ideas and directions. With access to museum staff and firsthand contact with the workings of the museum, the artists also gain invaluable career-building knowledge. During their six-month stint in Liverpool, artists receive a stipend and studio. Though they are not expected to produce work, many schedule open studio events and arrange to exhibit their art in the city.

The bookshop on the ground floor to the right of the entrance sells cards, posters, gift items and art books. The selection of books is not unique or extensive. At the opposite end of the lobby, you'll find a café-bar. The design is industrial-chic with steel as the material of choice. Try to get a seat in the boat-shaped mezzanine so you'll have a great view of the setting, inside and out.

Tony Cragg

Raleigh, 1986
Riverside Walk, Albert Dock

Walk around to the back of the Tate and you'll find a small, "leftover" parcel of land at the corner. Using granite architectural parts and cast-iron ship horns, Tony Cragg, the British sculptor famous for creating sculptures from found fragments of man-made objects, produced *Raleigh* for this space. The elements lie in a heap on the ground, reminders of a bygone era and of society's practice of throwing away products of its own making. In the context of this particular setting—a regenerated area that respected the old buildings—the sculpture also manifests recycling as integral to the process of art-making.

Bluecoat

School Lane, L1 3BX
0151-709-5297 f: 707-0048
gallery: 0151-709-5689
bluecoat@dircon.co.uk
gallery: Tues–Sat, 10:30–5;
closed Mon
admission: free
metro: Central Station

Located one block below Church St, behind Littlewoods department store.

Behind the wide pedestrianized road-ways of the downtown shopping area is a maze of narrow streets. One of these, School Lane, is where you'll find the arts complex called Bluecoat. (In its first incarnation as a charity school, students wore blue coats, hence the name.) Despite the proper veneer of the archi-tecture—a historic Queen Anne brick building (1717)—it's a lively place day and night. If nothing else, stop by to get information, meet the locals and try to find out what's going on about town. (There's no city arts guide listing all the current shows and events.)

On the one hand, Bluecoat functions as an art center promoting a wide range of activities. These include dance, music, theater and live art perfor-mances, poetry readings, exhibitions, festivals, fairs and lectures. On the other, it houses a large number of cul-tural organizations, workshops, artists' studios, a craft center, café-bar, garden, art supply shop, rehearsal, meeting and reception rooms.

Bluecoat Gallery sprawls out in four rooms to the left of the main entrance. Exhibitions favor contemporary art and span the gamut of media and image ori-entations. Recent exhibitions: *Conrad Atkinson, Pete Frame, Furniture by Contemporary Artists, Glitter Plus, Trace—Liverpool Biennial, Tom Wood.*

Open Eye

28–32 Wood St, L1 4AQ
0151-709-9460 f: 709-3059
www.openeye.org.uk
info@openeye.u-net.com
Tues–Fri, 10:30–5:30; Sat, 1:30–5;
closed Mon
admission: free
metro: Central Station

Housed in its stylishly refurbished space since November 1996, the Open Eye Photographic and Media Arts Gallery was one of the pioneering art ventures in the now hip, regenerated Rope Walks Quarter. Though previously a communi-ty-based organization, it shifted gears once it was in its new space. Quite rapidly, Open Eye established a regional and national reputation as a premier center of contemporary photography. Its exhibitions tend to present artists who take a documentary or photojour-nalist approach, embracing a sociologi-cal orientation toward subject matter. You probably won't see gigantic Cibachrome prints of manipulated fig-ures or orchestrated scenes, but you will see riveting, exceptionally composed depictions of real-world people and sit-uations by photographers from Brazil, Chile, Hungary, Russia, Spain, the UK and the US. The gallery does occasion-ally show photo installations and mixed-media projects. Exhibition brochures provide the most incisive, lucid and helpful commentaries you're likely ever to find on photography in general and certain artists in particular.

Should you be in town on a Thursday, see if one of the popular video screenings is scheduled (7 pm, free admission). These usually highlight the work of a single artist on the order of Marina Abramovic, Vito Acconci, Nam June Paik, Bill Viola, William

Wegman, Ann Whitehurst, and other innovative figures in the field. Open Eye also organizes artist talks, live events and off-site projects (outdoor video projections, street posters).

Recent exhibitions: *Tony Catano, Steve Hale, Highflyers—Clubravepartyart, Paul Kenny, Paula Latham, Markéta Luskacová, David Mabb, Mari Mahr, Simon Norfolk, Martin Parr, Daniel Reeves, Sebastiao Salgado, Allan Sekula, Star dot Star* (sculpture, video, communications technology, robotics).

FACT Center

92 Wood St, L1 4DQ
0151-709 2663 f: 707 2150
www.fact.co.uk
fact@fact.co.uk
metro: Central Station

The relocation of FACT (Foundation for Arts and Creative Technology) from Bluecoat to a regenerated former tea factory was publicly announced in 1999. FACT—a powerhouse organization involved with new media—will finally have its own space in which to present the first-rate productions, installations, exhibitions and festivals it previously organized for other venues. The new arts and media center (scheduled to open in 2002) will include two galleries, a project and events space, creative design studio, media lab, media lounge, digital facilities, work units, artist-residency apartment, café-bar and a three-screen art-house cinema. With this addition to its roster of art sites, Liverpool becomes even more of a where-it's-happening city within the international art circuit.

Taro Chiezo

Super Lamb Banana, 1998
This giant, brightly colored, playfully bizarre, hybrid-image sculpture created for the *artranspennine* exhibition (1998) was so popular with Liverpudlians when

Tara Chiezo, *Super Lamb Banana*, 1998

it first appeared near Albert Dock, that the Liverpool Architecture and Design Trust purchased it for permanent display. Its location has changed several times and its eventual home is still not certain. As of 1999 it was installed on the Strand. If it's not there when you visit, you should have no trouble getting information about its current location. Beyond the sheer absurdity of the image, Chiezo puts it forth as a possible example of futuristic biotech cloning.

Walker Art Gallery

William Brown St, L3
0151-207-0001
Mon–Sat, 10–5; Sun, 12–5
admission: £3/1.50
metro: Lime Street Station

Located on a hilltop next to the City Museum and Central Library. All three are classic stone buildings.

This museum has one of Britain's major collections of European art from 1300 to the present with strong holdings of Victorian, Pre-Raphaelite and 20th-century British art. Vanguard work from the modern and contemporary eras is barely represented. The one event that brings art by young Brits into the museum is the John Moores biennial. This open, juried exhibition, now incorporated into the Liverpool Biennial, celebrated its 21st birthday in 1999. Since the exhibition only includes painting and since innovative artists now use so many other materials, often not favoring painting, the exhibition doesn't offer a just impression of contemporary art. Past prize-winners have included David Hockney, Richard Hamilton, Peter Doig, Bruce McLean, Lisa Milroy and Tim Head.

Birmingham

Reconstruction after World War II involved the tearing down of a lot of Victorian architecture and implanting highways around and through central Birmingham. The results were a disaster—so much so that the city decided to try again. Virtually the entire center city underwent redevelopment during the 1990s. This time people, not cars, were given primary consideration. Now pedestrian plazas, walkways, fountains, canals and public sculptures humanize the downtown. The area also integrates civic, cultural and office buildings with housing, sports arenas, stores and hotels. The concept of mixed-use planning is rigorously observed, even to the extent of conjoining the convention center with the symphony hall under one roof in a giant new mall-like structure.

Having acted hastily in its previous renewal efforts, the city now proceeded extra-cautiously. This not only meant conserving old architecture but being conservative with regard to new designs. Recently constructed buildings as well as public artworks might best be described as stylish and inoffensive. Nothing is boldly innovative. Especially in terms of the outdoor sculpture, a provincial character prevails. Train from London (Euston), 1 1/2 hr; from Liverpool, 1 3/4 hr; from Leeds, 2 1/4 hr.

Ikon Gallery

renovation: LEVITT BERNSTEIN, 1998
1 Oozells Sq, Brindleyplace, B1 2HS
0121-248-0708 f: 248-0709
www.ikon-gallery.co.uk
art@ikon-gallery.co.uk
Tues–Fri, 11–7; Sat–Sun, 11–5;
closed Mon
admission: free

Brindleyplace borders the canal on the west side of the International Convention Centre, and Oozells Sq is off Broad St.

Ikon Gallery is one of a handfull of exhibition spaces in England with a truly international program. You can regularly see work here by young and midcareer artists who are being shown for the first time in the UK despite their international renown.

The gallery's move to Brindleyplace in 1998 situated it in the newly redeveloped center city together with Birmingham's leading cultural institutions. It is now housed in a nicely renovated old brick school replete with a historic tower and new glass elevator shaft. Especially on the top floor where rooms are intimately sized, the original architecture limits the scale of art that can be shown. In its favor, however, it offers (and actually encourages) a more concentrated viewing of individual objects. Because the 1st floor provides larger and interconnected open galleries, the building actually accommodates a wide range of work. Tall arched windows, exposed vaulting and other old details also establish a welcome change from the white-cube ambience of so many contemporary art spaces. There's a delightful café near the front entrance, and a bookshop—which stocks mainly monographs as well as cards, posters and gift items—is situated behind the reception desk.

Either two exhibitions take place simultaneously or one theme show occupies the entire space. Even if you don't like the art, the exhibitions are engaging because the objects are chosen and installed to highlight intriguing differences, similarities, progressions and contextual associations. Rather than object labels, Ikon has free leaflets and inexpensive (£1) brochures for each exhibition. In addition, a resource room on the top floor contains catalogues, books, videos and computers with materials relevant to the artists and art on display.

Recent exhibitions: *Babel—Contemporary Art & the Journeys of Communication, Gordon Bennett, Adam Chodzko, Claustrophobia, CSI—Contemporary Artists Investigate the Paranormal, Ellen Gallagher, Susan Hiller—Brian Catling—Wendy McMurdo, Callum Innes, Now—2000, Keith Piper, Martha Rosler, Secret Victorians, Yinka Shonibare, Sorted, Nancy Spero.*

Yinka Shonibare, *Affectionate Men*, 1999

Café Costa

architects: CZWG
Brindleyplace

When you leave the Ikon Gallery turn right and go to the end of Oozells St. You'll come to a modest public plaza, one of the nicest settings in the redevelopment zone. Walkways cross grass lawns and one path even cuts through the middle of a shallow pool with gentle cascades of water. Two black sculptural elements appearing like fragments of a colonnade, albeit minimalist in design with quirky irregularities, appear atop pathway entrances, and in the center sits a small but striking café. Its pointed-oval shape, glass-paneled walls and most especially its split-winged glass roof immediately catch your attention though the architecture is hardly bombastic. As in the award-winning lavatory–flower shop CZWG built in London (see p. 52), an innovative twist on the Art Nouveau–style glass canopy adds pizzazz to a relatively simple design.

Ron Haselden

Aviary, 1988–91
International Convention Centre

When the new Convention Centre–Symphony Hall complex was constructed, 1%-for-art funding was implemented. This served as the catalyst for additional funding which then supported numerous commissions within the building and outside in the grandiose new plaza, Centenary Square.

The multicolored neon sculpture at the main entrance of the center is by Ron Haselden. Using the blue steel framework of the canopy as a backdrop, he created a central cluster of knotted forms and a spread of linear shapes and flickering lights to suggest a tree and birds in flight. A computer governs the rhythms of color and movement. Though the work is a jazzy image at night, during the day when the complexity of the neon tubes is visible, it is far less effective.

Tess Jaray

Paving for Centenary Square, 1991

With orange, ocher, red and brown bricks as her medium, Tess Jaray developed a paving scheme for the whole plaza. Footstep-size patterns combine with large geometric shapes to both reduce and emphasize the scale of the area. Jaray also designed the lampposts, railings, benches, litter bins, tree grilles and boundary posts in the plaza.

Tom Lomax

Spirit of Enterprise, 1991
Centenary Sq

Located in the trefoil seating area overlooking the grass section of the plaza.

Three large disks leaning against one another and fronted by an expressive head are the focus of this bronze fountain sculpture. As was common in traditional public art, the figures are allegorical. Here they symbolize civic realms highly valued in Birmingham: Commerce, Industry, Enterprise.

David Patten

Monument to John Baskerville— Industry and Genius, 1990
Centenary Sq

Located in front of the large neoclassical building, Baskerville House, at the east end of the plaza.

A pair of stone blocks framing an alignment of six upright forms cut and shaped at the top like typepunches used in printing make up the structure of David Patten's sculpture. The meaning is not evident unless you go up close, read the inscription and see the letters "Virgil" embossed in reverse on the tops of the main stones. As noted, Baskerville was a Birmingham typographer, and Virgil's *Aeneid* was the first book to be printed in his celebrated typeface (1757).

Antony Gormley

Untitled (*Iron Man*), 1991–93
Victoria Sq

Centenary Square leads into a pedestrian overpass, Paradise Bridge, which in turn proceeds down to a monumental fountain in Victoria Sq. Gormley's figure is off to the right near the Trustee Savings Bank and Main Post Office facing New St.

Using his signature faceless, unidentifiably male-female image as a point of departure, Gormley created a 20 ft (6 m) high, cast-iron body-case (popularly called *Iron Man*) for Birmingham. Divided into four sections with heavy seams connecting the parts with wire-like lacing suggestively pulling the case taut across the body, the utterly constrained, totally covered-up figure is an ironic allusion to Victorian pomp and professed values. Buried in the ground up to its calves and leaning backward and to the left, *Iron Man* is also enigmatically rising and falling—a very appropriate dualism for a redeveloping city with a strong industrial past.

Antony Gormley, Untitled (*Iron Man*), 1991–93

Birmingham Art Gallery

🏛 Chamberlain Sq
0121-303-2834
Mon–Thurs, Sat, 10–5; Fri,
10:30–5; Sun, 12:30–5
admission: free, special exhibitions—£5/3.50 (variable)

The Birmingham Art Gallery does not specialize in modern and contemporary art but has a limited, conservative, exclusively British collection of representative examples. A typical display in the 20th-century room (#20) includes figurative paintings or pure abstraction by Gillian Ayres, Francis Bacon, John Dellamy, Paul Caulfield, Ewen Henderson, Barbara Hepworth, Howard Hodgkin, Shanti James, Ana Pacheco, Shanti Panchal, Bridget Riley, Francis Souza, John Walker. The display offers a good opportunity to see a survey of British art by a different cross section of artists than you're likely to see elsewhere.

If you're a Pre-Raphaelite fan, the Birmingham Art Gallery has a rich collection of their paintings and drawings. Edward Burne-Jones, a native son, is particularly well represented.

Walsall

Northwest of Birmingham, 20 min. by train.

New Art Gallery Walsall

🏛 architects: CARUSO ST. JOHN, 2000
139–143 Lichfield St, WS1 ISE
0192-265-3116 f: 265-3175
www.newartgallerywalsall.org.uk
newartgallerywalsall@walsall.gov.uk
Tues–Sat, 10–5; Sun 2–5

Walsall has constructed the New Art Gallery as a showpiece and cultural center for the community. Its main attraction—and the impetus for its creation—is the Garman Ryan collection, formed by Kathleen Garman, wife of the English sculptor Jacob Epstein, and her American friend Sally Ryan. In addition to 43 works by Epstein, the collection (which was donated by Garman to the city where she grew up) includes paintings, drawings and sculptures by Turner, Constable, Manet, Degas, Monet, van Gogh, Picasso, Matisse, Braque, Modigliani, Lucian Freud and other 19th- and 20th-century artists.

Positioned at the top end of the main shopping street and apex of a new canal basin, the building is a focal presence in the city. Its architecture, a five-story tower with windows of wide ranging sizes randomly distributed across its terracotta-tiled facade, makes it all the more striking. Inside, each segment has been expressly designed to accommodate a different part of the program: galleries for temporary exhibitions of contemporary art, a studio and project room for a guest artist, a children's discovery gallery, educational facilities and conference rooms, café-shop and rooftop restaurant.

The building officially opened its doors in February 2000 with the exhibition *Blue: Borrowed and New*, an exploration of the significance of the color blue in modern and contemporary art.

Richard Wentworth

👤 Untitled, 2000

Commissioned to design a permanent work for the exterior of the New Art Gallery Walsall, Wentworth created a pedestrian roadway uniting the linear area of the canal path with the oddly shaped spaces of open land around the gallery. Adding a theatrical effect, he striped the black asphalt path with a series of 20-ft (6-m) wide bands.

Woverhampton

West of Walsall, 15 min by train.

Wolverhampton Art Gallery

🏛 Litchfield St, WV1 1DU
01902-552-055
Mon–Sat, 10–5

Although boasts of a great collection of Pop art, Photorealism and contemporary work from the UK and US are exaggerated, you will find some strong examples from the 1960s–80s. Especially if you're not familiar with British artists like Conrad Atkinson, Tony Bevan, Peter Blake, Helen Chadwick, Richard Hamilton, Bruce McLean, Lisa Milroy and Richard Wilson, Wolverhampton will give you a sense of their creative modes and the general thrust of mid-20th-century British art.

Bristol

Even if you can only hop into town for a quick visit, you'll catch the flair of Bristol. It's a very upbeat city with a sizable population of creative people. The club scene is lively; there's lots of music and theater; artist-organized exhibitions regularly occur here and there within the city; and outdoor art projects are part of the environment in the summer. The cultural quarter around Narrow Quay and Harbourside is where you want to go. You can get there by bus from the train station.

Like many British cities, Bristol implemented an urban rejuvenation scheme during the late 1990s. It entailed the development of Harbourside as a leisure, education and entertainment area. Spring of 2000 marks its official inauguration though additional arts-related projects will follow. The initial plan included a striking new Centre for the Performing Arts designed by the up-and-coming Stuttgart architects Günter & Stefan Behnisch. It was a great shock to the city when this project didn't receive final lottery funding. Interestingly, the unconventional design of the building met with little resistance from the local community, in marked contrast to the vehement outcry against the innovative opera house proposal by Zaha Hadid for nearby Cardiff.

Train from London (Paddington), 1 1/2 hr; from Birmingham, 1 1/4 hr.

Arnolfini

🚪 architect: David CHIPPERFIELD, 1987
🏢 16 Narrow Quay, BS1 4QA
Mon–Sat, 10–7; Sun, 12–6
📖 0117-929-9191 f: 925-3876
www.arnolfini.demon.co.uk
arnolfini@arnolfini.demon.co.uk
admission: free

Located at the intersection of Wapping Rd and Prince St, where the waterway called Floating Harbor divides in two.

Founded in 1961, Arnolfini is one of Britain's premier contemporary art centers. Along with gallery exhibitions showing the latest developments in the visual arts, presentations of dance, theater, performance, poetry, music and film take place almost every night in the house auditorium. Indeed, the evening events are a dominant part of the program. For its exhibitions, Arnolfini tends toward one-person shows of midcareer, emerging or relatively unknown artists who are not so much trendsetters as individual voices. Commissioned work, especially new installations, enhance the exhibitions, and off-site projects add an important outreach dimension to the center's activities.

The building is a converted tea warehouse refurbished by David Chipperfield in 1987. The facade still retains the orig-

Joachim Koester, *Set Up*, 1999

inal 1830s character, but the gutted, restructured interior has a flexible white-box space with a large gallery, bookshop, auditorium and reception areas on the ground floor and two galleries upstairs. Though some segments of the building appear rundown and barren, others are elegantly styled with fine wood and stone. An inviting café-bar, entered from within the center or directly from the street, is a popular eating, drinking and meeting spot. Designed by the artist Bruce McLEAN, it has long, narrow tables set on a raised platform with views of the water, a bar spanning the length of the room and a multitude of captivating objects, some functional and others purely made as art. If you want to linger here, as most people seem to, you might want to visit the bookshop first. It carries a general selection of artist monographs, fiction, cultural theory, film, photography, design and architecture books as well as artist-made gifts and magazines.

Recent exhibitions: *Accelerator, Gordon Bennett, Tony Clark, Peter Doig, JK–JK (Joachim Koester, Janis Kerbel), John Frankland, Liam Gillick, John Hilliard, Kenny Hunter, Udomsak Krisanamis, Garry Fabian Miller, Tracy Moffat, Eilís O'Connell, Pictures of Pictures, Quay Designs, Rhapsodies in Black, Secret Victorians, Louise Short, Michael Snow, Jo Stockham, Voiceover.*

Arnolfini is in the process of developing plans for refurbishing and expanding its space, perhaps even constructing a new building.

Architecture Centre

Narrow Quay, BS1 4QA
0117-922-1540 f: 922-1541
Tues–Fri, 11–5; Sat–Sun, 12–5;
closed Mon
admission: free

Located next door to Arnolfini.

The aim of the Architecture Centre is to increase people's enjoyment of the built environment, hopefully thereby encouraging public demand for excellent design. Through a program of workshops, lectures, discussions, tours, exhibitions as well as available resources and a meeting place for professionals, the center tries to accomplish its ambitious goals. A high-energy, enthusiastic staff and rich variety of activities and events keep the ball rolling.

Unfortunately, the general space of the center is limited to a small shop on the ground floor and an inadequate exhibition gallery on the first floor with barely enough room for a few modestly sized objects or architectural models and an overcrowded display of drawings and plans on the walls. The paltry space is all the more disturbing since many exhibitions deal with topical, compelling themes. A better gallery and an upgrading of exhibition materials are necessary if the center expects this part of its program to contribute to its aims.

Recent exhibitions: The Art Nouveau of Riga, Bristol C20, The Harbourside Centre, Inside the Walls (English prisons), Mixed Use Urban Development, Mobile Villages, New Architects, Shaping Our Environment, Turning Green.

St. Augustine's Footbridge

designer: Eilís O'CONNELL, 1998
St. Augustine's Reach

This bridge provides a direct connection between the cultural institutions situated on either side of the intervening waterway. It also serves as a gateway to the new Harbourside development, linking it to the venerable Queen Square. The design, by the Irish sculptor Eilís O'Connell, has two enormous steel horns emanating from a gently curved deck at the point where the drawbridge hinges when raised to let high-masted boats pass through. Not only do the bell-shaped horns recall the imagery of funnels and ventilator spouts on ocean-going vessels, but they also serve a pragmatic function as counterweights to the segment of the bridge that rises.

Watershed

1 Canon's Rd, BS1 5TX
0117-927-6444 f: 921-3958
www.watershed.co.uk
info@watershed.demon.co.uk
gallery: daily, 12–8
admission: free, films—£4/2.50

Located at the water's edge (across the bridge from Arnolfini) in converted stalls on the dock, Watershed is a vibrant media center. The building is raw and simple, structured as a long concourse with separate compartments. It houses two theaters, a café-bar, gift shop, exhibition gallery and studio, darkroom facilities equipped for photographic and digital production. The theaters, affiliated with the British Film Institute, present a full schedule of films: animation, foreign films, classics, premiers, shorts and work by regional filmmakers. In addition, cinema festivals—like Brief Encounters, which features new short-subject films (November)—lectures, conferences and special events are part of the program. Performances of contemporary dance and music (especially jazz and experimental music) also take place in the auditoriums.

Exhibitions in the main gallery generally present new media and installation work. Often it's quite experimental, sometimes produced during residencies or as part of a research project. Artists are also commissioned to create animations, films and videos, which are then shown on a network of TV monitors placed around the building. In addition, Watershed displays photographs—from black-and-white to digital prints—in the concourse and offers a comprehensive program of photography workshops and classes. Web-based art is another aspect of the exhibition and training program

Recent exhibitions: Electric December, Here nor There, Invisible Geographies, Marlene Creates, October after Eisenstein—David Mabb, Michael Pinsky, Julia Spicer, Wingwalkers.

Wildscreen

 architect: Michael HOPKINS, 2000
Harbourside

Wildscreen and Explore are the primary focal points of the Bristol Harbourside development. The two centers, linked by new public squares and landscaped open spaces, add a pedestrian-friendly, civic-activity zone to the city.

Wildscreen is promoted as "the world's first purpose-built wildlife and environment media attraction, incorporating an electronic zoo, the ARKive inter-active database of endangered species, a large-format cinema and the first museum of wildlife film and photography." Even if you don't go inside, you can peer into the botanical house— a veritable rainforest with free-flying birds and butterflies—through the curving glass wall that stretches impressively across the building's long facade. Indeed, Hopkins's design has accommodated the exterior setting of plazas and waterfront views even as it inventively reshaped and expanded what was a derelict Victorian leadworks factory into a high-tech indoor nature park.

Explore

 architect: Chris WILKINSON, 2000
Harbourside

Explore is an interactive, experiential science center in the mode of the celebrated Exploratorium in San Francisco. It comprises a range of discovery-oriented exhibits about the human mind, body and senses, scientific principles and natural phenomena. As with Wildscreen, the architecture gives an enticing view of the interior. Here the whole length of the facade is an interactive glass wall showing images of experiments and activities going on inside in real time. In a corner of the building you can also observe the advanced eutectic thermal storage system—the energy-efficient heating and cooling device that sustains an even temperature inside. Look for a huge, transparent tower filled with small plastic balls. The balls contain special crystals that melt and harden and change color as the temperature goes up and down.

The building encompasses the old Great Western Railway shed but adds new parts, like the free-standing sphere that houses a planetarium-theater.

Spike Island

 133 Cumberland Rd, BS1 6UX
0117-929-2266 f: 929-2066
adm@spikeislandart.demon.co.uk

From the outside, the Spike Island building is nothing special. But when you enter, the glass-vaulted roof over the spacious center hall with side aisles below and a louver-enclosed balcony above, all painted white, has a cathedral-like aura. Lottery funds financed the renovation, transforming what was formerly a tea-packing factory into "a national center for visual art production." More specifically, the mammoth structure houses low-rent studios for about 100 artists, an atrium space available for exhibitions and performances, two small galleries and workshops for sculpture fabrication and printmaking.

Spike Island has no established policy for exhibitions, and they occur on a rather irregular schedule. You'll see posters around town when something is happening, and it's worth a visit to check it out. This is especially true for the annual show of work by the Henry Moore Spike Island Fellow. For example, when Mariele Neudecker was a resident fellow in 1998 she created a captivating, mystical installation in the atrium space. A glass tray filled with a white liquid emitting a frosty haze covered the entire floor area and in its midst was an ice-clad mountain range. Not only did the surrounding white walls and diffused light intensify the eeriness of the imagery, but the freezing temperature (required to sustain the artwork) actualized the wintry imagery.

Mariele Neudecker exhibition, 1998

Forest of Dean

Sculpture Trail

info: Forest Enterprise, Bank House,
Coleford, GL16 8BA
0159-483-3057 f: 483-3908
www.shu.ac.uk
daily, 8–dusk; closed Jan–Feb
(exact dates vary)

Buses into the forest run from Coleford and Cinderford. The nearest urban area is Gloucester (30 min by train from Bristol; 1 hr from Birmingham). If you're hearty, Coleford is a pleasant 2 1/2-mi walk (B4226) through the English countryside.

Forest of Dean is a favorite haunt of the British, renowned for its scenic drives, medieval heritage and mysterious character. Especially in the fall when the leaves of oak trees are ablaze with colors, it's a tranquil, sylvan paradise. If you plan to hike about or even take a short walk, wear waterproof shoes or boots since the trails are likely to be muddy.

Head for the Beechenhurst Lodge to gain access to the sculpture trail. (You can get a brochure-map here for 50p.) Open since 1986 and developed in two phases, this 4-mi circular path meanders through the center of the forest. Of the 18 works specifically created for and inspired by the setting, 12 remain. Since the work is mainly created from natural materials that respond to weather and time, some of it survives only a few seasons. New works are added but the trail is not meant to develop into an art park with numerous displays. Though there's not a lot of art to see, it's strong work and the artists are not the same familiar names. It's a pity the selection is so insular, averting the chance to intermix quality British and international creativity.

What makes the situation here special is that each piece is sensitive to the incredible landscape and vistas and attuned to contemporary art issues. (Arnolfini's involvement in the project surely played a role in this.) Amazingly, the sculptures actually enhance rather than disrupt the experience of walking through the forest. This is a rarity, well worth even a short visit. Should you not be an outdoorsy type or have limited time to spare, it's possible to make an abbreviated circuit, walking only about a third of the distance.

Magdalena JETELOVA, *Place*, 1986. Set atop a hill overlooking a valley, this gigantic oak form dwarfs people near it. Although it looks at first to be a chair, it lacks a seat and thus takes on the character of an entrance gate, especially when viewed from the rear, where the simple side posts and cross bar recall the Japanese tori (gate) located in front of temples and sacred places. In creating an image merging a gate—the passageway into a place—and chair—an object used for resting and positioning oneself in a place—Jetelova evokes an intriguing sense of *Place*.

Carole DRAKE, *Dead Wood/Bois Mort*, 1986. By her alignment of five steel plates sunk like coffins in shallow holes dug into a forest floor covered with the seasonal sheddings of deciduous pine trees, Drake confounds human, man-made and natural connotations of death.

Tim LEES, *The Heart of Stone*, 1986. Placing a circular stone between two upright blocks so it appears to be cutting into the earth, Lees alludes to the drift mine that once existed on this site. The image also suggests a protected core that can't be destroyed.

David NASH, *Black Dome*, 1986. As he typically does in his sculptures, Nash creates an image out of found natural elements, especially burned, broken or decomposing pieces of wood. Here he piles over 900 charred morsels of larch pine from the Dean in a slightly domed circle. Over time the image will disappear and the charred wood will be reintegrated into the forest.

Keir SMITH, *Iron Road*, 1986. Appropriating a disused railway line, Smith sets timbers carved with suggestive images atop 20 transverse bars on the old track. The work revivifies the industrial activity that once occurred in the forest even as it memorializes it as a vision from a past era.

Ian Hamilton FINLAY, *Grove of Silence*, 1986. Repeating his signature mode of outdoor sculpture, Finlay places engraved stone plaques on tree trunks. Here the word "silence," written in

Magdalena Jetelová, *Place*, 1986

many languages, takes the place of scientific terms identifying particular species. It becomes an unspoken, poetic evocation of the quietude in the setting.

Peter RANDALL-PAGE, *Cone and Vessel*, 1988. In one of the few literal references to the forest, Randall-Page sculpted giant stone images of a pinecone and the cap of an acorn from an oak tree. The objects lie on the ground amid their real counterparts.

Miles DAVIES, *House*, 1987. This tiny house atop four extremely tall poles has the witty character of a dwelling for birds set appropriately high off the ground and equipped with stilt legs so it blends into the surrounding woodland of spindly trunked trees. Constructed in steel, the image also recalls a mine shaft like those that once existed in the forest.

Bruce ALLAN, *Observatory*, 1988. Basing his sculpture on the idea that different heights give different perspectives of an environment, Allan has created a staircase-pulpit structure. Even through the elevation is not great, just being within an enclosed observation platform focuses vision and glorifies the act of viewing. Functional aspects aside, the reductive, triangular form of this work gives it character without making it an offensive object within the natural setting.

Kevin ATHERTON, *Cathedral*, 1986. Unfortunately, this work is often illustrated in connection with the sculpture trail. Unlike most of the other works, which are inventive forms integrated with the environment, this stained-glass window that depicts a forest scene and hangs on a pole above the trail appears egregiously out of place. Blatantly announcing itself as an art object and illustrative of the surroundings, it reduces the art-forest project to the level of kitsch. Espousing the forest-as-cathedral analogy via the title is a further travesty.

Cornelia PARKER, *Hanging Fire*, 1988. Transforming familiar objects into something magical is a common feature of Parker's art. Here she dangles red leaflike images from a hoop and suspends the hoop in space around the upper part of a tree trunk. The object itself bears a likeness to a festive whirligig. In the spring it stands out brightly against the green leaves; in the fall it blends with the forest colors; and in winter when trees are bare its circular frame seen from below suggests the image of a giant sun moving across the sky.

Peter APPLETON, *Melissa's Swing*, 1986. Imaginative and simple, this swing is a visitor favorite and a clever, winsome design. Composed of a steel arch and wooden seat, it hangs by a cable from an umbrella-like object high above, which in turn is attached to a tree. No matter what your age or play quotient, if you don't try this you'll be missing a few minutes of pure pleasure.

West Country

Exeter

This is a historically charming and people-friendly city with wonderful hidden courtyards, public greens, old inns, a Roman city wall and gothic cathedral. Train from Bristol, 1 hr; from London (Paddington, Waterloo), 2 1/4 hr.

Spacex Gallery

45 Preston St, EX1 1DF
01392-431786 f: 213786
www.spacex.co.uk
mail@spacek.co.uk
Tues–Sat, 10–5; closed Mon
admission: free

Located in the center of town. Take High St (which becomes Fore St) toward the river; turn left onto King St, then right onto Preston.

It's hard to imagine an audience for unconventional contemporary art in this very British, out-of-the-way region, but the unassuming Spacex Gallery has been presenting an impressive roster of distinguished artists for years. Indeed, it's the only place around where you can see work by such artists as Gary Hume, Richard Long, Lari Pittman, Bridget Riley and Gillian Wearing. Unfortunately, the exhibition space, renovated in 1996, is a compact conglomerate of small rooms oddly arranged on different levels. The architect has squeezed gallery space from every corner, but the disjunctive layout interferes with the cohesiveness of an exhibition and compromises the art.

Recent exhibitions: *Gustav Metzger, Tim Noble & Sue Webster, John Virtue.*

St. Ives

If you like the rugged coasts of Brittany or New England, you'll love Cornwall. Here too you can wander atop barren rocky cliffs or along sandy stretches of open beach, through fishing villages or crowded tourist havens once vibrant as secluded art colonies. Its Celtic heritage gives Cornwall a distinctive charm, and the narrow cobblestone streets winding up and down steep hills covered with tiny, weatherbeaten houses and alluring shops have made St. Ives a popular seaside attraction. The establishment of a component of the Tate Gallery here in 1993 greatly enhanced the region's appeal and called attention to its role in the history of British art.

Although a few modern artists began going to St. Ives in 1929, it was not until war broke out in 1939 that the group centered on Ben Nicholson, Barbara Hepworth and Naum Gabo settled here. The town then became a veritable outpost for abstract art of the type favored by Brancusi, Mondrian and the Russian constructivists. After the war, a younger generation of British artists brought new blood into the colony, though their work had far less vanguard, international cachet. The main figures were Peter Lanyon, John Wells, Roger Hilton, Bryan Wynter, Patrick Heron, Terry Frost, Wilhelmina Barns-Graham. What is sometimes called the St. Ives School usually bears the end date of 1975 with the death of Hepworth. Clearly this date marks the end of an era. However, artists continue the heritage by working in Cornwall. A second aspect of the St. Ives tradition, relating to ceramics, stems from the studio established by Bernard Leach and Shoji Hamada in 1920.

Train from Exeter, 3 hr; from London (Paddington), 5 1/2 hr.

Tate Gallery St. Ives

architects: Eldred EVANS and David SHALEV, 1993
Portmeor Beach, TR26 1TG
0173-679-6226
www.tate.org.uk
Tues–Sun, 10:30–5:30; closed Mon except July–Aug
admission: £3.90/2.30

The Tate St. Ives has the specialized mission of displaying 20th-century art in the context of Cornwall. Astutely, the museum did not define itself as a showplace for St. Ives's artists but instead set out to view the historical community from a multiplicity of perspectives, especially as these suggest relevant links to other artists, ideas, traditions and even current work. Past presentations have, for example, explored relationships between artists in St. Ives and the constructivist and De Stijl groups; the abstract painting of Serge Poliakoff and Pierre Soulages—two postwar artists from Paris; the work of John Wells, a relatively unknown St. Ives artist; the public art commissions by Patrick

Evans & Shalev, Tate St. Ives

entrance—a large, open-air rotunda—the dominant feature of an undistinguished facade sheathed in a white marble-chip surface simulating the white sand of the beach across the street, the building barely stands out as a museum. Once inside you proceed through several rooms, one empty except for a brightly colored abstract landscape by Patrick HERON in the form of a stained-glass window-wall, and the next another stories-high rotunda—an elegant space but overwhelming to art displayed in it. From there you can go up to a small shop on level 2. (It only sells books about St. Ives's artists and modernist art.) Further up is a gallery on level 3 that leads up to a courtyard and additional galleries or down to terrace galleries. On top, level 4, there is a coffee shop and roof terrace. Keep tract of the gallery numbers or you're likely to miss some displays.

The austere white or gray flat surfaces assert a minimalist sensibility, although repetitive rhythms and shapes are often manifest as decorative patterns not reduction. Various rooms are permeated with natural light shining through glass-bricks or windows cut into overhead areas. The most dramatic space is the circular front gallery, which has a sweeping balcony lined with exhibition vitrines. It overlooks the entrance rotunda and offers a spectacular view of the ocean. As elsewhere in the building, the architecture here features spaces within, through, beyond and around other spaces.

Heron; and new work by artists presently living in Cornwall. At any given time the program comprises displays from the Tate collection (these change annually), exhibitions (e.g., *Wilhelmina Barns-Graham, John Wells*) and artists' projects (e.g., *John Beard, Anthony Benjamin, Lubaina Himid*). All are of modest size and tend to merge together due to the common St. Ives focus and because of the nonlinear layout of the galleries.

Indeed, the arrangement of the five main galleries and other spaces is eccentric. Each room has a different, irregular shape and there is no clear path through the exhibition rooms and connecting passageways. The architecture is striking in places but often competes with the art or showcases captivating ocean vistas, which detract from viewing the art.

Set into the hillside with the

Barbara Hepworth Museum

Barnoon Hill, TR26 1TG
0173-679-6226 f: 679-4480
Tues–Sun, 10:30–5:30; closed Mon
except July–Aug, 10:30–5:30
admission: £3.50/1.80

Located up the hill behind the Tate at

the corner of Ayr Lane and Barnoon Hill. Just follow the signs.

Situated in the modest house that served as Hepworth's live-work setting from 1939 until her death in 1975, this museum presents a biographical and artistic synopsis of one of Britain's leading sculptors. The small lobby displays photographic documentation, catalogues, reviews and memorabilia, and a tiny adjacent room has some wood sculptures and tools on exhibit. Upstairs another small room is meant to give a sense of Hepworth's domestic environment. But it's so antiseptic and bland, there's not much trace of human life in it. The studio, entered from the back garden, includes some plaster models and sculpting tools. As in the house itself, there's very little suggestion of the artist's ideas or personality, unlike Brancusi's studio at the Pompidou Center in Paris, where his positioning of objects, pedestals, lights and background elements were central to his concerns and aesthetics.

The most interesting part of the museum is the back garden, which Hepworth used as a showroom for her work. It's overgrown with plants and jam-packed with bronze sculptures and unfinished or abandoned stone blocks arranged in accordance with instructions left in the artist's will. A walking path leads up and around the spacious plot, passing in front and behind the objects. A side greenhouse also contains some sculpture.

Newlyn

Train from St. Ives to Penzance, 20 min. Newlyn, a modern fishing port, is about 1 mi from Penzance.

Newlyn Art Gallery

 24 New Road, Newlyn TR18 5PZ
01736-363715
Mon–Sat, 10–5

This gallery, located in the first building on the way into town from Penzance, generally shows local artists. During the tourist season, it often appeals to a broader audience with exhibitions of a more vanguard nature. In 1999, for example, James Turrell transformed the space into one of his signature three-dimensional light environments (*Arcus*). The exhibit also included seating in the form of *Eclipse*, the elliptical bench in wood and steel by Langlands & Bell. This project was followed by exhibitions of the video-artist Tacita Dean and the photogram-artist Susan Derges.

St. Austell

Train from Penzance, 1 hr; from London (Paddington), 4 hr.

Eden Project

architect: Nicolas GRIMSHAW, 2000
Bodelva
01726-222900 f: 222901

Located 1 mi north of the road (A390) between St. Austell and Lostwithiel.

The established horticulture and prideful garden traditions of Cornwall bolstered the idea of locating the world's biggest greenhouse in the area. Needless to say, this is one of the mega–Landmark Millennium Projects. Built at the bottom of a steep quarry in a wasteland left from clay mining, the new Eden encapsulates the four key climatological regions on Earth. A complete range of plants and trees showcasing global biodiversity fills four gargantuan "biomes." These dome-shaped greenhouses, each capable of containing 13 cathedrals, and a visitor center snake along a half-mile distance.

As with other Landmark Millennium Projects, Eden is a grandiose structure conceptualized and promoted with superlative terminology. The hope is that these projects will regenerate derelict zones of land; provide thousands of jobs in economically depressed regions; give a new identity and focus to bygone, atrophied communities; and attract hundreds of thousands of tourists from all over the world. It remains to be seen whether some or all of the projects will turn out as planned. If so, Britain may well become the dominant tourist haven of the 21st century.

wales

Cardiff

Most visitors travel to Wales to explore the appealing natural landscape. To say there hasn't been much vanguard activity in the realm of the visual arts and architecture here is a generous understatement. The conservative bent of the Welsh was exemplified by their rejection of a captivating proposal for a new Cardiff Bay Opera House (1994), which was to be one of Britain's landmark millennium buildings. The competition-winning design, created by one of the world's most innovative architects, Zaha HADID, caused a national uproar even though it was internationally praised and scrutinized by a predesignated jury as well as a second review panel. With its gravity-defying, crystalline segments arranged as a necklace, the building would have given Wales a world renowned, must-see icon and crowned Cardiff's regenerated waterfront with a striking centerpiece.

A bright spot in Cardiff's future is the new Centre for Visual Arts. To its credit, the city has also supported a rash of public artworks as part of the bay-front redevelopment projects. However, as might be expected given the Hadid controversy, most of the projects are benign designs that add a bit of interest to the environment but warrant little attention as innovative art.

Train from Bristol, 45 min; from London (Paddington), 2 hr.

Centre for Visual Arts

Working St, The Hayes, CF10 1GG
029-2039-4040
www.cva.org.uk
Tues–Wed, Sat, 11–6; Thurs, 11–9;
Sun, 11–5; closed Mon
admission: £3.50/2.50

Located in the heart of Cardiff, on the west side of St. David's Centre (a pedestrianized shopping area), this contemporary art space reinvigorated the old library when it opened in September 1999. The refurbished building has a spacious ground-floor gallery with a high vaulted ceiling and a second exhibition area in a roomy underground gallery. Fantasmic—an interactive gallery exploring the world of art and seeing—is on the upper level together with a shop, café and conference and event facilities.

Billed as a place where one can enjoy new and historic works of national and international art, the center has more than lived up to its publicity with its inaugural presentations. It began with a dazzling installation by *Jessica Stockholder* and followed this with *Unconvention*—an inventive exhibition featuring artists (Francis Bacon, Frank Capa, Martin Kippenberger, Edvard Munch, Pablo Picasso, Jackson Pollock,

Jessica Stockholder, Untitled, 1999

Jenny Saville, the Situationists, Andy Warhol, Lawrence Weiner, etc.), poets, posters (from the Spanish Civil War and Vietnam) and other materials that have inspired themes of love and revolution for the popular Welsh band the Manic Street Preachers; and *Claustrophobia*— an exhibition in which 16 contemporary artists from Kosovo to Los Angeles (Uta Barth, James Casebere, Mona Hatoum, Matthius Muller, Rachel Whiteread, etc.) explore the way we feel about our homes. Other exhibitions: *Las Vegas, Oil/Water, David Nash, Terra Mirabilis* (6 young Australian artists).

Ffotogallery

31 Charles St
029-2031-4667 f: 2034-1672
info@ffotogallery.freeserve.co.uk
Tues–Sat, 10:30–5:30
admission: free

As with other photography centers in Britain, this is a publicly funded, community-oriented space with an active education program of classes and workshops. The gallery, which has limited exhibition space, shares the premises with darkroom facilities, an archive and a small bookshop.

In addition to showing photographs and occasional films and videos, Ffotogallery also commissions work for traveling shows and a collection relating to Wales. For example, one project (1997–98) invited the esteemed Czech artist Josef Koudelka to document the radically changing landscape of Cardiff Bay and the industrial belt of southeast Wales. And a millennium project called *Just Another Day* invited 24 photographers specializing in fashion, landscape, documentary and portrait imagery to record experiences in Wales during the 48-hour period from December 31, 1999, through January 1, 2000.

Gallery shows are typically monographic, though theme projects like Sleuth, which explored the influence of film noir on contemporary photography and video artists, are arguably the best shows. Recent exhibitions: *Stephanie Bolt, Toril Brancher, Ian Breakwell, Avant Gardenner—Peter Finnemore, Hart Island—Melinda Hunt and Joel Sternfeld, Josef Koudelka, Alison Marchant, Marzena Pogorzaly, Sleuth (Adam Chodzko, Cheryl Dunye, Zoe Leonard), Alexa Wright.*

National Museum of Wales

Cathays Park, CF1 3NP
029-2039 7951 f: 2037-3219
Tues–Sun, 10–5; closed Mon
admission: £4.25/2.50

Art, science and history museums coexist in a large, stately building, one of many equally bland civic edifices in the Cathays Park area. The encyclopedic art collection, located on the fourth floor, is generally lackluster with the exception of some choice impressionist paintings. Contemporary art is limited to one room (#16) and focuses on British artists. Included is a strong early sculpture by David Nash, *Table with Cubes* (1971–72). Twentieth-century offerings (#14, 15) include some terrific paintings: *The Weaver* (1912–13) a vibrant composition by the Russian futurist Natalia Gontcharova; a not-so-familiar Vincent Van Gogh, *Rain* (1890); superb surrealist works by Max Ernst (*The Wood*, 1927) and René Magritte (*Empty Mask*, 1928); and fine British paintings by Paul Nash, *Plage* (1928), and Graham Sutherland, *Trees with Green-shaped Form, I* (1972).

From time to time, special exhibitions feature contemporary art. *David Hockney: Photoworks and Reconnaissance: Josef Koudelka* were both part of the 1999 program.

Chapter Arts Centre

Market Rd, Canton, GF5 1QE
029-2031-1060 f: 2031-3434
www.chapter.org
enquiry@chapter.org
gallery: Tues–Sun, 12–5 and 6–9
admission: free

Located in the Canton area (about a 15-min walk or short bus ride from down-town Cardiff), Chapter Arts Centre is the place where innovative talents in dance, theater, film, music, literature and the visual arts gather. Established in 1971, it now occupies four buildings containing a theater, three performance spaces, four cinemas, a gallery, two bars, a café, seminar rooms and studio or office space for over 30 artists or companies.

Gallery exhibitions focus on work deemed challenging and are particularly committed to support emerging artists. Typically the shows are adventurous and worth a visit. The Art in the Bar program features local and young artists. Recent exhibitions: *Adam Booth, Mikala Dwyer, Ffresh 2, Jane Grant, Paul Granyon, Lucy Gunning, Melanie Jackson, Nobuhira Narumi, Sleuth (Victor Burgin, Willie Doherty, Hugo Glendenning, Tim Etchells, Julia Scher)*.

John Gingel

Power Box/Blue Flash/Mesh Chips, 1994–96
Tyndall St electricity substation

At the very busy intersection of Tyndall Street and Central Link (behind Atlantic Wharf), John Gingel's brightly colored, bold artwork cleverly transforms the appearance of a highly visible, mundane, industrial setting. Rising above the roofline is a giant red box, a sharply angled blue lightning flash and a sweeping arc of darting yellow sparks. These elements were created as part of the expansion of the substation when the artist joined the design team of engineers and architects. Even as the imagery effectively camouflages the building, it emphasizes the power and dynamic character of electricity and upgrades the visual environment.

Pierre Vivant

Landmark 1992
Traffic circle, juncture of East Tyndall St and Ocean Way.

Recognizing the need to have a notable image at a major juncture, situated between an industrial site and a large residential area, the Cardiff Bay

John Gingel, *Power Box/Blue Flash/Mesh Chips*, 1994–96

Development Corporation commissioned the colorful, eye-catching proposal by Pierre Vivant. Known locally as "the magic roundabout," the work emblazons a traffic circle with five geometric shapes (sphere, pyramid, cube, cylinder, spiral) covered with standard road traffic signs and five evergreen topiaries in matching forms. Not only is the work a landmark during the day, but at night the reflective surfaces of the signs light up when caught in the headlights of passing cars.

Eilís O'Connell

Secret Station, 1990–92
Rover Way near Alexandra Gate

Located at the eastern approach to Cardiff Bay (junction 29 from M4/A48-M), this sculpture launched the public art commissions undertaken as part of the waterfront regeneration projects. Simple in form, the work is composed of two tall bronze cones (39 ft/12 m) with steel arcs balanced atop their apexes. Intermittently a cloud of steam issues from a slit near the top of the cones. This is meant to signify past technology associated with Cardiff Bay in contrast to the blue fiber-optic light—the birth of new technology—which illuminates the sculpture at night. Though the symbolism stretches the imagination and is hardly discernible, the glowing forms create a striking beacon against a darkened sky.

Millennium Waterfront

As with the Isle of Dogs project in London, Cardiff sought to regenerate its derelict docklands during the 1990s. Plans entailed a total transformation of the appearance and use of a prominent stretch of waterfront and its reunification with the city. A new street plan with open squares, green areas and embankment walkways was created to accommodate new residential, office, retail, cultural, entertainment and civic buildings as well as areas devoted to outdoor sport and leisure activities. Some landmark structures, like the brick Pierhead Building of 1896 and the timber Norwegian Church of 1867, were retained, but these are a small minority. Attention now centers on places like Techniquest, a hands-on, discovery science center, and Mermaid Quay, a huge shopping mall.

A civic focus was added to the waterfront redevelopment after Wales voted in September 1997 to create its own National Assembly. Following this historic separation from British rule, an international competition for the design of a National Assembly building (1998) resulted in the selection of a handsome, utterly non-governmental-looking proposal by Richard Rogers. The edifice will greatly enhance the Inner Harbour landscape, adding a distinctive architectural gem. Sadly, the Wales Millennium Centre—the edifice that ultimately replaced the ill-fated Opera House design of Zaha Hadid—contributes little to the setting or architectural history.

By far the biggest and most costly project undertaken as part of the harbor transformation was the construction of an enormous barrage across the Severn estuary stretching from the Cardiff docks west to Penarth. The 500-acre freshwater lake created by the dam was meant to give the city a nonurbanized character in line with that enjoyed by the Welsh hinterlands.

Buses run frequently from the downtown area (Queen St, Churchill Way, Wood St) to the waterfront, or you can catch a shuttle train at the Queen St or Cardiff Bay Stations (except Sun).

Wales Millennium Centre

architect: Percy THOMAS, 1999–
After the Hadid debacle, the original plan for a national Opera House was considerably revised. The reformulated proposal called for a multipurpose building amenable to the presentation of various music, dance and cultural programs. It's also home to the Welsh National Opera as well as contemporary dance companies, amateur music federations, literary organizations and other creative groups promoting Welsh culture, identity and talent.

The core of the building, a 1,700-seat auditorium, is emphasized by a sweeping, low-arched roof with truncated sides. But the dominant feature is the structure's white sterility, which has given it the nickname "Sellafield," a reference to a huge nuclear reprocessing plant in Cumbria.

National Assembly

architect: Richard ROGERS
Harbour Dr and Pierhead St
As proposed, the architecture of the National Assembly will stand in diametric contrast to the adjacent Millennium Centre. (At the time of this publication, the building was still in a concept stage. The scheduled opening is 2002.) Whereas the latter has heavy walls like a medieval castle, the former is open and refined like the Mies van der Rohe museum in Berlin, its source of inspiration. The spare modernity of Rogers's design is also dramatically different from his high-tech signature style, exemplified in such renowned creations as Lloyd's in London and the Pompidou Center in Paris.

Composed of glass and slate, the structure will rise in stepped levels from the shores of Cardiff Bay. Window walls will make the interior visible, though visitors will also get a bird's-eye view into the debating chamber by walking across its high glazed ceiling, which will double as a rooftop terrace, itself covered by a lightweight, billowing expanse of steel net.

In the words of lord Callaghan, chair of the design competition panel, Rogers's proposal is "simple, straightforward, elegant and economical. It allows for light and transparency and will provide generous public spaces. In symbolic form, it represents the open modern democracy which the National Assembly for Wales must be."

Brian Fell

Merchant Seafarers' War Memorial, 1996
next to the Pierhead Building
At first sight, this object looks like a large chunk of steel from a shipwreck. Then it takes shape as a face (or mask) turned downward as if asleep, comfortably resting on a circular patch of cobblestone pavement. The dualism appropriately signifies the sculpture's function as a war memorial for merchant seafarers.

Visitor Centre

architects: ALSOP & STORMER, 1990
currently located at the end of Harbour Drive
Designed as a temporary structure to house exhibitions about the regeneration of Cardiff Bay, this unconventional building—known as "the tube"—will hopefully become a permanent part of Cardiff's landscape. Its status and location after March 2000 (when the Development Corporation ceases to exist) have yet to be determined.

A seemingly simple, ovoid shape with window walls at both ends, the tube floats above the ground on scissor legs. Structured by steel ribs, it is clad with plywood panels weatherproofed by an

Alsop & Störmer, Visitor Center

outer covering of gleaming white poly-
ester fabric. Inside, the continuous curvature of the building's form is also
manifestly evident, although some
rooftop cutouts, patterned a bit like
seagulls, create spots of diffused light.

Harvey Hood

Celtic Ring, 1993
Start of Taff Trail at Inner Harbour
Marking the seaside beginning of a 55-
mile bicycle and walking trail linking
Cardiff with Brecon, this ring-form
sculpture raised off the ground on three
legs creates a meeting place and serves
as a viewpoint for the bay. Its wide,
curving shape fabricated from bronze is
cut to recall a Celtic torque (metal col-
lar). The artist further historicized the
work with surface details referring to
tidal charts, seafaring instruments and
industry associated with the old Cardiff
Docks. He also sculpted a Braille map of
the Taff Trail on four adjacent boulders.

St. David's Hotel and Spa

architect: Patrick DAVIES, 1999
Havannah St, CF10 6SD
Its flying winged roof and setting on a
promontory jutting into Cardiff Bay
make this nine-story building a dominant element in the harbor landscape. It
also stands out as the first and only five-
star hotel in Wales. Luxury abounds in
the atrium-centered structure whose
rooms all have balconies or terraces
overlooking the sea.

Llanarthne

Located in south-central Wales; the
nearest train station is Swansea.

The Great Glasshouse

architect: Norman FOSTER, 2000
National Botanic Garden of Wales
Middleton Hall, SA32 8HG
01558-668768 f: 668933
www.gardenofwales.org.uk
thutton@gardenofwales.org.uk
Once again, a British millennium project

has opted for a superlative by creating the largest single-span glasshouse in the world. The oval dome by Norman Foster does not, however, exude monumentality. Its curvature complements those of surrounding valley slopes, and it is surrounded by grass to give the appearance that it is rising out of the hillside. When opened in the spring of 2000, the structure will feature a complete representation of the Mediterranean floras of the world with particular attention paid to endangered ecosystems. As with most contemporary public enterprises, it will also contain a hands-on educational exhibition, this one called Bioverse.

The Great Glasshouse will be the heart of the National Botanic Garden of Wales. It is one of several new or restored buildings and environments associated with Middleton Hall—a once glorious 18th-century estate with fine landscaped gardens and parklands that were lost in scrub and marshes for more than 100 years.

Norman Foster, The Great Glasshouse

scotland

A bimonthly contemporary art guide for Scotland is available free in most galleries or on-line at dspace.dial.pipex.com/collective. You can also buy *The List* (£1.90), a biweekly magazine with an events guide for Edinburgh and Glasgow.

Edinburgh

Edinburgh is a charming, friendly though somewhat reserved city most known in the arts for its extraordinary International Festival. The entire city comes alive and thrives each August when the famous festival—or more accurately festivals—takes place. Virtually all cultural institutions are involved with performances, exhibitions and events, and these occur in every available or makeshift space in the city and beyond. A good source of information about the various festivals is www.go-edinburgh.co.uk or www.edinburghfestivals.co.uk.

Even off-season (any time other than August), there's a fair amount of notable contemporary art activity in Edinburgh. What's more, during the rest of the year you won't have to reckon with the zillions of festival patrons who form a voracious, impassioned mass of certifiable culture-vultures. Don't be surprised if you encounter some other citywide promotion in the arts. From time to time, there are thematic celebrations, like the Japanese Festival planned for 2001, or collaborations like *Ambient Light*, an exhibition held simultaneously at various contemporary art venues (1997–98).

Although there is paltry evidence of prime exemplars of contemporary architecture in Edinburgh—the new Museum of Scotland is a striking exception—a panoply of vintage Georgian and Victorian buildings gives character to the urban landscape. In addition, Edinburgh Castle, perched dramatically and dominantly atop a craggy cliff (volcanic rock formed during the Ice Age) in the very center of the city, is unique as an urban phenomenon.

Train from London (King's Cross), 4 1/2 hr; from Glasgow, 48 min.

Edinburgh International Festival

Festival Office & Visitor Centre
The Hub, Castlehill, EH1 2 NE
0131-473-2001 f: 473-2002
www.eif.co.uk
eif@eif.co.uk

Launched in 1947 as a postwar initiative to reunite Europe through culture, the Edinburgh International Festival has become the centerpiece of the world's largest arts festival. Held annually for two to three weeks beginning in mid-August, it's a cornucopia of high-caliber performances of opera, classical music, theater and ballet. In any given year, the program features the most respected companies from a wide range of countries; legendary stars as well as new celebrities; premieres, traditional favorites and rediscovered or unusual compositions.

Since many events sellout well in advance, it's best to order early. Usually the program is announced in late March and bookings begin soon thereafter. Should there be unsold tickets, these can be purchased on the day of the performance at half-price from either the festival box office or at the particular venue.

All the visual art spaces in Edinburgh schedule their most important exhibitions to coincide with the festival. Often there are also special events. For example, the Scottish National Gallery of Modern Art opened a major show of the acclaimed avant-garde artist Mona Hatoum in late August 1998, and she presented a live performance that became part of the Fringe Festival.

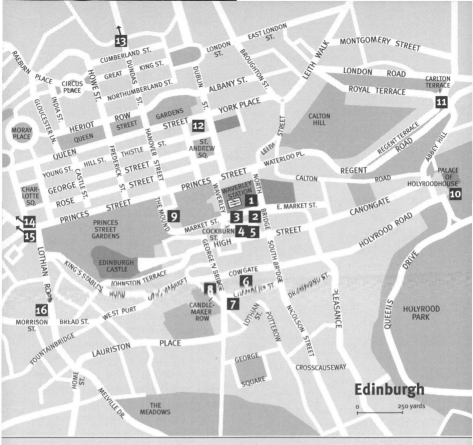

Edinburgh

0 ———— 250 yards

1. Fruitmarket Gallery
2. City Art Centre
3. Stills
4. Collective Gallery
5. Beyond Words
6. Matthew Architecture Gallery
7. Museum of Scotland
8. Portfolio Gallery
9. National Gallery of Scotland
10. Scottish Parliament
11. Ingleby Gallery
12. Scottish National Portrait Gallery
13. Inverleith House
14. Scottish National Gallery of Modern Art
15. Dean Gallery
16. Filmhouse

Although some exhibitions are listed in the various festival brochures, numerous others take place in all sorts of ad hoc venues and don't appear on the official lists. Extended hours are in effect at some museums and galleries, so if you're pressed for time you may be able to squeeze in a few extra visits.

Fringe Festival

Festival Fringe Society
180 High St, EH1 1QS
0131-226-5257 f: 220-4205
www.edfring.com
admin@edfringe.com

The same year as the main Edinburgh International Festival began, six Scottish and two English companies decided to show up uninvited and take advantage of the gathered crowd and press. The Fringe Festival thus emerged.

Some consider it a lowbrow alternative, but it's really an amazing potpourri of diverse, often very daring and innovative comedy, dance, music, theater and live art performances. Composed of professional and amateur productions, the range is widespread. Be prepared for a scintillating experience, an unbearable ordeal and everything in between. The Fringe tradition of total artistic freedom still rules even when confronted with controversy. A recent (mid-1990s) uproar was elicited by a feminist, intermittently nude version of Mozart's *Don Giovanni*.

From its initial, haphazard organization and small size, the Fringe Festival now boasts a year-round staff, central coordination, a pre-arranged program (yet still able to accommodate last-minute additions) and a mind-boggling number of events. In its 23-day run in 1999, there were 607 companies, nearly 1,500 shows and 15,699 performances. Unlike the main festival, which uses large, specially equipped concert halls, Fringe productions customarily are in small, unconventional theaters.

The program is announced in June or July and here, too, popular events sell-out in advance. Tickets are less expensive than for the main festival and can be ordered from the Fringe box office.

International Film Festival

88 Lothian Rd EH3 9BZ
0131-228-4051 f: 229-5501
www.edfilmfest.org.uk
info@ edfilmfest.org.uk

Not to be outdone, film is highlighted in the Edinburgh International Film Festival held annually during the same few weeks in late August. Like its sister festivals, it dates back to 1947. Similarly, it is a mammoth undertaking comprising more than 350 films, star-studded galas, world premieres and a full array of related events. Documentaries,

shorts, animation, retrospectives, a British focus and director's focus are featured aspects of the program.

International Book Festival

Scottish Book Centre
137 Dundee St, EH11 1BG
0131-228-5444 f: 228-4333
www.edbookfest.co.uk
admin@edbookfest.co.uk

The last weeks of August are also a time when writers and readers come to Edinburgh to partake in the International Book Festival. Billed as a celebration of the written word, this festival features over 350 authors (famous names, unknowns, local favorites) and 400 events. Geared to both adults and children, the program includes readings, workshops, lectures, debates, dialogues and special performances. Events occur daily from 10 in the morning until midnight. A preview listing comes out in April and the final plan is released in mid-June.

1 | Fruitmarket Gallery

45 Market St, EH1 1DF
Mon–Sat, 11–6; Sun, 12–5
0131-225-2383 f: 220-3130
www.fruitmarket.co.uk
info@fruitmarket.co.uk
admission: free

Located next to Waverley Station.

Fruitmarket not only is the leading contemporary art space in Edinburgh but has one of the foremost contemporary exhibition programs worldwide. Well-conceived, well-presented, challenging exhibitions are the rule here. Adventurous topics are explored before they become clichés; known artists are encouraged to take risks with new ideas; unfamiliar or young artists are showcased for the first time; and foreign artists from large and small countries are given UK premieres. It's not that every exhibition is a knock-out, but they inspire discovery and perpetually reshuffle prevailing categories and instinctive responses.

Don't expect mega-exhibitions since there are only two modest-sized galleries—one on the ground floor and a second above. However, works are carefully chosen and strategically installed to heighten their visual and communicative potency. Usually a single exhibition fills both galleries.

As part of its exhibition program, Fruitmarket commissions art from time to time. A new series, *Visions for the Future*, begun in 1999, added to this practice by determining that new bodies of work commissioned from Scottish artists would be featured.

Artist talks are a regular, popular highlight of activities that accompany exhibitions. There are also workshops, literary evenings and forums keynoted by leading figures in diverse disciplines. These events customarily lead to lively discussions and debates on pressing social issues. If your stay in Edinburgh coincides with one of these, be sure to include it in your schedule.

Although the gallery spaces are relatively simple, Richard MURPHY, the architect who did the renovation in 1993, punctuated the interior with his utterly handsome design of the lower staircase. Not to be missed is his equally appealing, ingeniously conceived reception desk (likewise in steel and wood). Without undue splash, these elements fit comfortably into the open layout of the entrance area, which also houses the bookshop—a great place to browse for recent texts on contemporary art, science, philosophy, poetry or art magazines—and café—a very pleasant setting with large windows looking onto the street and an enigmatic light projection of a functioning clock on the wall. Another projection that animates the wall with waving movements is difficult to see in daylight hours.

Recent exhibitions: *Continental Drift—Europe Approaching the Millennium,*

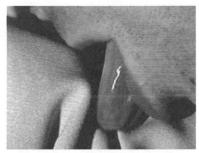

Smith/Stewart, *Gag*, 1996

Peter Doig/Udomsak Krisanamis, Evolution Isn't over Yet, Flower Show, The Mag Collection, Yoko Ono, Kiki Smith, Smith/Stewart, Tales of the Sands—Israeli Art, Visions for the Future—(1) Martin Boyce, Ross Sinclair, (2) Anne Bevan, Graeme Todd.

2 | City Art Centre

🏛 | 2 Market St, EH1 1DE
0131-529-3993 f: 529-3977
www.cac.org.uk
Mon–Sat, 10–5; Sun, 12–5
admission: £3/2

The enormous brick Victorian building across the street from Fruitmarket is the City Art Centre. A huge collection of Scottish art, arranged variously by media, period, subject matter and style, fills all four floors. There's not much vanguard work and even the special exhibitions offer a conservative or craft-oriented sense of the present.

Should you decide to visit the center, take a look at the immense abstract composition (1973) by Eduardo Paolozzi in the escalator corridor on the top floor. It's a virtuoso wall relief combining the artist's familiar machine-derived motifs with a collage of curved and checkered segments. Curiously, the aluminum-colored cast panels bear a strong affinity with the architectonic design of Art Deco (1930s), rather than recalling Pop art, the movement that brought Paolozzi renown in the 1950s.

3 | Stills

23 Cockburn St, EH1 1BP
0131-1622-6200 f: 622-6201
www.stills.demon.co.uk
info@stills.demon.co.uk
Tues–Sat, 10–6
admission: free

Cockburn Street, a steep, winding road-way, is partially gentrified but still gives evidence of the gloomy, crammed ambi-ence that once characterized Old Town. Its location near Fruitmarket in an affordable rent district has made it a hub for artists.

Stills—a photography center with two spacious galleries, a tiny but attrac-tive café, a small gift shop and public-access production facilities (darkrooms and a digital-imaging lab)—is one area magnet. Since reopening after a major refurbishment (1997), the center gives evidence of a more vanguard exhibition program. The broadened perspective embraces video, conceptual and radi-cal-image photography in addition to classic and documentary work. Recent exhibitions: *Emily Bates, Neville Blaszk, Tracey Emin, Nicky Hoberman, Alexander & Susan Maris, Cornelia Parker, Richard Prince, The Queen Is Dead (Australian and Scottish artists), Nina Saunders, Tomako Takahashi, Taking Snapshots— Amateur Photography in Germany from 1900 to the Present, Joel-Peter Witkin.*

4 | Collective Gallery

22–28 Cockburn St, EH1 1NY
tel/fax: 0131-220-1260
Tues–Wed, Fri–Sat, 11–5:30;
Thurs, 11–7; Sun, 2–4; closed Mon
admission: free

The Collective is an artist-run organiza-tion dedicated to the support of emer-gent artists and new art. Within Edinburgh, it is an important informa-tion and gathering center for artists as well as a launching pad for burgeoning members of the local art community. It also has its finger on the pulse of adventurous art from elsewhere in Scotland and sporadically shows work by London's reigning stars. Many exhibi-tions reveal the gallery's penchant for new media and radical modes of pre-sentation. As with many such art spaces, the character and quality of the work are at times below par, but the high-energy ambience and openness to experimentation overpower this.

In April 2000, when the Collective

Tracey Emin, *Sobasex*, 1998

opens again after a major refurbishment, it will undoubtedly lose its previously grungy-chic appearance. Plans call for enhanced galleries and a new lounge area incorporating a video viewing space, artists' computer resource and "mind bar." *British Art Show 5* will inaugurate the renewed gallery. This will be followed by *New Work Scotland* (a series of 3 exhibitions showcasing 6 young Scottish artists) and *Glass Box* (a show focused on Paris). Exhibitions are accompanied by free handouts or little brochures with statements by the artists.

5 | Beyond Words

42–44 Cockburn St, EH1 1PB
0131-226-6636 f: 226-6676
Jan–Mar: Tues–Sat, 10–6;
closed Mon
Apr–Dec: Tues–Sat, 10–8;
Sun–Mon, 12–5

This bookstore focuses on photography, mainly taking a classic approach to the medium. As a subspecialty, it offers a large selection of books concentrating on landscape images of Scotland. The store has a small exhibition space showing work in line with the tenor of its books.

6 | Matthew Architecture Gallery

University of Edinburgh
20 Chambers St, EH1 1JZ
0131-650-2306
matthew.gallery@ed.ac.uk
Mon–Fri, 10–4:30;
Sat–Sun, 10:30–2:30
admission: free

Located in the center of the university (which sprawls throughout Old Town), in one of its oldest buildings, the Matthews Architecture Gallery occupies a few rooms on the ground floor just to the right of the main entrance. There are no bold signs denoting its presence,

and little has been done to transform the dark-paneled setting from its former use (it appears to have been some sort of private study or sitting room) into a gallery. Nevertheless, the exhibition program includes some quite interesting shows relevant to contemporary art and current developments in architecture.

Of particular note is an ongoing series titled *Making/Thinking: Artists Build*. Thus far, it has featured buildings designed by Siah Armajani, Erwin Heerich and Per Kirkeby. Regardless of your background, the exhibitions are accessible owing to clear explanatory labels and issue-oriented materials that elaborate the design concepts. The program alternates touring exhibitions with displays of work by Scottish architects.

7 | Museum of Scotland

architect: Gordon BENSON and
Alan FORSYTH, 1998
Chambers St and George IV Bridge,
EH1 1JF
0131-225-7534 f: 247-4027
www.nms.ac.uk
Mon, Wed–Sat, 10–5;
Tues, 10–8; Sun, 12–5
admission: £3/1.50;
free—Tues, 4:30–8

This building redeems one's faith in contemporary architecture in a city otherwise devoid of outstanding examples. (Hopefully the new Parliament by Miralles will do likewise.) It's not revolutionary when compared with other 1990s buildings, but it is a superb example of the period with its own flair for historicism, captivating features and precisioned craftsmanship.

Dominated by a high, sharply angled perimeter wall with sunken windows (slits, horizontal spreads) and a few bold protrusions, the structure looks like a fortress. A freestanding tower, positioned at a major street intersection and serving as the museum entrance, reiterates this association with Scotland's medieval heritage. The whole is clad in sandstone blocks whose beige, rose and brown tones and wind-gust markings are meticulously arranged to articulate the surface.

After entering the round tower and walking down a long hall, you emerge into a covered triangular courtyard of epic scale. The drama is accentuated by daylight streaming down from the roof. Display cases are set into the thick walls, and the eccentric protrusions and odd forms seen on the exterior are now seen to be particularized spaces for featured objects in the collection. The windows, moreover, have been specifically sized and placed to frame marvelous views of the city. On top, a timber-decked garden and restaurant give a panorama of Edinburgh.

For the basement court, the architects commissioned Edward PAOLOZZI to create robotic-styled figures denoting people of prehistory. The figures, whose chests double as display cases for archaeological finds, add imaginative humor to the installation. Artist-designed display settings were also made by Andy GOLDSWORTHY for artifacts of Roman implements. Here the exhibit cases are part of the slate and clay wall structures. You'll find additional walls by Goldsworthy on the roof terrace.

The Museum of Scotland tells the 5,000-year history of the country using objects and images, interactive and multimedia displays. Sometimes the Scottish significance is exaggerated and curatorial finesse is often wanting. But then, the museum is only newborn and still establishing its mission and orientation. When planning began in 1991, it was envisioned as merely an extension of the adjacent Royal Museum of Scotland whose collection covers geology and fossils, Egyptology, Chinese, Islamic and European decorative art. The two museums are now separate entities though they are connected by passageways. Even if you're not interested in the Royal Museum's holdings and special exhibitions, at least walk into this museum to get a glimpse of its incredible, unexpected interior. The heavy Italianate facade doesn't prepare you at all for a long oval atrium (with great round radiators!), surrounded by three stories of balconies, the whole delicately constructed in cast iron and glass in the style of Joseph Paxton's 1851 Crystal Palace, its source of inspiration.

8 | Portfolio Gallery

43 Candlemaker Row, EH1 2QB
0131-220-1911 f: 226-4287
www.ednet.co.uk/~portfolio
portfolio@ednet.co.uk
Tues–Sat, 12–5:30

Candlemaker Row is a winding hill street bordered by an oddity of shops, such as Bagpipe Supplies, Deadhead Comics, Sheeppish Looks. On the right side near the bottom is Portfolio Gallery. Don't be misled by its appearance. The exterior may give the impression of a genteel boutique selling old-master etchings, and the interior—with its narrow, two-level space—has a sedate, domestic ambience. It may not look or feel like the typical contemporary art space, but Portfolio has an exhibition program featuring photographers who are among the most esteemed names in the international art circuit. Artists: Helen Chadwick, Rineke Dijkstra, Detlef Henrichs, Marie-Jo Lafontaine, Andres Serrano, Hiroshi Sugimoto, Jeff Wall, Joel-Peter Witkin.

In addition to its exhibitions, the gallery publishes *Portfolio*, a seminal magazine on innovative photography being created or shown in Britain.

National Gallery
9 of Scotland

🏛 The Mound, EH2 2EL
0131-624-6200
pressinfo@natgalscot.ac.uk
Mon–Sat, 10–5; Sun, 2–5
admission: free

Located in the heart of the city in an august, neoclassical building with a palatial-styled interior (highlights include a grand, circular staircase, lushly colored walls and octagonal rooms), the National Gallery houses a collection of European and Scottish art from c. 1300 to 1900. More than a comprehensive survey, the display presents selective gems. You won't find anything from the contemporary era here but will see outstanding work by artists who are still influencial: Gainsborough, Hals, Poussin, Rembrandt, Rubens, Terborch, Tiepolo, Tintoretto, Titian, Van der Goes, Van Dyck, Watteau. There's even a major American landscape by Frederic Church (an oddity in European museums) and an unusual, secular-themed painting by El Greco, *Allegory (Fabula)*, depicting a figure blowing on burning embers while a man and a monkey watch. Among the late-19th-century holdings are paintings by Cézanne, Degas, Monet, Van Gogh, and Gauguin's great *Vision after the Sermon*. Labels with short texts accompany each work but the content tends toward the mundane and superficial.

Scottish art, arranged by subject matter—still life, portrait, landscape, genre, mythology—hangs in galleries on the basement level. You probably won't recognize any of the artists' names, and the styles are very academic. Yet don't give up before seeing the vibrantly colored, elegantly patterned series of paintings by Robert Burns (c. 1926), commissioned for exclusive tea rooms on Princes Street.

10 Scottish Parliament

🏛 architect: Enric MIRALLES, 2001

Like Wales, Scotland voted to create its own parliament (1997), thereby opting for legislative authority over local government and education. Elections took place in May 1999 and the first session convened in 2000. The selection of an architect for the new lawmakers resulted from an international competition held in 1999. The winning design came from Enric Miralles, a Catalan whose major buildings are in Spain.

Rather than a big structure symbolizing power and authority, Miralles conceptualized an organic-styled building with an egg-shaped entrance and open public area in front. He aimed for an image that signified democracy. By spreading the component elements among a group of buildings and emphasizing integration with the surrounding landscape, he further sought to create a parliament that did not look like a big office building or corporate headquarters.

Located at the end of the Royal Mile (the historic road beginning at Edinburgh Castle) behind the palace of Holyroodhouse (the queen's official residence in Scotland), the building relates both to the historic center of Edinburgh and the glorious green space of Holyrood Park. In his turn, Miralles has produced a design that takes advantage of the views and setting. He moreover establishes an affinity with the past by reusing old materials in some segments and by echoing Old Town in his development of an ensemble with various shapes and heights.

The building is scheduled for completion in 2001.

11 Ingleby Gallery

🖼 6 Carlton Terr, EH7 5DD
0131-556-4441 f: 556-4454
inglebygallery@dial.pipex.com
Wed–Sat, 10–6

From the east end of Princes St, continue on Waterloo Pl which then becomes Regent Rd. Follow this up the hill and turn left near the top onto Carlton Terr, a residential street lined with Georgian town houses. The walk will take about 15 min.

Ingleby Gallery, open since 1998, brings to Edinburgh a different range of artists. The specialty here is contemporary Scottish and early-20th-century British art including ceramics. Unlike galleries that establish themselves as gathering places, this one is off the beaten track and has the gloss of a private domain. But don't be intimidated. Just ring the bell and enter.

Artists: Craigie Aitchison, Jeffrey Blondes, Richard Bray, Richard Cook, George Dannatt, Susan Derges, Ian Hamilton Finlay, Emma Ford, Andy Goldsworthy, Harriet Mena Hill, Howard Hodgkin, Callum Innes, John McClean, Patricia Macdonald, Danny Markey, Margaret Mellis, Craig Murray-Orr, Hylton Nel, Tim Nicholson, Ian McKenzie Smith, Rupert Spira, Julian Stair, Emily Young.

12 | Scottish National Portrait Gallery

🏛 | 1 Queen St, EH2 1JD
0131-624-6200 f: 332-4939
natgalscot.ac.uk
Mon–Sat, 10–5; Sun, 2–5
admission: free; special
exhibitions—£2.50/1.50

Along with its collection of portraits of people who have played a significant role in Scottish history from the 16th century to the present, Scotland's Portrait Gallery also houses the national photography collection. Unfortunately, only a very limited selection is displayed in one small gallery (near the café). However, photography exhibitions figure prominently in the grand-scale, temporary shows presented at the

museum. Recent exhibitions: *William Klein—New York, Annie Leibowitz, Magna Brava—Magnum's Women Photographers*.

Don't overlook this venue just because there's no big-name photography project being headlined. Often a small show is a surprising treasure. This was true of *Little Sparta, Portrait of a Garden*, a collaboration between Ian Hamilton Finlay and the photographer Robin Gillanders (1998). Using poetry and images of Hamilton's private garden (a dense expanse of trees, plants, pathways, figurative sculptures and carved inscriptions), the exhibition conveyed ideas about the struggle between nature and culture that lie at the root of Hamilton's art.

13 | Inverleith House

▭ | Royal Botanical Garden
20A Inverleith Row, Arboretum Pl, EH3 9LR
0131-248-2943 f: 248-2901
www.rbge.org.uk/inverleith-house
Wed–Sun: 11–3:30 (Nov–Feb) ;
11–5 (Mar–Apr); 10–5 (May–Oct);
closed Mon–Tues.
admission: free

One mi (1.6 km) north of the center city. Buses 8, 19, 23, 28, 37, 39 will leave you at the East Gate entrance to the garden on Inverleith Row.

A visit to this exhibition space has the added bonus of allowing you to meander through the splendor of Edinburgh's Botanical Gardens. Its location in a late-18th-century mansion with great views of the city is another plus. Despite having served as the home of the Scottish National Gallery of Modern Art until 1984, little has been done to alter the domestic ambience. The space presently appears run-down, and though it isn't suited to all types of contemporary art, the exhibition program is specifically geared to work that teases the boundaries between art and science, making reference (often obtusely) to the natural world. Most all the art, as well as the installations, are planned with an awareness of the house and garden.

The schedule from past years reveals a mix of solo shows highlighting established international artists (especially New Yorkers) and emerging Scottish or British artists. Occasionally, watercolors and drawings from the botanical archives are also displayed in Inverleith House. Recent exhibitions: *Carl Andre, Graham Fagen, Family, Christine Frew, Angus Hood, Callum Innes, Melissa Kretschmer, Myron Stout, Richard Tuttle.*

A few works by Andy Goldsworthy and Alan Johnson, originally created for exhibitions, are located on the grounds around the building. Two sculptures by Barbara Hepworth, part of the national collection, also are in the garden.

Scottish National
14 Gallery of Modern Art

🏛 | Belford Rd, EH4 3DR
📧 | 0131-556-8921
Mon–Sat, 10–5; Sun, 2–5
admission: free; special exhibitions £2.50/1.50
Bus 13 from George St to Belford Rd; bus 32, 40, 41, 52, 82 to Queensferry Terr.

It's a good 20-min walk from the west end of Princes St to the museum. Take Queensberry St until it forks; the left fork is Belford Rd, which will curve around through a residential area, climb up and down a hill, cross a river in a deep ravine (just past the Hilton Hotel), climb up another incline bordered by a stone wall enclosing a park. The museum is on the left just after the road enters the park.

Founded in 1959, the gallery was originally located in Inverleith House (see above) until a new building could be constructed, preferably on Queen Street, opposite the Portrait Gallery. Forestalled by bureaucratic indecisive-

ness, the museum ultimately decided to take up residence in an old school building a distance from the city center. The austere stone edifice with a decidedly institutional, neoclassical exterior was renovated and the move was completed in 1984.

From its inception, the gallery recognized the impossibility of developing an in-depth survey collection and instead decided to concentrate on acquiring single, major works by seminal artists. At this time, you'll find strengths in certain areas (like German Expressionism), some extraordinary objects and some discernible gaps. Among the outstanding treasures are works from the modern period by Bacon, Balthus, Bonnard, Braque, Delaunay, Derain, Dix, Dubuffet, Gabo, Goncharova, Jawlensky, Kirchner, Larionov, Léger, Lipchitz, Matisse, Mondrian, Nicholson, Nolde, Picasso, Popova, Vordemberge-Gildewart, Vuillard.

Without question, the keynote of the gallery's collection is its Dada and surrealist art. Having already established itself as a leading resource in this area, the museum's holdings catapulted to indisputable world-class stature in 1995 when it acquired 26 exceptional paintings and sculptures, as well as the archive and library, from the Roland Penrose estate. Even if you're not a big fan of Surrealism, you'll surely marvel at the imaginative character and exquisite artistry of many of the objects on display. Included are exemplary works by the celebrated leaders—Arp, Breton, Dalí, Delvaux, Ernst, Giacometti, Magritte, Man Ray, Masson, Miró, Picabia, Schwitters, Tanguy—as well as superb creations by lesser-known artists. This collection alone is worth a visit, even a special trip to Edinburgh! (Dada and surrealist art is now separately installed across the street in the Dean Gallery. See below.)

The museum's holdings of contemporary art offer a strong selection.

Mona Hatoum, *Light Sentence*, 1992/1998

Again, it's not a comprehensive collection, but there are many intriguing objects by such artists as Stephan Balkenhol, Georg Baselitz, Joseph Beuys, Boyle Family, Marcel Broodthaers, Günter Brus, Anthony Caro, Helen Chadwick, Tracey Emin, Dan Flavin, Lucien Freud, Hamish Fulton, Gilbert & George, Antony Gormley, Damien Hirst, David Hockney, Donald Judd, Sol LeWitt, Roy Lichtenstein, Richard Long, Marc Quinn, James Rielly, Kerry Stewart, Catherine Yass. The prevalence of quality British and Scottish art offers a good opportunity to broaden and deepen your sense of recent developments in the UK—especially those not centered on the trendy activities dominating the headlines.

Be sure to meander outside to see sculptures by Anthony Caro, Barbara Hepworth, Henry Moore, Eduardo Paolozzi, George Rickey and William Turnbull installed on the lawns around the gallery.

Special exhibitions are a major part of the museum's program, and these bring to Edinburgh first-rate works of both modern and contemporary art. Most of the large, temporary shows are now presented in the Dean Gallery.

15 | Dean Gallery

renovation: Terry Farrell, 1999
73 Belford St, EH4 3DS
0131-624-6200
www.natgalscot.ac.uk
information@natgalscsot.ac.uk
Mon–Sat, 10–5; Sun, 2–5
admission: free; special exhibitions—£2.50/1.50

Located on the right side of Belford St across from the Scottish National Gallery of Modern Art.

In March 1999 the Scottish National Gallery of Modern Art expanded into a neighboring neoclassical building that used to be an orphanage. The move was largely driven by two important gifts: Gabrielle Keiller's collection of surrealist art and Eduardo Paolozzi's donation of the entire contents of his Chelsea studio.

On the ground floor, the Dean Gallery (as the new building is called) houses the Dada and Surrealist Collection and Study Centre and two galleries permanently devoted to Paolozzi. The upper floor is used for major temporary exhibitions, and usually there is more than one scheduled at any given time. Some temporary exhibitions shows are still presented across the street. Recent exhibitions: *Eileen Agar, Avidor Arikha, Joseph Beuys— Multiples, Elizabeth Blackadder, Henri Cartier-Bresson, John Coplans, Salvador Dalí, Andreas Gursky, Mona Hatoum, Nigel Henderson, Gary Hume, René Magritte, John Maxwell.*

16 | Filmhouse

88 Lothian Rd, EH3 9BZ
0131-228-2688 f: 229-6482
www.filmhouse.demon.co.uk
admin@fimhouse.demon.co.uk

Located in the block just past the Sheraton Hotel and before Morrison St.

Besides being a major venue for the Edinburgh International Film Festival, Filmhouse runs a year-round program of art, classic and new films. Guest appearances, special events, retrospectives and premieres complement the three daily screenings presented in three theaters. The café-bar is also a popular gathering place.

Dundee

Train from Edinburgh, 1 1/4 hr.

Dundee Contemporary Arts (DCA)

152 Nethergate, DD1 4DY
0138-243-2000 f: 243-2294
www.dca.org.uk
dca@dundeecity.gov.uk.
galleries: Tues–Wed, Sat–Sun, 10:30–5:30; Thurs–Fri, 10:30–8; closed Mon
admission: free

DCA, which opened in March 1999, is an interesting partnership between the city, the university and a nonprofit contemporary arts organization. With its multiple facets, the center serves and brings together various sectors of the local community. Through its exhibitions and productions, it also aims to open dialogues with the national and interna-

Andreas Gursky, *Rhine*, 1996

tional art world.

The building houses two spacious galleries, two cinemas, activity rooms, a print studio, research center, shop (selling original works of art) and café. The galleries show innovative work by Scottish and international artists, mainly from the current period. Both new and classic films are featured in the cinemas, and the Visual Research Center (VRC) includes production facilities for television, imaging, fine arts and design plus Centrespace, a place for events and experimental work.

In addition to being an exhibition and research center, DCA has a major education program for adults and children alike. Recent exhibitions: *Christine Borland, Tacita Dean, Olafur Eliasson, Frank O. Gehry—The Architect's Studio, Stephen Partridge, W. Eugene Smith*.

Maggie's Centre

architect: Frank O. GEHRY, 2001

This Cancer Caring Centre, located adjacent to Niewells Hospital overlooking the Tay River, will be Frank Gehry's first building in Britain. The announcement of his selection was made in July 1999 and plans call for completion about 2001. If you're in Scotland thereafter, it will probably be worth visiting Dundee to see a work by one of the world's most celebrated contemporary architects. It won't be a monumental edifice but is likely to reveal signature aspects of Gehry's design vocabulary: eccentric forms, sunlit spaces and an intriguing use of industrial materials.

M8

M8 Art Project

In an attempt to visually transform the dreary M8 highway between Edinburgh and Glasgow, this project (begun in 1992) has been encouraging corporations in the area to join with local authorities and cultural groups in commissioning major artworks for the roadway. To date three proposals have been implemented and others are in the pipeline.

Louise SCULLION and Matthew DALZIEL, *The Horn* (1997), Polkemmet Country Park, West Lothian. This work

Tacita Dean, *Disappearance at Sea*, 1996

consists of a funnel-shaped element positioned horizontally at the end of a 75-foot-high (22.5m) pole. Located at the edge of the park alongside the highway, the sculpture is a curiosity that arouses interest as well as being a beacon and signpost for Polkemmet. Inside the park, the horn emits a soundtrack of voices, music, familiar and odd noises at irregular intervals.

Patricia LEIGHTON, *Sawtooth Ramps* (1993), Bathgate, West Lothian. The artist has created a notable presence on the highway with this 1,000-foot-long (300 m) environmental sculpture. Its massive, serrated mounds of earth covered with grass catch and hold your attention. They are unnatural forms and yet they are composed of natural, not man-made materials so they become an integral part of the landscape. Attuned to ecological considerations, the artist specified that the grass be kept trim by grazing sheep—indigenous animals that were reintroduced to the area as a result of this artwork. Also located on the property, though not visible to passing motorists, is a new Motorola factory. As the corporate sponsor for the project, Motorola wanted to have a memorable landmark for itself on the M8. Leighton's sculpture fits the bill without being a commercial sign.

David MACH, *Big Heids* (1999), Mossend, Lanarkshire. This project, located on the future site of Eurocentral (a freight terminal for trains from mainland Europe), consists of three huge portrait heads set atop monumental pedestals. The pedestals are actually upended shipping containers, and the heads are made of scrap materials from steel yards. To further defy elitist notions of sculpture, Mach has configured his portraits as common people rather than famous, heroized individuals.

Glasgow

Whereas Edinburgh has the reputation of being a beautiful, cultured city, Glasgow is often thought of in industrial, working-class terms. Such clichés aside, Glasgow is permeated with the legacy of Charles Rennie Mackintosh (a renowned architect-designer-artist of Art Nouveau style), has long been a magnet for innovative theater and has recently become the cradle for exciting young talents in the art world. Moreover, it's a high-energy, friendly city with lots going on day or night.

Low-rent studios and production spaces for painting, sculpture, photography, TV, film and video, as well as training programs, workshop facilities and project grants are impressive indices of local government support of the arts. Not surprisingly, this has resulted in a large artist population, many of whom are graduates of the esteemed Glasgow School of Art. Also notable is the high degree of interchange and collaboration among organizations and individuals in various disciplines—fine arts, dance, music, writing, live and recorded performance, etc. Citywide events and festivals are the most obvious manifestation of this. The success it brings was hammered home during 1999 when virtually all the arts communities participated in Glasgow's reign as the City of Architecture and Design. A mind-boggling range of creative, entertaining, educational and pragmatic activities took place throughout the entire year. Notably, the overriding theme was not a commemorative or futuristic concept but explorations into the way architecture and design affect everyday life.

Because so much goes on informally, look for announcements of exhibitions and performances in studios or off-the-wall spaces. Also, keep your eyes open for street and storefront performances, especially in the Trongate district. These typically feature ironic, witty behavior and mimes who are easily mistaken for store mannequins.

Train from London (King's Cross), 5 1/4 hr; from Edinburgh, 48 min.

Centre for Contemporary Arts (CCA)

1

renovation: PAGE & PARK, 1999–2001
350 Sauchiehall St, G2 3JD
0141-332-7522 f: 332-3226
www.cca-glasgow.com
gen@cca-glasgow.com
center: Mon–Wed, 9am–11pm;
Thurs–Sat, 9am–12pm; Sun, 12–6
gallery: Mon–Wed, Sat, 11–6;
Thurs–Fri, 11–8; Sun, 12–5
admission: free
tube: Cowcaddens

Holding forth in the Sauchiehall (pronounced socky-hall) area is the CCA, a hotspot of avant-garde activity. It's a sprawling space, where art exhibitions share attention with a full schedule of performance events, dance and music programs, lectures, conferences and cultural debates. If you just want to hang

out, the CCA has a terrific bookstore, large café-bar and ever-bustling lobby.

The center views itself as a breeding ground for new ideas and has a deserved reputation for enterprise and innovation. It regularly commissions work and is open to bold, experimental projects. Though the emphasis is on young Scottish artists, an international perspective rules and art by foreigners is often featured. Generally there's one major exhibition (with catalogue) and various smaller shows each season. Sometimes a theme (more conceptual than image-based) prevails for a whole season, unifying all facets of the gallery and auditorium programs.

Taking advantage of lottery funds, the CCA is undergoing a major redevelopment of all three floors in its current building is expanding laterally into adjacent premises. The renovated center, scheduled to open in early 2001, will have additional and upgraded exhibition and performance spaces, multipurpose areas, a room specially equipped for showing films, a restaurant, enlarged bookshop and other amenities. During the interim, CCA has relocated to the McLellan Galleries, a few blocks up the street.

Eva Rothschild, *Levitation*, 1999

1. Centre for Contemporary Arts
2. McLellan Galleries
3. Glasgow Film Theatre
4. Willow Tea Room
5. Glasgow School of Art
6. Mackintosh Gallery
7. Gallery of Modern Art
8. The Lighthouse
9. Mark Firth (public sculpture)
10. Intermedia Gallery
11. Street Level Photoworks
12. Transmission Gallery
13. Tron Theatre, Bar, Restaurant
14. Tramway
15. Burrell Collection
16. Art Gallery and Museum
17. David Mach (public sculpture)
18. Scottish Exhibition and Conference Centre

Recent exhibitions: *Brussels/Bruxelles, Continuum 001, Earth and Everything—Recent Art from South Africa, Slipstream.*

2 | McLellan Galleries

270 Sauchiehall St, G2 3EH

This city-owned space is variously used for temporary exhibitions. During 2000, CCA is presenting a rich program of exhibitions, performances, dance, music and talks here while its own building is being renovated (see above).

3 | Glasgow Film Theatre

12 Rose St, G3 6RE
0141-332-6535 f: 332-7945
www.scot-art.org/gft
tube: Cowcaddens

GFT is a repertory, two-hall cinema showing the classics of British and independent film, with a bias toward Scottish productions. Its program includes special series or single screenings coordinated with exhibitions or festivals taking place in the city. One such program was the highly creative *Cinema as Architecture*, which explored the relationship between architecture, design and film.

Café Cosmo, a popular meeting place in the area, also doubles as a space for art exhibitions.

4 | Willow Tea Room

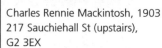

Charles Rennie Mackintosh, 1903
217 Sauchiehall St (upstairs),
G2 3EX
Mon–Sat, 9:30–5; Sun, 12–4:30
tube: Cowcaddens
The ground floor is occupied by
Henderson The Jewellers.

If you don't have the time or inclination to visit the full scope of Mackintosh buildings in Glasgow, you can come here for a snack and simultaneously get a taste of his design modality. Of course, you'll have to ignore the updated nature of the setting and realize that some important features were removed when the structure, closed since 1926, was restored for commercial use in 1980.

What you will see in the interior is the full flair of Mackintosh's sinuous architectural style and use of violet and silver organic ornamentation against plain white surfaces. Don't miss the magnificent doors of the Salon de Luxe up the stairway in the front. Indeed, try to wander around (not easy to do since it's a crowded tourist spot) so you can see how the architect organized the space on several interrelated levels with screens subdividing them. He actually didn't design the building from scratch, only remodeled it. His work on the exterior produced the very minimalized, white stucco facade with broad horizontal openings.

5 | Glasgow School of Art

Charles Rennie Mackintosh,
1897–99 and 1907–09
167 Renfrew St, G3 6RQ
0141-353-4526 f: 353-4746
www.gsa.ac.uk
tours: Mon–Fri, 11 and 2;
Sat, 10:30; only when classes
are in session
admission: £3.50/2
tube: Cowcaddens

If you're expecting to see the kind of Art Nouveau created on the Continent with linear curves and decorative floral imagery, you'll be taken aback when you arrive at the Glasgow School of Art (GSA), Mackintosh's best-known work. It's an austere, gray granite building (heavily blackened with age) whose facade is defined by large studio windows on two levels and the asymmetrical organization of the main entrance. The only real ornamentation is the ironwork, and it's rather plain and insignificant.

The left (east) side of the school was constructed first, followed seven years later by the west wing. If you walk around the corner of Scott Street, you'll see how Mackintosh created a vertically oriented, more stylized facade on the steep slope of the hillside, in contrast to the horizontality of the front facade. Three long bay windows, gridded and set into tall projecting blocks, are the dominant elements here. Remarkably, the back (north) wall, which faces the center city, is so dramatically blank, articulated only by a few windows, that it looks like a medieval fortress.

You can go inside to the art gallery (see below) but can only access to the extraordinary public rooms, designed and furnished by Mackintosh, if you take a tour. These, and a room containing a display of other pieces of furniture, give evidence of a more classic, albeit British, mode of Art Nouveau.

(Tickets are sold in the gift shop just inside the front door.)

With such a simple, straightforward facade, you'd presume to find a corresponding interior. Although it's similarly austere and geometric, the volume is divided into four floors—not the two levels implied externally by the windows—with a few double-height rooms. Moreover, complex interconnections and divisions are created by winding staircases and subsidiary corridors. The dark wood paneling used throughout the building attains its greatest expression in the library, an amazing, refined, totally unified design.

6 | Mackintosh Gallery

Glasgow School of Art
167 Renfrew St, G3 6RQ
0141-353-4525 f: 353-4746
www.gsa.ac.uk
Mon–Thurs, 9:30–8:30; Fri, 9:30–5;
Sat, 10–12; between semesters,
Mon–Fri, 9:30–5; Sat, 10–12
admission: free
tube: Cowcaddens

Located in the center of the first floor, the gallery is readily accessible to both the general public and students. Its exhibitions of design, architecture, fine and applied arts offer a diversified program even as they feed into the disciplines taught in the school. Despite the school's current reputation for producing avant-garde artists, the gallery takes a more conservative approach. Recent exhibitions: *Otl Aicher, Susan Cohn, Paul Cosgrove, Cross Currents, Scott Kilgore, Chuck Mitchell, Made in Brussels, Representations of Death, Dying and Disposal in Art, James Robertson, Ettore Sottsass, Thinking through Drawing.*

If you want to see what's going on within the up-and-coming generation, check out the Newbery Gallery in the dreary-looking building directly across the street. This is where exhibitions of student work are presented.

7 | Gallery of Modern Art

Royal Exchange Sq (Queen St),
G1 3AZ
0141-229-1996 f: 204-5316
Mon–Sat, 10–5; Sun, 11–5
admission: free
tube: Buchanan Street

Thomas Joshua Cooper, *Landfall—Vinland—near farthest North Ice flow along the Atlantic...*, 1998–99

Yes, the classical building with the massive columns that looks like a Greek temple, bank or seat of governmental authority is Glasgow's Gallery of Modern Art. In fact, it formerly housed the Royal Exchange. But in 1996 it acquired a new identity and transformed aura. The *Mirrored Room* installation of glass fragments and *Tympanium*, a fanciful chandelier, both by Niki de Saint-Phalle, greet you as you cross the darkened threshold, emphatically establishing an atmosphere somewhere between an entertainment spectacle and decorator kitsch. Unfortunately, this atmosphere prevails throughout the museum.

The main gallery, with its stone columns, coffered ceiling and large arched windows, is a majestic room though not very amenable to contemporary art. To compensate, temporary walls with steel frames and stone-block bases have been installed for paintings, and spreads of white pebbles are set on the floor around sculptures. The effect is discordant with the grandeur of the old interior but also looks designer-tacky and demeans the artwork.

Despite promoting itself as a gallery for work by living artists, the collection is almost exclusively centered on a narrow stream of contemporary (largely Scottish) creativity: figurative, narrative imagery. Moreover, the art has been selected and organized thematically by the elements—fire (basement), earth (ground floor), water (1st floor), air (2nd floor). The displays include work by Craigie Aitchison, John Byrne, Stephen Campbell, Ken Currie, Andy Goldsworthy, Alexander Guy, Alvin Davie, Jim Dine, Neil Hawksworth, Peter Howson, David Kemp, Felipe Linares, Ron O'Donnell, San Reed, Bridget Riley, Paul Waplinton, Alison Watt. Recent exhibitions: *Alvar Aalto,*

Tony Cooper, Flesh + Stone—Building a Scottish Identity.

The Lighthouse— Centre for Architecture, Design
8 and the City

 renovation: PAGE & PARK, 1999
11 Mitchell Lane (56–76 Mitchell St), G1 3LX
0141-221-6362 f: 221-6395
wwww.thelighthouse.co.uk
enquiries@thelighthouse.co.uk
Mon, Wed–Fri, Sat, 10–5:30;
Tues, 11–5:30, Thurs, 10:30–7;
Sun, 12–5
admission: free
tube: Buchanan Street, St. Enoch

The national Centre for Architecture, Design and the City, opened in 1999, is appropriately housed in the former Herald office building, the first major public edifice (1893–95) by a most favorite son, Charles Rennie Mackintosh. Although the conversion of the old structure, abandoned since the 1980s, preserved the original red sandstone facade, new features have dramatically reshaped the exterior. There is now a tower (hence the name Lighthouse) on the side and a prominent glass and copper extension (termed "a battery pack" by the architects) that provides a new entrance and roof platform with incredible views of the city.

The interior is composed of two main exhibition galleries, display areas, a conference room, education facilities, study centers—including one devoted to Mackintosh—and a café. In all its activities and programs, Lighthouse takes a people-based approach to design. On a grander scale, it aims to make Glasgow an architectural magnet in the 21st century.

Recent exhibitions: *Building Design Partnership, Jack Cunningham, Droog Design, Glasgow Collection, Identity*

Crisis—The 90s Defined, The Shape of Colour—Red, Philippe Starck, Alexander Thomson.

9 | Mark Firth

Chthonic Columns, 1996
St. Enoch Underground

Glasgow's subway system is the third oldest in Europe after those of London and Budapest. To mark its centennial in 1996, the Underground authorities commissioned two permanent artworks for busy concourses at the St. Enoch and Patrick stations. Mark Firth's sculpture celebrates the technological and engineering achievements used to create the original tunnels. In particular, it draws attention to the complex structural system and the hydraulic rams supporting the roof by presenting a pair of sturdy high-polished pumps, sized for a floor-to-ceiling fit, but frightfully positioned on a diagonal.

10 | Intermedia Gallery

18 King St, G1 5QP
Tues-Fri, 11-6; Sat, 2-6;
closed Mon (variable)
admission: free
tube: St. Enoch

Artists or groups apply to use this city-owned space for exhibitions or performances. It's a rent-free arrangement in which all aspects of the project (installation, publicity, opening, etc.) are the responsibility of the artist(s). Projects generally last about two to three weeks. They get excellent exposure since the gallery is located alongside notable contemporary art venues in the midst of a neighborhood filled with artists' studios.

11 | Street Level Photoworks

26 King St, G1 5QP
0141-552-2151 f: 552-2323
info@streetlevl.ndirect.co.uk
Tues-Sat, 10-5:30; closed Mon
admission: free
tube: St. Enoch

As Glasgow's center for photographic art and lens-based media, Street Level Photoworks organizes exhibitions, lectures, conferences and events. It also runs darkroom facilities that are heavily used by postgrad artists and art students. As with nearby galleries on King Street, the ambience is low key. But don't let this deceive you. A high-energy passion lies just beneath the surface. The storefront location with its narrow exhibition space is also deceptive until you realize there's a second, larger space in back with big window walls facing Parnie Street. (It's easy to miss the back space since the connecting passage is not very obvious.)

Exhibitions try to blur the boundaries of photography while also upholding the aesthetics of the medium. You're therefore just as likely to see classic, documentary and experimental photography as installations, videos and multimedia performances. Featured artists span the gamut from emerging to high profile, local to international. Recent exhibitions: Ian Breakwell, Dettie Flynn, Richard Gallen, Patrick Jamieson & Andrew Whittiker, Eric Lesderna, Reflections-Five German Photographers, Lesley Shearer, Andrew Stone, Streetworks, Ewen Sutherlund, Tower of Babble, Elizabeth W'rnde.

12 | Transmission Gallery

28 King St, G1 5QP
0141-552-4813 f: 552-1577
101346.422@compuserve.com
Tues-Sat, 11-5; closed Mon
tube: St. Enoch
Located corner of Parnie St,
1 block from Trongate.

Established in 1983, this is a veritable alternative space. Begun by young artists who had no place to exhibit their work, it's still membership-based and run by a volunteer committee of six who serve for up to two years. Though interested in showcasing local work, the gallery recognizes the need to be connected with the outside art world. The program therefore aims to frame local, less established artists within the context of an international peer group. It does so by organizing group shows, one exchange project and one solo show by a local artist each year. Past exchanges have been arranged with Barcelona, Antwerp, Belfast, Toronto, London, Chicago and Sydney.

The gallery itself is a very raw storefront with a main gallery on the ground floor and two project spaces downstairs. You never know what you'll find on display but it's inevitably worth a look. Just having the opportunity to see new work by a diversity of artists exploring new ideas is a big plus. A small selection of art magazines, catalogues and CDs, including Transmission projects and some off-beat publications, are for sale. Ask to see a gallery newsletter to get a sense of the art scene in Glasgow. Recent exhibitions: *Eurocentral, Four Projects (Nicolas Floch, Liam Gillick, Clara Ursitti, Beata Veszely), Jim Lambie, Never Been in a Riot, Tobias Rehberger, Haley and Sue Tompkins, Atelier van Lieshout*.

Tron Theatre, 13 Bar, Restaurant

architects: RMJM, 1997-99
Trongate and Chisholm Sts, G1 5BR
0141-287-5511
www.tron.co.uk
tube: St. Enoch

The Trongate (or Merchant City) district is a rundown area slowly undergoing regeneration. An anchor and catalyst in the process has been the Tron, which has itself been engaged in an extensive renovation project. Its building is an oddly segmented collage comprising a steeple from a church built on the site in 1528; two sides of the 18th-century church that replaced the original one, destroyed by fire; a facade from the late-19th-century church that supplanted its predecessor; and the new glass, stone, wood and tile components that are part of the recent refurbishment.

When church operations ceased in 1946, the Tron Theatre, whose focus is on new Scottish writers and actors, came into existence. Its auditorium was, and still is, the former worship hall, replete with a stained-glass window in back of the stage. Even if you don't go inside, you can view the interior through the floor-to-roof glazed wall that forms a second facade and lobby, set well behind and separate from the stone frontage of the old church. Lighting and color sequences on the walls add tonal and spatial nuances to the box office area. The whole design is quite creative and handsome.

The theater extends back along Chisholm Street, where a new cube structure houses a bar-café and offices. The chic interior combines natural lighting and open space with projecting and receding elements, ceilings of differing heights, stylish furnishings, wood paneling and walls painted with off-beat colors in a minimalist, geometric mode. Almost as soon as it opened, the Tron Bar became a favorite place for people to meet, eat and drink. Be forewarned, it's packed day and night.

The Tron Restaurant, located behind the new bar-café, is a large room of classic Victorian decor. Most striking is the all-pervasive dark wood and high pitched roof. At times the restaurant is the setting for dinner music events and performances.

14 | Tramway

renovation: ZOO, 1998–2000
25 Albert Dr, G41 2PE
0141-287-5429 f: 287-5533
www.tramway.org
info@tramway.org
Wed–Sun, 12–6 (may
change when reopened)
admission: free
train: Pollokshields East

Don't be put off by the out-of-the-way location in a grungy industrial district across the river (south of the city center). This is a must-see place, worthy of its widespread reputation for having an innovative program and "reckless ambition."

The building, an old tram shed, was saved from demolition in 1988 by the playwright Peter Brook, who transformed it into a theater to present *Mahabarata*. Vast expanses for art exhibitions, project rooms, performance spaces, studios, reading areas and a café-bar were subsequently added, and management passed to the city. Taking advantage of National Lottery funds,

Tramway underwent major redevelopment during 1998–2000 to upgrade the facilities, open the back area and enhance the setup with new and improved amenities. The layout is now based on a system of internal streets aimed to provide better access routes and greater spatial flexibility. Despite the changes, the raw, industrial feel and former ambience have been preserved. Tram lines still cross the floor, and brick and iron work from the original shed still embellish the main theater.

The exhibition program features internationally celebrated artists and unknowns, both young and midcareer. Some works are commissioned, and shows range from grand-scale to modest presentations. Similarly, the theater hosts leading avant-garde companies of acting, music and dance from all over the world and premieres are a notable aspect of the schedule. Recent exhibitions: *Marina Abramovic, Anya Gallaccio, Ulay*. Tramway will reopen in the summer of 2000 with two group shows: *Dark Lights Commissions and Mirror's Edge*.

Anya Gallacio, Untitled, 1993

15 | Burrell Collection

2060 Pollokshaws Rd, G43 1AT
0141-649-7151 f: 636-0086
Mon-Sat, 10-5; Sun, 11-5
admission: free
bus: 45, 48A, 57, exit at the park
gates off Haggs Rd, then walk
(10 min) or take the shuttle to
the museum.

Located 3 mi (5 k) south of the city center in the middle of Pollok Country Park, this museum is Glasgow's most popular attraction. Its setting, at the edge of a woodland, rivals its eclectic collection of decorative and fine arts from all over the world. Tapestries, Chinese ceramics, embroidered furnishings, stained glass and paintings by the likes of Cézanne and Renoir are among the treasures, all gathered by the wealthy shipowner and industrialist William Burrell and donated to the city in 1944. There's something for everyone, and when you need a rest you can relax in the glass-enclosed café and look at the serene natural environment outside. Special exhibitions don't tend to focus on contemporary art, although Glasgow 1999, the year of architecture, brought a Mies van der Rohe show to the premises.

16 | Art Gallery and Museum

Kelvingrove Park, G3 8AG
0141-287-2699 f: 287-2690
Mon-Sat, 10-5; Sun, 11-5
admission: free
tube: Kelvin Hall

Located near the university in the West End, the west end of Argyle St at Kelvin Way.

Looking like a Victorian castle with its decorative, red stone facade and endless splay of subsections, the building reiterates an aura of excess in the central hall dominated by organ pipes. Displays of arms and armor and natural history objects on the ground floor may cause you to wonder if you're in the right place, but don't give up. Just head for the stairs or elevators and you'll find the art galleries on the upper level. The collection is admittedly uneven. Nevertheless, it includes some fine British and European paintings by Botticelli, Rembrandt, Millet, Monet, Van Gogh, Picasso. There's also a comprehensive representation of Scottish painters, landscape and still-life imagery. From the contemporary era, you'll find art by Brits (Edouard Paolozzi, Bruce McLean, David Hockney, et al.) and a few foreigners, like Jasper Johns. If you enjoy furniture and decorative art objects typical of Mackintosh and his contemporaries (they're superb treasures!), don't miss the permanent display, Glasgow 1900.

Among the special exhibitions at Kelvingrove, some occasionally make forays into the modern era. In 1999, for example, the museum participated in Glasgow's year as the City of Architecture and Design by presenting Design Machine, Going Out in Style-Coffins from Africa and Frank Lloyd Wright.

17 | David Mach

Some of the People, 199
Patrick Underground station

Ever fascinated with common objects, unusual materials and kitsch, Mach here turned to snapshot photos and postcards. The work has a floor-to-ceiling glass-and-steel-framed rectangular box as its form. On each side panel there is a larger-than-life-size portrait photograph of someone you'd be likely to see on the Underground: a young mother and her two daughters, an older woman with shopping bags, a student and a fisherman with rod and stool. Each photo has been vertically sliced, reassembled and remounted onto a background of 3,000 identical picture postcards. You still see the original image but also have the sensation of movement.

Scottish Exhibition and Conference
18 Centre

 architect: Norman FOSTER, 1995-97
train-SECC station; bus-SECC terminal

Located west of the city center, off the Clydeside Expressway.

This recent addition to the city's architecture finally broke the ice in terms of Glasgow's receptivity to vanguard contemporary design. The building, known as "the armadillo," has a bold form somewhat like the famous Sydney Opera House. The roof, structured as a sequence of shells, encloses the central auditorium and five exhibition halls of varying sizes. Slots between the shells bring daylight into the interior, and a glazed wall, sheltered from sun by the wide overhang of the first shell, extends across the entire front facade. The image is both eccentric and impressive, all the more so because of its isolation on the banks of the River Clyde.

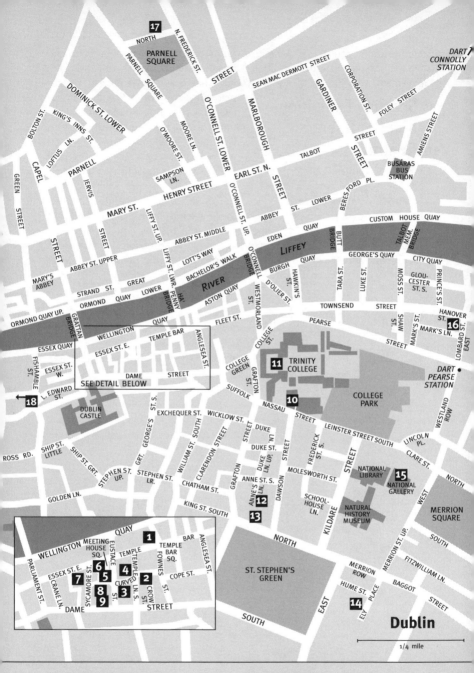

1. Temple Bar Gallery and Studios
2. Maud Cotter, mural
3. Arthouse
4. Temple Bar Music Centre
5. The Ark
6. National Photographic Archive
7. Project Arts Centre
8. Gallery of Photography
9. Irish Film Centre
10. Douglas Hyde Gallery
11. Trinity College
12. Kerlin Gallery
13. Rubicon Gallery
14. Royal Hibernia Academy
15. National Gallery of Ireland
16. Green on Red Gallery
17. Hugh Lane Gallery
18. Irish Museum of Modern Art

republic of ireland

In the past, the most vanguard Irish artists tended to become part of the London scene. But the late 1990s saw the blossoming of significant activity on Irish soil, especially in Dublin and Belfast. Both cities are alive with creative energy. It's a great time to visit before too much institutionalization and commercialization sets in. You can find a good listing for current museum and gallery exhibitions in both the Irish Republic and Northern Ireland on the web at www.entertainmentireland.ie/exhibitions/index.htm. *Circa* is the major contemporary art magazine for Ireland (£3.75); *Source* is Ireland's photographic review (£3).

Calls to the Republic of Ireland use the area code 353; Northern Ireland uses the UK area code 44.

Dublin

As an urban environment, Dublin is pretty grim looking due to the prevalence of dark gray stone, not to mention dilapidated streets and derelict buildings. The country's strong economy in recent years has, however, accelerated renewal efforts. New construction, conservation and the pedestrianization of neighborhood zones are markedly transforming the city's appearance in a very positive direction. Increased support for the arts and artists is also notable and impressive. Indeed, the arts community is emerging as a lively, formidable presence within Dublin and internationally.

▥| Temple Bar

This tightly packed area on the bank of the River Liffey—roughly bordered by the Bank of Ireland (originally built as the Irish Parliament) to the east, Parliament Street to the west and Dame Street on the south—dates back to the first Celtic settlements (c. 300 B.C.). It

officially became Dublin's cultural quarter in 1991 when the city sanctioned a renewal framework devised by Group 91 (a conglomerate of talented young architects) for developing what was then a badly run-down, neglected zone, albeit laden with a valued, bohemian ambience. Over the course of the next eight years, the plan was instrumental in promoting change. Cobblestone streets, old warehouse and craftsmen's habitats were restored; imaginative new structures with exhibition, performance and studio space were erected; housing units were incorporated throughout; two public squares were inserted into the network of narrow streets; and the neighborhood was enlivened by cafés, pubs and shops. In addition, artists were involved in the creation of street furniture, lighting installations and designs for cobbling and paving slabs. The results are world-class!

Perhaps most amazing was the decision to develop the new plaza, Meeting House Square, as an outdoor performance spot replete with a stage and projection screen built into two adjacent buildings. The use of these resources has not gone to waste and the square has become a center of art activity. During the winter, the large screen is treated as an alternative gallery venue for which artists create slide or video programs that are presented nightly (dusk to 11) for two-week runs. In the summer, both screen and stage are fully utilized in the evenings for open-air movies, theater, dance and music events. The square is also the site of street theater at noon on weekdays, food and book markets on Saturdays, and games and circus performances on Sundays. Everything is free though some events are ticketed. (Programs and tickets are available at Temple Bar Information Centre, 18 Eustace St, 01-671-5717, info@temple-bar.ie.)

You won't find many public spaces so well developed for public art. Some planned and spontaneous events also occur at Temple Bar Square, the second new neighborhood plaza. Having the advantage of being located right on Temple Bar, a major cross street, and surrounded by housing and shops, it has emerged as the community's, ever-bustling social spot.

With all its urban renewal success and appeal as an arts quarter, it is hoped that Temple Bar doesn't turn into a too-chic, too-touristy, high-end residential and business zone like Soho in New York.

1 | Temple Bar Gallery and Studios

architects: McCULLAGH MULVIN, 1994

5ñ9 Temple Bar, 2
01-671-0073 f: 677-7527
www.paddynet.ie/tbgs
tbgs@indigo.ie
MonñSat, 10–6; Sun, 2–6
admission: free

Located on the corner of Temple Bar and Fownes St across from Temple Bar Sq.

The architects have nicely masked the fact that this building incorporates an old shirt factory and a new section by wrapping the entire structure in a continuous white facade. The lively window design and cutout and extended elements also create a hybrid of interconnections Indeed, the geometric arrangement of large and small shapes, horizontal and vertical rhythms and red, yellow and blue panels is Mondrianesque—inflected with an industrial aesthetic and a 1990s architectural zaniness. (Note the steel windows and arbitrary curiosities.)

Inside an industrial and art-studio rawness prevails. The architects have added a wide central stairway that doubles as a meeting hub. An oval atrium cuts through this space, bringing in

added daylight and increasing communication among the various levels. Moreover, it serves as an eccentric point of spatial theatrics.

The building houses four exhibition rooms on the ground and first floors plus 30 studios. It's an artists' cooperative providing workspace for emerging and established artists (one studio is reserved for an international invitee) and exhibition space for artists who are not affiliated with commercial galleries. Usually two shows are presented simultaneously, and though you can't predict what you'll find, the work tends toward the high creative end of contemporary art. The public spaces are also used for interdisciplinary exhibitions, performance and music events.

Recent exhibitions: Paul Bradley, International Print Show, Annabel Konig, Ronan McCrea & Paul O'Neill, Rosie McGurran, Amanda Ralph, James Scanlon.

2 | Maud Cotter

Absolute Jellies Make Singing Sounds, 1994
Green Building, Temple Ln S, 2

For the entrance area of this building, Maud Cotter has created a composition using cut pieces of steel, glass, Plexi, copper and lead. The materials are set within geometric subsections, each having a different size, texture and visual character. A drape, formed by bands of metal, sweeps across the surface producing a vibrant rhythm. In the lower right, wooden boards cover a section that includes the door.

The Green Building stands out not only because of its sculptural entrance but also because it has wind propellers and solar panels on its roof. As its name suggests, it was created as a state-of-the-art energy-efficient urban structure. Indeed, Cotter's sculpture, like many other components of the interior and exterior, is made of recycled materials.

Among the most clever and attractive are the balcony balustrades, created by James GARNER from old bicycle frames.

3 | Arthouse

 architects: Shay CLEARY, 1995
Curved St, Temple Bar, 2
01-605-6800 f: 605-6801
www.arthouse.ie
Mon–Fri, 9–6:30; Sat, 10–6
admission: free

Curved Street, a new pedestrian roadway uniquely curved as its name implies, is formed by the two buildings that front it. On the south side, the four-story structure with a concave white facade riddled by diversely sized windows variously placed is Arthouse—Multimedia Centre for the Arts. It's an inviting building whose ground-floor exhibition space is visible from the outside. The exhibition area continues on the first floor, and the center also contains a residency studio, performance space, training facility (for web, audiovisual, digital technology), offices, meeting rooms and Cyberia (an Internet café). There's even a computer database of contemporary Irish artists that anyone can access from a kiosk in the lobby.

Arthouse aims to explore and expand the use of new technologies as a means of creation, presentation and promotion of art. These activities notwithstanding, the center also presents innovative, non-technology-based work in its exhibitions. Indeed, you're just as likely to come upon some compelling paintings or conceptual objects as interactive video projects. Recent exhibitions: Mark Dickinson, Freeze, Inconsistency.

Temple Bar
4 | Music Centre

 architects: Niall McCULLOUGH & Valerie MULVIN, 1996
Curved St, Temple Bar, 2

In contrast to the freely dispersed windows on the Arthouse facade, the Music Centre, across the street, has one big stretch of window wall in the center of its convex white exterior. The building encompasses an auditorium, practice rooms, recording studios, a school and office space for music-based enterprises and a café-bar. As with many of the seemingly new buildings in Temple Bar, screen facades and new structures hide and envelop old industrial and artisanal facilities. Here, for example, the auditorium is a former warehouse redesigned as a "black box." (It's clad in black steel louvers.) Standing separate from but connected to its new surrounds, it's also barely visible behind the frontage of the Music Centre on Curved Street.

Shay & Cleary, Arthouse

5 | The Ark

architects: Shane O'TOOLE &
Michael KELLY, 1995
Eustace St and Meeting House Sq,
Temple Bar, 2

The Ark, a children's cultural center, contains a large activity room, gallery, workshops and a 150-seat theater. The main entrance is on Eustace Street, where the original brick facade of the 1728 Presbyterian Meeting House still stands. Prior to recent construction work, the building had become a warehouse and printing plant, its interior gutted and back wall disfigured. In line with the Temple Bar plan to develop Meeting House Square for outdoor events, the architects developed a second, rear frontage for the building. Dominated by a giant theater curtain, set within a bold, blue-green copper frame, this facade is explicitly oriented to the exterior. Indeed, Ark's semicircular performance space, surrounded by bleachers and a balcony recalling the original meeting house, doubles as a stage for outdoor performances when the big curtain is raised. Ingeniously designed, the curtain—created by Santiago CALATRAVA, the extraordinary Catalan architect- engineer—slides up while folding in half along a curved, horizontal ridge and projecting outward to form an awning over the proscenium.

O'Toole & Kelly, The Ark; Santiago Calatrava, theater curtain

National
6 | Photographic Archive

architects: Sheila O'DONNELL &
John TUOMEY, 1998
Meeting House Sq, Temple Bar, 2
01-603-0371 f: 677-7451
photoarchive@nli.ie
Mon–Fri, 10–5; Sat, 10–2
admission: free

This building houses the photography collection previously held in the National Library of Ireland. It also includes an exhibition area on the ground floor and balcony, where prints from the collection are displayed. For the most part, these are documentary photos, but as in many such archives they include hidden treasures that are far more than visual chronicles of history and culture. If you're so inclined and have the time, the reading room (open to the public) has all sorts of books on photography (past and current).

The archive building is another of the curious amalgams in Temple Bar. The ground floor, whose entrance is on a narrow walkway leading from Essex Street East to Meeting House Square, belongs to the archive, but the upper levels, whose entrance is around the corner, is the Dublin Institute of Photography. In addition, there's a projection room on the side facing the square for open-air screenings. Clad in red brick with lead trim, the building is simple and refined. Its most striking feature is the low, sweeping arch that marks the archive's main door.

7 | Project Arts Centre

architect: Shay CLEARY, 2000
39 Essex St E
01-671-2321
www.project.ie
nfo@project.ie
admission: free

Established in 1966 as the first artist-run center in Ireland, Project Arts existed for decades in a dilapidated structure. It now has a purpose-built new home with a gallery, auditorium and multiuse space in which to conduct its active program. Strongly committed to new, innovative and experimental work, the exhibitions aim to show art that explores new paths or challenges existing ones, regardless of media, style, content or approach. Likewise, the auditorium presents numerous art forms including live-art and multimedia performances, contemporary dance, new music and theater. The new building is scheduled to open in late spring 2000.

8 | Gallery of Photography

architects: Sheila O'DONNELL & John TUOMEY, 1994–96
Meeting House Sq, Temple Bar, 2
01-671-4654 f: 670-9293
www.irish-photography.com
gallery@irish-photography.com
Mon–Sat, 11–6
admission: free

Like the Ark, this building provides a key element for open-air art projects and events in Meeting House Square. In this case, it's a silver screen that slides down to cover the enormous picture window in the center of its facade. The screen thus converts the plaza into an outdoor cinema, video or slide-projection space.

In addition to its grandiose window, the white Portland stone facade is eccentrically marked by a narrow, vertical slit on the left (a stairwell window) and a diagonally cut, recessed window wall on the bottom center right (the reception lobby). Even if you're not drawn inside by images seen through the window, the design of the facade provokes curiosity.

As a space for displaying photography—in fact, this is Ireland's premier and only gallery exclusively devoted to the medium—the interior is regrettably wanting, all the more so because of the engaging exterior design. To be sure, the layout is distinctive with its double-height main gallery overlooked by a balcony and two side galleries. But the rooms are few and quite small and there's very little hanging space. This sometimes necessitates the disastrous solution of stacking images Salon-style, where they're impossible to see close-up, or at all. And if the photographs are hung only at eye-level, or if the images are oversized (as is the case with much contemporary work), the space barely accommodates even a modest exhibition.

In all fairness, the architects had only a narrow plot of land at their disposal, and they set their boxlike building right against the structure behind (the Irish Film Centre). Fortunately, the large window in front faces north, thus reducing the problem of direct, strong sunlight, an important consideration for photography, a highly light-sensitive medium.

The gallery's exhibition program focuses on Irish photography, presenting about 12 shows annually. It also offers a complementary series of talks and conferences and has darkroom facilities available for public use. Recent exhibitions: *Liam Blake*, *Michael Boran*, *Bright Young Things*, *Robert Capa*, *Elliott Erwitt*, *Exploring Identity*, *Hoping for Heroes*, *Ireland at the Millennium*, *Jacques-Henri Lartique*, *Lightning Strike and other stories*, *Gareth McConnell*,

O'Donnell & Tuomey, Gallery of Photography

Patrick McCoy, Pádraig Murphy, Osman Collection, Martin Parr, Pictures from the Garden, Jürgen Schadeberg, Tom Wood.

9 | Irish Film Centre

renovation: Sheila O'DONNELL & John TUOMEY, 1987–92
6 Eustace St, Temple Bar, 2
01-679-5744 f: 677-8755
www.iftn.ie/ifc
fii@ifc.ie
daily, 11 am–12 pm

If you look left when exiting the Gallery of Photography, just ahead you'll see a neon sign denoting the Irish Film Centre (IFC). This entrance path, up a stairway and along a tall narrow portico, has not a shred of resemblance to the wide-open, marquee-embellished facades of most cinemas. Although this route is somewhat of a back-door passage, in actuality the IFC has no major street frontage since it's located in the middle of a city block. The main entrance off Eustace Street, similarly marked by a neon sign, leads down a long corridor through a barrel-vaulted hallway with illuminated panels set into the floor (intended to suggest a strip of film).

Regardless of which path you take, you ultimately emerge into a marvelous, glass-covered courtyard: the center of the IFC complex. From here you have access to the box office, a restaurant-bar (one of Dublin's liveliest, most popular hangouts), the Irish Film Archive, library and bookshop (it's small but has a superb selection of magazines, books, cards and videos) plus, of course, the two cinemas. The main theater is in a 17th-century Quaker meeting house that still has many original features but has been reshaped by the addition of a balcony. Cinema 2 is upstairs in a space with an old timber roof. Both present a varied program of new releases, classics and rare or forgotten films with a particular focus on movies unlikely to receive commercial distribution in Ireland. The center also organizes retrospectives, special events and guest appearances, as well as film festivals.

The architects have masterfully

organized a difficult conglomerate of partite units into a functional, appealing entity. Indeed, IFC is a highly valued, widely used social, entertainment and educational resource within the Temple Bar community.

10 Douglas Hyde Gallery

Trinity College, 2
01-608-1116 f: 670-8330
dhgallery@tcd.ie
Mon–Wed, Fri, 11–6;
Thurs, 11–7; Sat, 11–4:45
admission: free

Enter the campus from Nassau St through the gate opposite Dawson St. The gallery is under the arch immediately on the left in a dreary concrete building.

Named for Douglas Hyde (the first president of Ireland and a big supporter of Irish culture), the gallery opened in 1978 and was the major contemporary art exhibition space in Dublin until the creation of the Irish Museum of Modern Art in 1990. Over the years, it has accrued a remarkable track record of pioneering, impressive exhibitions that feature the work of midcareer and young artists from Ireland, Europe and America.

From its reputation, you might expect a big, impressive space. On the

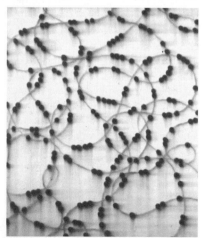

Mark Francis, *Hyphae*, 1999

contrary, it's quite unassuming, even generically bland, and moderately sized. Because the exhibition room is set below the ground floor with a double-height ceiling, you look down into it and get an odd—or tantalizing—perspective from above before entering. Fortunately, the gallery is creative in its installations, often taking advantage of the height and openness.

The gallery publishes a "newsletter" for each exhibition containing an excellent commentary on the art, artist and relevant historical, contextual ideas. These are available for free at the reception desk. A lecture series on contemporary art, art theory and culture is also part of a season's program. The speakers address current issues regarding multimedia, architecture, psychoanalysis, feminism, photography, design and other subjects having a vicarious or direct impact on contemporary art. If your stay overlaps with one of these talks, it's a good way to spend an evening and experience the illustrious Trinity College ambience.

Recent exhibitions: *Behind the Mask—Mexican Devotions, Louise Bourgeois, Carmen Calvo, Shane Cullen, Marlene Dumas, Jimmy Durham, Keith Edmier, Günther Forg, Felix Gonzalez-Torres, Joseph Grigely, Hungry Ghosts, Jaki Irvine, Kazuo Katase, Wolfgang Laib, Annette Messager, Pieter Laurens Mol, Mike Nelson, Guiseppe Penone, Annelies Štrba, Paul Thek, Luc Tuymans, Utopias, Bill Viola, John Virtue.*

11 Trinity College

If you walk past the gallery further into the campus, you'll soon come upon a black-painted steel sculpture, isolated on a circular cobblestone base on the lawns of Fellows' Square. It's one of the more playful Alexander CALDER stabiles (1967). Curved planar elements spread out like fluttering wings, and in the center one segment narrows into an attenuated neck held straight up in the air with a tiny sphere at its apex.

Return to the main walkway and proceed toward the campanile, one of the historic campus monuments. Nearby is a bronze Henry MOORE sculpture. Composed of a large, hollow, curvilinear form enclosing both angular and rounded shapes, the work recalls the artist's maternal figurations, though here the imagery is decidedly abstract.

If you continue down the main green walking east, to your right just past the building at the end is the new Berkeley Library with a sculpture by Arnaldo POMODORO in front. Sphere with Sphere (1982–83) is a large, polished bronze circular mass with deep fissures lined with jagged components and an interior cavity containing a similar form.

A visit to Trinity College wouldn't be complete without seeing the Book of Kells—the spectacular 9th-century illuminated manuscript that is one of the world's great treasures. It's housed in the old library, the long, stately building across from the new library. (Just follow the crowds.) June–Sept, Mon–Sat, 9:30–5; Sun, 9:30–4:30. Oct–May, daily, 12–4:30. (01-608-2320)

12 | Kerlin Gallery

Anne's Ln, Anne's St S, 2
01-670-9093 f: 670-9096
www.kerlin.ie
gallery@kerlin.ie
Mon–Fri, 10–5:45; Sat, 11–4:30

Anne's Ln is a back alley off Anne's St S, which runs between Dawson and Grafton Sts. It mainly has delivery entrances to shops, so you might assume you have the wrong address. Don't despair. Near the end on the left side, there's an innocent-looking door and the gallery's nameplate. Take the stairs to the top (two flights up).

Unexpectedly, the main gallery space

Paul Seawright, *Shaft #2*, 1999

is a spectacular, large, white-walled room with a high-pitched roof and wonderful light. It looks like something out of the Chelsea district in New York. Indeed, Kerlin is the most upscale, internationally connected gallery in Dublin. Though it represents only Irish artists, they are the leaders of cutting-edge creativity on the local scene, if not recognized and emerging stars abroad. If you haven't seen much contemporary Irish art, this is a good place to become acquainted with it. For starters you might seek out photographs by Seawright and Doherty, or the erotically charged objects by Cross, or abstract paintings by Egan, Francis and Ní Chiosáin.

Artists: Barrie Cooke, Dorothy Cross, Willie Doherty, Felim Egan, Mark Francis, David Godbold, Richard Gorman, Siobhán Hapasha, Stephen McKenna, William McKeown, Elizabeth Magill, Brian Maguire, Fionnuala Ní Chiosáin, Kathy Prendergast, Sean Scully, Paul Seawright, Seán Shanahan.

In addition to shows by these artists the gallery intersperses its program with exhibitions of powerhouse international figures, like Francesco Clemente, Richard Hamilton, Howard Hodgkin, Martin Kippenberger, Mimmo Paladino, Albert Oehlen, Hiroshi Sugimoto, Andy Warhol.

13 | Rubicon Gallery

⌂ | 10 St. Stephenìs Green, 2
01-670-8055 f: 670-8057
rubi@iol.ie
Mon–Sat, 11–5:30

Located on the north side of St. Stephen's Green, one block down from Grafton St. on the 2nd floor.

There's both a mature, refined strain and an experimental, youthful expression conveyed in the artwork exhibited at the Rubicon Gallery. If anything unifies the artists, it's an intense sensitivity to materials and texture. This is particularly significant in the work of Clear, Cotter, Drummond and Harding. All of the artists shown are from Ireland, though some now live elsewhere. Be sure to look at the announcement cards posted in the hallway since these give a snapshot of past shows and local artists.

Artists: Veronia Bolay, Felicity Clear, Clifford Collie, Eamon Colman, Diane Copperwhite, Maud Cotter, Blaise Drummond, Nathalie Du Pasquier, Mary Avril Gillan, Anita Groener, Marie Hanlon, Alexis Harding, Aoife Harrington, Ronnie Hughes, Eithne Jordan, Michael Kane, Nick Miller, Tom Molloy, Margaret Morrison, Hughie O'Donoghue, Vivienne Roche, Donald Teskey, Samuel Walsh.

14 | Royal Hibernia Academy

▭ | Gallagher Gallery, 15 Ely Pl, 2
01-661-2558 f: 661-0762
homepage.tinet.ie/~rhagallery
rhaglallery@tinet.ie
Mon–Wed, Fri–Sat, 11–5; Thurs, 11–8; Sun, 2–5

In its spacious gallery, the Royal Hibernia Academy (RHA) presents a varied program embracing both traditional and innovative artwork. Exhibitions have tended to be conservative but this may change. There's a new director whose past record is dominated by support for a challenging program, including shows of young artists who are just emerging as international figures. Recent exhibitions: An Artist's Century—Masterworks from Private Collections, William Crozier, Florence Biennale in Dublin, Kingdom of Heaven, Melanie le Brocquy, William McKeown, Thomas Ryan, The Sea and the Sky.

15 | National Gallery of Ireland

🏛 | Merion Sq W, 2
01-661-5133 f: 661-5372
www.nationalgallery.ie
artgall@tinet.ie
Mon–Wed, Fri–Sat, 10-5:30;
Thurs, 10–8; Sun, 2-5
admission: free

Like most of Europe's national museums, this one has a rich collection of treasures. The art spans the 14th–20th centuries, including choice works by Vermeer, Caravaggio, Vélasquez, Picasso and a stream of other great talents. Almost every major development of 19th-and early-20th-century European art is represented There's also a comprehensive selection of Irish art.

16 | Green on Red Gallery

⌂ | 26–27 Lombard St E, 2
01-671-3414 f: 672-7117
greenred@iol.ie
Mon–Fri, 10–6; Sat, 11–5

Westland Row, the eastern boundary of Trinity College, becomes Lombard St E after it crosses Pearse St. The gallery is on the left, above some storefronts, in the block before Townsend St.

Located off the beaten track, the Green on Red Gallery occupies a spread of rooms with a central, high-ceilinged space that has the ambience of a workshop. A broad range of media is represented—painting, sculpture, photography, prints, environment art, installations—and, as with most galleries in Dublin, the artists are almost exclusively Irish. If it's not too crowded, ask to see some images or works by such rising stars as Cullen, Maher and Rolfe.

Artists: John Aiken, Basil Beattie, Jim Buckley, Liadin Cooke, John Cronin, Shane Cullen, Fergus Feehily, Mary FitzGerald, Terry Frost, Andy Goldsworthy, Paddy Graham, Pat Hall, Robert Janz, Finola Jones, Mark Joyce, Alice Maher, Fergus Martin, Abigail O'Brien, Eilís O'Connell, Maurice O'Connell, James O'Nolan, Vivienne Roche, Nigel Rolfe, Joel Noel Smith, Corban Walker, Michael Warren, Catherine Yass.

Hugh Lane Municipal Gallery of Modern Art

17

🏛 Charlemont House, Parnell Sq N, 1
01-874-1903 f: 872-2182
📖 www.hughlane.ie
hughlane@iol.ie
Tues–Thurs, 9:30–6; Fri–Sat,
9:30–5; Sun, 11–5; closed Mon
admission: free
bus: 3, 10, 11, 13

Located just off O'Connell St Upper next to the Dublin Writers Museum; a 5-min walk from the river.

Hugh Lane, a successful art dealer in London, established this museum (1908) and furnished it with some choice impressionist paintings so that Ireland would be able to see their native artists alongside Europeans. The collection, housed in an elegant 18th-century town house (expanded back to provide additional space), now comprises art from the 19th century to the present including Manet's *Le Concert aux Tuileries* (*The Concert in the Tuileries*) and paintings by Courbet, Millet, Degas, Renoir, Monet, Burne-Jones,

Bonnard, Vuillard, Rouault and a large selection by Dublin's own Jack B. Yeats. Contemporary holdings are limited in number but encompass strong examples of work by Joseph Beuys (a blackboard object from a lecture he gave in the gallery in 1974), James Coleman, Dorothy Cross, Willie Doherty, Mark Francis, Edward and Nancy Kienholz (a superb assemblage relief), Sarah Lucas (a provocative panty-hose figure on and as an office chair), Agnes Martin, Kathy Prendergast, Niki de Saint-Phalle, Sean Scully.

Special exhibitions are located upstairs in rooms still decorated with fireplaces and Waterford chandeliers from the original house. There's a bookshop in the lobby where you can find some useful books and catalogues on contemporary Irish art. Recent exhibitions: Alice Maher, Michael Minnis, Janet Mullarney, Perry Ogden, Aloysius O'Kelly, Catherine Owens, Tidal Erotics—Vivienne Roche & John Buckley, Mick Wilson.

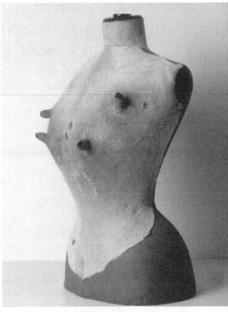

Dorothy Cross, *Bust*, 1992

The big excitement currently at Hugh Lane is the Francis Bacon studio, donated to the gallery by the artist's heir in 1998 and scheduled for a grand public opening as part of a larger exhibition in November 2000. Bacon, who was born in Dublin (1909) lived in London and worked in this studio from 1961 until his death in 1992. The contents have been described as "a diary of the last 30 years of his life." They include drawings, canvases, old paint brushes, rags, bottles of pigment, stacks of books, magazines and collected images, assorted debris and the last, unfinished self-portrait, which was on the artist's easel at the time of his death. The reconstruction process entails removing and meticulously reassembling all the objects as well as the paint-splattered plaster from the walls, floor, ceiling and door. The gallery hopes the display of the studio will shed light on Bacon's work. (The model for this is Brancusi's studio at the Centre Georges Pompidou in Paris.) A new Hugh Lane annex at 7 Reece Mews will permanently house the Bacon studio.

18 | Irish Museum of Modern Art (IMMA)

Royal Hospital, Military Rd, Kilmainham, 8
01-612-9900 f: 612-9999
www.modernart.ie
info@modernart.le
Tues–Sat, 10–5:30; Sun, 12–5:30
admission: free; New Galleries exhibitions, £3/1.50, free on Sat
bus: 68, 68A, 69, 78A, 79, 123, 90–Dart to Heuston, then an 8-min walk

If you're hardy and want to see a side of Dublin not on the tourist trail, walk west from Dame St following a continuous path (the street name keeps changing) from Lord Edward St to High St to Thomas St to St. James's St. You'll soon come to a place where St. James's St veers to the left and Bow Ln goes straight ahead. Take Bow Ln. You should see Stevens Ln immediately on the right. Turn right a short bit farther onto Military Rd. IMMA is on the left.

It's a shame that IMMA is located such a distance from the city center. It's downstream to the west, bordering a run-down industrial area. On a positive note, it's close to the National College of Art and Design—a major training ground for Irish artists—and down the road from one of the city's major monuments: Guinness Breweries.

The choice of this location was dictated by the availability of a historic 17th-century building, constructed as a hospital for retired soldiers and modeled after Les Invalides in Paris. The hospital closed in 1927, and until 1950 the edifice was used as a military headquarters. In the mid-80s the government restored the building, but it remained empty until IMMA moved in, opening its doors to the public in 1991. Apart from a new glazed lobby, the original building remains pretty much intact. (Preservation laws allow only a limited amount of transformation.) The exterior presents a dignified, three-story stone structure, utterly classical with exacting symmetry and rational order. These characteristics are even more apparent when you enter the large center courtyard around which the quadrangle building is positioned. The setting—an incredible expanse of parkland encompasses a formal garden, meadow, medieval burial grounds and various historic buildings—adds a romantic tone to the picture.

Like the facades, the interior is a rigorously repetitive design. But here the lack of fine detail makes for institutional austerity. The openness of the renovated double-height lobby shifts dramatically to a methodical layout of a long, wide corridor behind which lies a stream of rather small rooms connected one to the next with intermittent outlets back to the main corridor. Fortunately, there are a lot of rooms so the museum can spread out the art to provide good viewing conditions. However, this arrangement isolates each object, greatly diminishing the potential for an artist or curator to use juxtapositions and combinations as a means of communication. More problematic still is the lack of spacious galleries for the large-scale objects and multipartite installations favored by many contemporary artists.

Collection galleries are situated in the west wing. Considering that purchases and donations only began in 1990 when the museum was established, the objects present a meandering, disjunctive view of modern art. The mandate is to show Irish and international work, emphasizes the years from 1947 onward, and there's great pressure to build a strong collection without delay. As it is now, you can see a good selection of the leading names in the Irish contemporary art world, plus a few examples of European and American artists. Among those represented are Janine Antoni, Stephan Balkenhol, Jean-Michel Basquiat, Maud Cotter, Mark Francis, Gilbert & George, Antony Gormley, Alice Maher, Vong Phaophanit, Paul Seawright, Beverly Semmes, Rachel Whiteread, Bill Woodrow.

Because a chronological organization makes no sense when there are so many gaps, the museum creates thematic groupings that are like mini-exhibitions which change every three to four months. *Lifescapes*—works referring to a sense of place, to mental and physical locations and how we relate to them—was one such grouping, and *Half Dust*—works dealing with identity, spirituality and the body—was another.

As a means of representing points of origin in works of major 20th-century

Michael Landy, *Costermonger Stall No. 3*, 1991

artists in the context of ongoing exhibitions of contemporary work, IMMA opened the former Deputy Masters' House on the northeast terrace—now called the New Galleries—in February 2000. It will be used for a series devoted to special collections, both public and private. The inaugural exhibition features works on paper from the Picasso Museum in Paris and works on paper attributed to Francis Bacon from the Barry Joule Archive.

This series complements the established program of special exhibitions located in the east wing of the main building. In addition to presenting major 20th-century figures and mid-career artists, IMMA organizes group exhibits that include work by the leaders of the younger generation of international artists. Dubliners have therefore been exposed to art by Ellen Gallagher, Wolfgang Tillmans, Gillian Wearing, Yukinori Yanagi and others. Another program begun in 1999 is called New Projects of International Art. It offers a more extensive, in-depth focus on a single young artist and sometimes involves the creation of a work in situ. Callum Innes and Olufur Eliasson launched this series. IMMA also presents an annual exhibition coordinated with the Glen Dimplex Prize (£15,000), Ireland's version of the Turner Prize, except that this one's open to artists from any country. Past winners were Janine Antoni, Willie Doherty, Siobhán Hapaska, Alanna O'Kelly, Paul Seawright and Catherine Yass.

Recent exhibitions: . . . and start to wear purple, Art Unsolved, Joseph Beuys—Multiples, Come to the Edge, Olafur Eliasson, 50/50—Irish Artists 1950–2000, Leon Golub, Callum Innes, Ilya & Emilia Kabakov, Hughie O'Donoghue, Dennis Oppenheim, Kathy Prendergast, William Scott, Peter Shelton, Kiki Smith, Hannah Starkey, Alfred Wallis & James Dixon, Veronica's Revenge—Contemporary Perspectives in Photography, Wall of Myths, Andy Warhol. Catalogues and information sheets accompany most exhibitions. A shop next to the lobby sells some related publications though its stock is mainly books on Irish artists and general books on modern art.

The long building adjacent to the museum, formerly a coach-house block, has been converted to studios for the artists' work program, an international studio-residency project. Designed to provide artists with the opportunity to develop their work and ideas using the museum as a resource, the program emphasizes the creative process rather than the product. The public also gains awareness of the process through the talks, workshops, panel discussions and open studios organized as part of the residency program. The museum has also created the Nissan Art Project to give artists an opportunity to make a major temporary work for the public domain. In 1997, the first award to Frances Hegarty and Andrew Stones resulted in putting neon texts from Molly Bloom's Ulysses monologue in nine city center locations. The second project, realized by Dorothy Cross in February 1999, was the creation of Ghost Ship, a luminous lightship anchored in the bay near Dublin.

As is evident, IMMA is exploring and developing many different types of programs and activities to connect with artists, the local public, museum visitors and the international art world.

For those curious about the printed text "Sticks & Stones . . . Water & Sand" located on around the archway into the courtyard, this is a work by the conceptual American artist Lawrence WEINER. The tall, timber-and-steel sculpture of minimalist aesthetic situated on the front grounds is by the Irish artist Michael WARREN.

northern ireland

Belfast

The sense of a village community comes across in many areas of Belfast, but this metropolis, like Liverpool and Manchester, was at the forefront of the Industrial Revolution. Similarly, it has fallen on hard times. Renewal efforts geared toward strengthening the economy and transforming the city's appearance and identity began in the 1990s and are slowly taking hold. To be sure, the political-religious conflicts exacerbate the situation. As elsewhere in Britain, establishing a cultural infrastructure has played a key role in urban revitalization. With Van Morrison as a favorite son and a spirited music and club scene already in place, these facets of contemporary culture have received more attention than the visual arts. Nevertheless, the arts community is quite lively and building its presence within and beyond the city.

A percolating ground swell of activity is most apparent in temporary public projects and events. These take the form of artist billboards (see Ormeau Baths Gallery below), street interventions (see Catalyst Arts) and storefront displays (see Proposition Gallery). There was also The Irish News project. For this, three artists—Yoko Ono, David Shrigley, Wolfgang Tillmans—were commissioned to create work (photos, drawings, texts or whatever) specifically for the city newspaper, which then ran them on the three Fridays during the big Belfast Festival in 1998. A more ongoing phenomenon is the work of Grassy Knoll Productions, a two-artist team that integrates its creations with existing public spaces and commercial products. For example, it created handmade cigarette boxes and put them alongside brand-name ones in actual cigarette machines.

These distinctive efforts intentionally break with tradition regarding the placement of art within the community and its interface with the public. Most particularly, the focus is not on a museum or exhibitions seen by a circumscribed art-world population. The legacy of the esteemed artist Joseph Beuys, who developed a social concept of art and had a fondness for Ireland—especially Northern Ireland—is notable here. He, and a seminal series of his drawings and gouaches, The Secret Block for a Secret Person in Ireland (1936–72), traveled to Belfast in the mid-1970s, and an outpost of his Free International University for Creativity and Interdisciplinary Research (FIU) was established in the city.

In many ways, Belfast's art scene is like an energetic, impatient teenager. It's bursting with enthusiasm and potential but is still rough around the edges and not yet sure how it wants to develop.

Train from Dublin (Connolly), 2 hr.

Belfast Festival at Queen's

25 College Gardens, BT9 6BS
028-9066-7687 f: 9066-3733
www.qub.ac.uk/festival
festival@qub.ac.uk

This festival is Ireland's answer to the Edinburgh Festival. Although it's not as large, it's well established—2000 marks its 39th year—and likewise attracts some of the world's leading artists in the realms of music (classical, rock, pop, jazz, folk), theater, opera, comedy, dance and literature. The program is chock-full of events that take place over the course 2 1/2 weeks each November at some 20 venues all around the city. Queen's University administers everything. Artists and the visual arts institutions participate with major exhibitions, performances, projects and special events.

Belfast Fringe Festival

Crescent Art Centre
2–4 University Rd
028-9066-0515

With the growth of the festival at Queen's, a complementary Fringe Festival began in 1998. As in the situation at Edinburgh, it is an open festival aimed at a younger audience. Aiming to support "fresh ideas, new perspectives, alternative approaches as well as the plain, weird and wonderful," it doesn't hesitate to show a seamy side, such as an erotica weekend. Thus far, most of the participating acts are from Belfast. Events mainly take place in the Cathedral quarter.

Ormeau Baths Gallery

18a Ormeau Avenue, BT2 8HQ
028-9032-1402 f: 9031-2232
ormeaubathsgallery@btinternet.com
Tues–Sat, 10–6; closed Mon
admission: free

Only established in 1995, Ormeau Baths Gallery (OBG) is the major venue for contemporary art in Belfast. It's located in a renovated Victorian building, originally a municipal bath. The gallery's presence may not be obvious on the exterior, since it's one of several entities sharing the building, but the interior is a wonderful environment for exhibitions. The layout has four spacious, attractive rooms with natural overhead lighting. One has a barrel-vaulted roof and another is a two-story room with a surrounding balcony.

The program focuses on both Irish and international art, alternating between large exhibitions occupying all four spaces and shows featuring four different artists, one in each space. A small reading area and bookshop complement the art on display and the general gallery program.

Considering its short life, OBG has an impressive exhibition history, including well-known and emerging international artists working in a wide variety of media as well as Irish artists oriented toward both vanguard creativity and the ethnic, craft traditions of the region. Recent exhibitions: *Archetype (John Ford, Don Prince, Michael Warren)*,

Yoko Ono exhibition, 1998

David Byrne, *Better Living Through Chemistry*, 1998

Architecture 20/00, David Byrne, Henri Cartier-Bresson, Drawings & Sculptures (Helen Frik, Arno Kramer, Tjibbe Hooghiemstra), John Duncan, Gilbert & George, House in the Woods, Iontas, Janet Ledsham, Brian McGuire, Yoko Ono, Status of the Object (Ian Dawson, Laura Godfrey-Isaacs, Jon Langan), Tracings/Walldrawings (Leo de Goede, Simon Patterson, Colin Drake, Sol Le Witt), Bill Viola, 0044-20 Contemporary Irish Artists.

Notably, OBG has expanded its reach by organizing off-site projects in tandem with its exhibitions, especially during the Belfast Festival. In the fall of 1998, for example, it presented extraordinary shows by Yoko Ono and David Byrne in the gallery as well as Byrne's billboard project, *Better Living through Chemistry*, in various sites within the city and Bill Viola's video installation, *Nantes Triptyph* (1992), at the Portview Trade Centre, an industrial space on the east side of Belfast.

Catalyst Arts

5 Exchange Pl, BT1 2NA
028 9031-3303 f: 9031-2737
info@catalystarts.dnet.co.uk
Mon–Fri, 11–6; closed Sat
admission: free

Exchange Pl is a narrow alleyway in the area just south of St. Anne's Cathedral between Donegall and Hill Sts, one block before Waring St. The gallery, located on the north side of the alley, is behind a wooden door with huge locks and up a steep flight of stairs.

As you might surmise from the blight and destitution in the area, it's suffered the brunt of the Northern Ireland conflicts and economic adversity. The cathedral quarter, however, is a hip neighborhood alive with music, dance and performance clubs, film screening places, café-bars favored by writers and artists' studios.

Catalyst Arts began in 1993 by five artists rebelling against the commercialism of art and the lack of space and support for experimental projects in Belfast. It's still an artist-run, low-budget, against-the-grain organization, strongly committed to widening access to contemporary art. Indeed, a dominant aspect of the gallery's program involves events and projects that take place in the city at large: in storefronts, public buildings, streets, pubs, etc. In addition to giving local artists exposure, Catalyst Arts networks with artists and artist spaces elsewhere in the UK and Europe and then presents work from abroad in Belfast.

The gallery space, which used to be a factory, has two rooms for displaying art. It's a raw space and if it's winter when you visit, wear a warm coat, hat and gloves since there's no central heating. Off-beat approaches to art are common, including sound and text-based work or conglomerate objects formed from eccentric components. Painting is sometimes the medium of choice, but more often it's installation, multimedia, video or performance art. Recent exhibitions: *Ireland/Slovenia Exchange, Martin, (play) & (record), Right Place Wrong Time Friend, Tongue Tied* (collaboration with Valencia, Spain)

Proposition Gallery

Unit 22, North St Arcade
Thurs–Sat, 1–5; closed Mon–Wed
028-9023-4072
www.proposition.freeserve.co.uk
info@proposition.freeserve.co.uk
admission: free

Located in the downtown pedestrianized area adjacent to the tourist information center.

This gallery takes advantage of its location in a store in a shopping arcade by positioning eye-catching and provocative artwork front and center as window displays. It's a fairly lackluster arcade, so the art really stands out. The public nature of the gallery allows for an interaction with various segments of the community and serves as a challenge to artists. Proposition invites local and international artists working in all

media to create works for its space. They are typically young and just beginning their careers. Recent exhibitions: *Acerbarparc, Tom Bevan, Burmuda Triangle, Ian Charlesworth, Fear, Darragh Hogan, Alice Knox & Mitsuhisa Yoshida, Philip Lindey, Stephan Nilsson, Isabel Nolan, Jennifer Odem, Mitch Robinson, Joonas Sirvio, Matthew Walmsley.*

Waterfront Hall

architects: ROBINSON McILWAINE, 1997
2 Lanyon Pl, BT1 3LP
028-9033-4400 f: 028-9033-4467
Located off of Oxford St opposite the Royal Courts of Justice.

A major revitalization plan recently transformed the river-front area around Lanyon Place from an old meat and fish market into a high-class culture, office, hotel complex. The new buildings have undeniably enhanced the cityscape and also seem to be contributing to an economic upturn. The hope is that they will spearhead Belfast's attempt to redefine itself as a European city.

At the center of the project lies Waterfront Hall, a concert and convention center. The building is a striking circular form with a domed roof clad in copper. It contains a huge 2,235-seat auditorium, geared for symphony, opera, rock, pop, dance and theater, as well as a 400-seat studio, bars, restaurants, gardens, meeting and reception rooms. There's lots of public space, arranged on three levels around the auditorium with views toward the city and across the River Lagan.

Though a gallery for art exhibitions and product displays was an integral part of the architectural design, this hasn't been developed as a contemporary art space. However, three artists— Ceal Floyer, Barbara Freeman, Catherine Yass—were invited to respond to the building with temporary creations during the Festival of 1998, the first year the hall was open. Floyer's clever, ambiguous word compositions, discretely hung in unexpected places, added a nice, non-decorator touch.

Ulster Museum

Botanical Garden (Stranmillis Rd), BT9 5AB
028-9038-3000 f: 9038-3003
Mon–Fri, 10–5; Sat, 1–5; Sun, 2–5
admission: free
bus: 69 to Stranmillis Rd

Located south of the city center near Queen's University.

The Ulster Museum houses collections relating to natural history, archaeology, botany, ethnography, geology, zoology, history, antiquity, applied and fine art all under one roof. The art collection has bits of everything with no particular emphasis on the contemporary period. However, there are occasional exhibitions that pay noteworthy attention to recent developments, for example, *Joseph Beuys in the Celtic World* and *Contemporary Irish Painting & Sculpture*.

Derry (Londonderry)

Bus from Belfast, 1 3/4 hr.

Orchard Gallery

Orchard St, BT48 6EG
028-7126-9675 f: 7126-7273
Tues–Sat, 10–6; closed Mon
admission: free

Located near the Foyleside Shopping Centre.

Open since 1979, Orchard Gallery has established itself as one of the premier, most innovative contemporary art spaces in Ireland. It also is a respected, engaged member of the city and surrounding communities due to its energetic, imaginative array of educational programs and promotion of an ongoing dialogue between artists and the public. Works in all media are featured, and the schedule includes monographic and thematic exhibitions as well as commissioned works created by resident artists. Approximately one-third of the shows each year focus on Irish art while the rest are international. Recent exhibitions: *Maloisa Boyle, Anne Carlisle, Willie Doherty, Christoph Draeger, David Mabb, Phillip Napier, Miguel Navaro, New Media Projects (Nigel Rolfe, A.K. Dolvin, Marie-Jo Lafontaine, Dorothy Cross, Tacita Dean), Adrian O'Connell, Mike O'Kelly, Once Is Too Much, Jose Sanloon, Tom Woods.*

Context Gallery

Playhouse Community Arts Centre
5–7 Artillery St, BT 48
028-7137-3538 f: 7126-1884
Mon–Sat, 10–5:30
admission: free

The mission of Context Gallery is to provide a platform for young and emerging Irish artists. Far from being provincial, it presents innovative work by talented artists who go on to develop successful careers. Recent exhibitions: *Beyond Borders Plus, Maloisa Boyle, Susan MacWilliam, Alistair Wilson.*

Antony Gormley

Untitled, 1987
City walls, Bogside

The city walls were built in the early 17th century to shelter Protestants from a Catholic siege. In 1987, when Antony Gormley was commissioned to create a public sculpture for the city of Derry, the religious-political division symbolized by the walls was just as intense.

For this project, he made three pairs of cast-iron cruciform figures, 6 1/2 feet tall (2m). The figures are identical and the pairs are inextricably joined back to back and entirely sealed except for gaping eye sockets that look off in diametrically opposite directions. The imagery powerfully captures the essence of the conflict in the city (and Northern Ireland). Gormley's explicit positioning of the three sculptures intensifies this implied meaning. One pair overlooks the Protestant cathedral and nearby Fountain Bastion, a Protestant housing estate inside the walls. The second overlooks the Catholic cathedral and the destroyed Walker monument, blown up by the IRA in 1973. The third faces the barracks occupied by the British army across the River Foyle.

Referring to the figures as "poultice," Gormley views them "as a catalyst for some kind of healing."

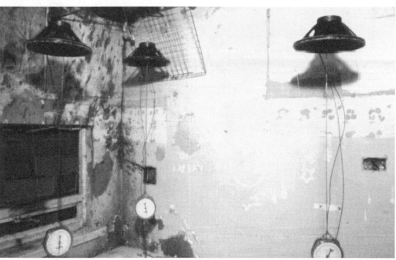

Phillip Napier, *Guage*, 1999

subject index

architecture

SUBJECT INDEX

sculpture parks

arts bookstores

index

Page numbers in **bold** refer to illustrations.

photo credits

cover and p. 60, Graeme Peacock, courtesy Gateshead Council

p. 26 courtesy Victoria Miro Gallery, London

p. 30 courtesy Marian Goodman Gallery, NY

p. 33 courtesy Anthony d'Offay Gallery, London

p. 36 courtesy Laurent Delaye Gallery, London

p. 38 courtesy Jay Joplin/White Cube, London

p. 40 courtesy Marian Goodman Gallery, NY

p. 41 courtesy the artist, Anthony Reynolds Gallery

p. 47 courtesy Photographers' Gallery

p. 52 courtesy Robert Prime Gallery

p. 55 courtesy Lisson Gallery, London

p. 56 Stephen White, courtesy Lisson Gallery, London

p. 63 courtesy Alexander & Bonin, NY

p. 64 Hugo Glendinning, courtesy Serpentine Gallery, London

p. 74 Edward Woodman, courtesy National Galleries of Scotland, Edinburgh

p. 82 Hayes Davidson/Tate Gallery, courtesy Foster and Partners, London

p. 85 courtesy Delfina, London

p. 93 Dennis Gilbert, View, courtesy Foster and Partners, London

p. 103 courtesy Jay Joplin/White Cube and Whitechapel Art Gallery, London

p. 106 courtesy Maureen Paley Interim Art, London

p. 108 courtesy Jay Joplin/White Cube, London

p. 120 courtesy Laure Genillard Gallery, London

p. 121 courtesy Andrew Mummery Gallery, London

p. 126 courtesy Sculpture at Goodwood

p. 126 courtesy Southampton City Council

p. 129 courtesy Museum of Modern Art, Oxford

p. 138 Nigel Young, courtesy Foster and Partners, London

p. 151 courtesy Maureen Paley Interim Art, London

p. 156 courtesy Art on the Riverside, Gateshead

p. 161 courtesy Art on the Riverside, Gateshead

p. 164 courtesy Sunderland Arts Council

p. 170 Richard Davies, courtesy Michael Wilford, London

p. 171 David Clark, courtesy Irwell Sculpture Trail, Salford

p. 174 courtesy Tate Gallery Liverpool and ARS, NY

p. 179 courtesy Stephen Friedman Gallery, London

p. 183 courtesy Arnolfini Gallery, Bristol

p. 187 courtesy Forest Life Picture Library, Edinburgh

p. 194 courtesy Centre for Visual Arts, Cardiff

p. 200 Nigel Young, courtesy Foster and Partners, London

p. 205 courtesy Fruitmarket Gallery, Edinburgh

p. 206 Stephen White, courtesy Jay Joplin/White Cube, London

p. 212 Philippe Migreat, courtesy National Galleries of Scotland

p. 213 courtesy National Galleries of Scotland

p. 214 courtesy Frith Street Gallery, London, and Marian Goodman Gallery, NY

p. 216 courtesy Centre for Contemporary Arts, Glasgow

p. 219 courtesy Anthony Meier Fine Arts, San Francisco and Sean Kelly, NY

p. 223 courtesy Blum & Poe, Santa Monica

p. 234 courtesy Kohn Turner, Los Angeles

p. 235 courtesy Kerlin Gallery, Dublin

p. 237 courtesy Kerlin Gallery, Dublin

p. 239 courtesy Irish Museum of Modern Art

p. 247 courtesy Orchard Gallery, Derry

All other illustrations courtesy of the author.

we appreciate your help

If you found errors regarding information about a site we discussed or know about sites we missed, please tell us.
art·SITES, 894 Waller Street, San Francisco, CA 94117 USA
fax: 415-701-0633, website: www.artsitespress.com

also available

art-SITES FRANCE

art-SITES PARIS

art-SITES SAN FRANCISCO

art-SITES SPAIN

art-SITES™

ORDER FORM

Check your local bookstore or order directly from us.

NAME

STREET

CITY   STATE   ZIP

COUNTRY   TEL(   )

PLEASE SEND (show quantity of each title)

_____ BRITAIN & IRELAND @ $19.95 $_____

_____ FRANCE @ $19.95 $_____

_____ PARIS @ $19.95 $_____

_____ SPAIN @ $19.95 $_____

_____ SAN FRANCISCO @ $19.95 $_____

sales tax ($1.70 per book) for CA residents $_____

shipping

    in US, $4 for the first book, $1.00 for each additional book $_____

    international airmail ($7 per book) $_____

                                       TOTAL $_____

PAYMENT

○ Check or money order (payable to **art-SITES** in US dollars drawn on a US
   bank. Send to: **art-SITES,** 894 Waller Street, San Francisco, CA 94117 USA

○ MasterCard   ○ Visa

CARD NUMBER   EXP DATE

EXACT NAME ON CARD

SIGNATURE

ORDER BY
telephone: 415-437-2456   fax: 415-701-0633   Internet: www.art-sites.com